P9-DEU-584

The Complete Encyclopedia of Cooking

Supercook

The Complete Encyclopedia of Cooking

Supercook

Marshall Cavendish
London Sydney New York

Introduction

Everything you will ever need to know about food – what to buy,
how to cook it, how to serve it and – most important of all – how
to enjoy it. You'll never need another cookbook.

'Supercook' is an important and valuable collection
which makes every other cookbook seem incomplete – or
even obsolete. As well as including thousands of recipes,
'Supercook' explains about raw ingredients, weights and
measurements and kitchen utensils, and details oven
temperatures and cooking times, basic cooking terms and
cooking and baking techniques. It shows you how to
plan a well-balanced menu and how to serve attractive
and delicious food from around the world.

Starting with 'A' and progressing through every letter of
the alphabet to 'Z', 'Supercook' builds into a complete
encyclopedia of international cooking. Each volume
contains about 200 recipes, as well as basic techniques
and instructions. Every volume includes starters, main
courses and desserts, so you have a wide choice of dishes
from which to create thousands of interesting meals. In
addition, there are recipes for snacks, cakes, pastries,
preserves and delicious home-made sweets, as well as
new ideas for picnic food and informal indoor get-
togethers. By arranging the volumes in alphabetical
order we have made it easier to find what you need –
especially in a hurry.

The 'Supercook' staff have combed the world to bring
you interesting recipes, so that you will never get bored
with cooking, and your family and friends will find an
even greater enjoyment in the meals you prepare. Each
recipe includes information on how the dish is served in
its native country and its traditional accompaniments.

The recipes also suggest suitable dishes to complete the menu and offer guidance about wines or other beverages to serve. The more you know about food, the more you will enjoy cooking and eating.

All the recipes have been tested, tasted and – if it met with the approval of our panel of experts and home economists – passed on to you with clear, easy-to-follow instructions.

Every recipe in *'Supercook'* is coded with coloured symbols that quickly indicate everything necessary for planning a meal: how long it will take to prepare, whether it is easy or complicated, and the relative cost of the main ingredients in season. Certain recipes are marked *Low-cal,* to guide you if you are watching your calorie intake. (See pages 8-9 for a full explanation to using the low-calorie recipes.)

Practical help for those who are learning to cook
'Supercook' recipes are easy to follow. They are written clearly with nothing left to chance and never include vague directions, like 'throw in a handful of flour' or 'add a little grated cheese'. Every stage of the preperation of a dish is explained in easy-to-follow detail. Many of the recipes are beautifully illustrated in full colour, and the more complicated ones have step-by-step pictures to guide you.

With *'Supercook'* as a guide, you really can't go wrong. Even the least experienced of cooks will be impressed by the ease with which they learn to produce perfect results every time.

Exciting ideas for the more experienced cook
Each volume of this unique encyclopedia includes hundreds of ideas for breakfast, lunch and dinner . . . ideas for simple family meals, or elaborate and impressive dinners . . . ideas for starters, main courses and desserts – and even fourth and fifth courses if you're really going to town! With *'Supercook'* in the kitchen you will never again be at a loss for an answer to the eternal question, 'What on earth am I going to feed them?'.

The World of International Cooking

A whole new world of culinary delights will open up and family mealtimes will acquire an international dimension when you use this illustrated A-Z encyclopedia of step-by-step recipes, cooking terms and techniques.

The aim of compiling this encyclopedia with more than 5,000 recipes from around the world has been to give all readers – from beginners to gourmet cooks – the knowledge, enthusiasm and understanding to help them become creative and exciting cooks. Foreign recipes and unusual ingredients are clearly explained. 'Agneau aux Tomates' may sound like a complicated dish from French cuisine, but don't be intimidated – the clear explanation and instructions in the recipe for this simple lamb casserole will turn it into a family favourite.

As your collection of *'Supercook'* volumes grows, so will your cooking repertoire – to include such diverse

international specialities as stir-fried Oriental dishes, Italian pastas and sauces, Irish fruit breads, spicy Eastern curries, sharp Mediterranean fish dishes, delicate French pastries and new versions of American favourites. Many of the recipes are accompanied by colour photographs, and the more complicated techniques are illustrated in step-by-step photographs. Every recipe includes an indication of how many average-sized portions it will make, and our home economists have included lots of suggestions for dishes

to serve with many of the recipes to turn an informal meal into a dinner party with an international flavour.

Learn how to turn an ordinary meal into a special one – and a special meal into a sensational one! Enjoy adding to your repertoire dishes you know you can cook with confidence, which will please your family and impress your friends and enhance your reputation as a cook and a host or hostess.

Every volume that follows includes interesting new tastes and additional helpful hints. Nothing could be more enjoyable than cooking your way through the alphabet until you reach the classic Italian dessert, Zabaglione.

'Bon appetit!'

Symbols in Supercook

'Low-Calorie' Recipes

The description 'low-calorie' has been given to recipes in *'Supercook'* which contain fewer calories than other comparable recipes in the book. For instance, the pudding recipes marked 'Low-cal' have the fewest calories when compared to other pudding recipes in *'Supercook'*. Some – but not all – of the recipes labelled 'Low-cal' would be suitable for people who are following strict slimming or low-calorie diets. Each recipe should be examined carefully to ascertain whether the ingredients are permitted for a particular special diet.

The labelling 'Low-cal' will be more helpful for those aiming to lose weight slowly by reducing their calorie intake slightly or those who frequently experiment with new recipes but wish to avoid a very high consumption of calories. These recipes can also guide the person entertaining for weight-conscious friends. However,

thought should also be given to what is to be served *with* the 'low-calorie' recipe. An over-enthusiastic combination of these recipes will not guarantee a low-calorie meal!

In deciding which recipes to consider in the 'low-calorie' category, each ingredient needs to be considered for its calorific contribution. Low-calorie ingredients such as vegetables, fruits, white fish and eggs may be combined with a moderate amount of fat or fat-containing foods and still be relatively 'low-calorie'. A generous combination of fats and fat-containing foods will produce a high-calorie recipe. Similarly, recipes which rely heavily on sugar, alcohol, flour or a combination of these foods with or without fat will be excluded from the 'low-calorie' rating.

In some recipes it may be possible to make further reductions in the amount of fats and sugars used, such as substituting low-fat yogurt for cream, or to grill [broil] food and drain off fat rather than frying, although the end results will differ slightly.

The calorie chart under the alphabetical heading CALORIES (p. 302) may be used to work out the approximate calorific value of individual recipes.

This is the guide to the amount of skill needed for each recipe.

Easy   **Needs special care**   **Complicated**

This is an estimated guide to the dish's cost, which will, of course, vary with the season.

Inexpensive   **Reasonable**   **Expensive**

This is an indication of the amount of time needed for preparing and cooking the dish.

Less than 1 hour   **1 hour to 2½ hours**   **Over 2½ hours**

Front Cover: Crown Roast of Pork, p. 511

**Published by Marshall Cavendish House
58 Old Compton Street
London W1V 5PA**

This Edition Published 1987

©*Marshall Cavendish Ltd 1987, 1986, 1985, 1979, 1978, 1977, 1976, 1975, 1974, 1973, 1972, 58 Old Compton Street, London W1V 5PA*

*Printed and bound by
L.E.G.O. Spa Vicenza*

Cataloguing in Publication Data

*Supercook
1. Cookery
1. Cameron-Smith, Marye
641.5   TX717   79-52319*

*ISBN (for set) 0 85685 534 0
ISBN (this volume) 0 85685 535 9
Library of Congress catalog card number 78-52319*

Cooking measures & terms

MEASUREMENT CONVERSIONS

Solid measures

(1 ounce = 28.352 metric grams, but for convenience it is usually calculated, as in this chart, 1 ounce = 30 grams)

½ ounce = 15 grams	3½ ounces = 100 grams
1 ounce = 30 grams	1 pound 1½ ounces = 500 grams
2 ounces = 60 grams	2 pounds 2 ounces = 1,000 grams
2½ ounces = 75 grams	(1 kilogram)

Liquid measures

20 fluid ounces = 1 pint (UK)
16 fluid ounces = 1 pint (US) or 2 cups (US)
 8 fluid ounces = 1 cup (US)

fluid ounces	Imperial	Metric	American
1	2 tablespoons	¼ deciliter	2 tablespoons
2	4 tablespoons	½ deciliter	¼ cup
4		1 deciliter	½ cup
5	¼ pint	1½ deciliter	⅔ cup
6		1¾ deciliter	¾ cup
8		2¼ deciliter	1 cup (½ pint)
10	½ pint	2¾ deciliter	1¼ cups
16		4½ deciliter	2 cups (1 pint)
20	1 pint	5½ deciliter	2½ cups
32		9 deciliter	4 cups (1 quart)
36	1⅓ pint, plus 1 ounce	1 liter	4½ cups

Frequently-used measurements

	Imperial	Metric	American
butter or margarine	½ ounce	15 grams	1 tablespoon
	4 ounces	120 grams	¼ cup
	½ pound	250 grams	1 cup
plain flour	1 ounce	30 grams	¼ cup
	2 ounces	60 grams	½ cup
	4 ounces	120 grams	1 cup
self-raising flour	1 ounce	30 grams	¼ cup
	2 ounces	60 grams	½ cup
	4 ounces	120 grams	1 cup
raisins	6 ounces	180 grams	1 cup
rice	8 ounces	240 grams	1 cup
brown sugar	⅓ ounce	10 grams	1 tablespoon
	3 ounces	90 grams	½ cup
	6 ounces	180 grams	1 cup
castor sugar	½ ounce	15 grams	1 tablespoon
	4 ounces	120 grams	½ cup
	8 ounces	240 grams	1 cup

The weights and measures equivalents are approximate only.

USEFUL KITCHEN TERMS

British equipment & terms	American equivalents
cake tin	cake pan
entree	main course
frying pan	skillet
heatproof baking dish	flameproof casserole
greaseproof paper	waxed paper
to grill	to broil
kitchen paper	paper towels
pudding	dessert
sieve	strainer
starter	appetizer
tea towel	dish towel
to whisk	to beat

British ingredients	American equivalents
aubergine	eggplant
bacon rashers	bacon slices
bicarbonate of soda	baking soda
biscuit	cookie
castor sugar	superfine sugar
cornflour	cornstarch
chutney	relish
cos lettuce	romaine lettuce
courgettes	zucchini
demerara sugar	pale brown granulated sugar

digestive biscuits	graham crackers
double cream	heavy or whipping cream
fillet steak	filet mignon
gammon slice	ham steak
haricot beans	dried navy beans
icing	frosting
icing sugar	confectioners' sugar
marrow	large zucchini or squash
Martini	vermouth
minced meat	ground meat
pancake	crêpe
pastry case	pie crust
plain flour	all-purpose flour
potato chips	French fries
potato crisps	potato chips
prawns	shrimp
salad cream	creamy salad dressing
salt beef	corned beef
scone	baking powder biscuit
self-raising flour	self-rising flour
single cream	light cream
sorbet	sherbet
sprats	smelts
spring onion	scallion
treacle	molasses
veal escalopes	veal scallops
wholemeal flour	whole-grain flour

Recipes in Volume 1

A

Abaisse

There is no English equivalent for *abaisse* (AH-bays), a French pastry-making term generally used to describe a sheet or piece of pastry which, depending on the use for which it is intended, has been rolled out to a certain thickness. The word *abaisse* is also used to describe a layer of sponge cake or the undercrust of pastry.

Abalone

A mollusc native to the waters of the Pacific Ocean, the shell of the abalone yields mother-of-pearl which is used in button-making and inlaying. Abalone meat has long been a popular food in China, Japan and in California.

Fresh abalone meat has a subtle flavour, but it is tough and must be tenderized. Most of the fresh abalone meat sold in California, for example, is ready to use. If, however, the meat has not been filleted and tenderized it can easily be softened by pounding thin slices with a wooden mallet. Today, tenderized canned abalone is exported all over the world and is readily available in speciality and Chinese provision shops.

Overcooking abalone will make it tough and disappointing. Fresh abalone, sliced thin, can be sautéed in melted butter for 45 to 55 seconds, turning once. Fresh abalone can also be cut into thin strips, dipped into batter and quickly deep fried.

This is the meat of small abalone which has been tenderized and canned. The shells of the mollusc, found in the waters of the Pacific Ocean, yield high-grade mother-of-pearl.

Abalone Chinese Style

Canned abalone is an ingredient of many Chinese dishes which are easy to prepare and quickly cooked.   4 SERVINGS

5 large Chinese dried, black mushrooms or $\frac{1}{4}$ lb. fresh mushrooms, washed and sliced
1 chicken stock cube dissolved in 15 fl. oz. [2 cups] boiling water
1 small can water chestnuts
2 tablespoons cornflour [cornstarch]
2 tablespoons cold water
1 lb. can abalone, drained and cut into very thin slices
4 spring onions [scallions], split in half and cut into 1-inch lengths
1 tablespoon soy sauce

If you are using Chinese mushrooms put them in a small bowl, cover with cool water and soak for 2 hours. Drain. Cut them in strips.

In a large, heavy frying-pan heat the chicken stock to boiling, add the water chestnuts, drained and sliced, and the mushrooms. Reduce heat and simmer for 5 minutes.

Dissolve the cornflour in the cold water and set aside.

Add the abalone, spring onions and soy sauce to the ingredients in the frying-pan and continue to simmer for 1 minute.

Slowly stir in the cornflour and cold water mixture. Lower the heat and stir continuously until the sauce thickens. Serve immediately in a warm serving dish accompanied by hot, boiled rice.

Abbacchio Brodettato

ITALIAN BRAISED LAMB

This Roman entrée (ahb-BAHK-ee-oe broh-det-TA-toe) is robust and delectable and is neither expensive nor difficult to prepare. It cannot be made quickly, however, for quite a bit of preparation is required and the meat must be cooked in the oven for about 1½ hours. It makes a delicious main dish for an informal dinner accompanied by lots of crusty Italian bread, a green salad and dry white wine.

6 SERVINGS

4 tablespoons diced fatty bacon
2 tablespoons oil
2 lb. lean shoulder of lamb, boned and cut into cubes
1 garlic clove, crushed
1 small onion, finely chopped
4 oz. [½ cup] canned, drained tomatoes
4 fl. oz. [½ cup] dry white wine
2 pints [5 cups] beef stock, fresh, canned or made with beef stock cubes
3 tablespoons flour
1 teaspoon salt
  freshly ground black pepper
1 bay leaf
½ teaspoon of dried oregano
½ teaspoon of dried basil
3 egg yolks
2 tablespoons lemon juice
3 tablespoons chopped fresh parsley

Preheat oven to moderate 350°F (Gas Mark 4, 180°C).

In a large, heavy frying-pan over high heat, fry the bacon, until crisp and brown. Stir frequently to prevent it from sticking. With a slotted spoon, remove the bacon and discard it.

Add the oil to the remaining fat and when it is hot lower the heat to moderate, add the lamb, a few cubes at a time and fry them until golden brown. As they brown, transfer them to a medium-sized, flameproof casserole.

In the remaining fat fry the garlic and onion for 8 minutes or until the onion is transparent. Stir in the tomatoes and add the wine and boil for about 10 minutes or until it is reduced by half. Pour in the stock, and with a wooden spoon stir well to mix. Bring to the boil again.

Sprinkle the flour, salt and 4 grindings of black pepper over the meat in the casserole. Place the casserole over moderate heat and, stirring all the time, cook until the meat and flour are blended.

Pour the wine and stock mixture over the meat in the casserole. Add the bay leaf, the oregano and basil. Bring to the boil over moderate heat, stirring occasionally.

Cover the casserole and transfer it to the oven. Braise for 1½ to 2 hours, or until the meat is tender.

With a slotted spoon, transfer the meat to a heated, deep, serving dish, cover with a lid or piece of aluminium foil and keep hot.

Strain the stock in the casserole into a medium-sized saucepan. Leave it to rest for a minute or two, then skim any fat from the surface.

In a small bowl beat the egg yolks and lemon juice together with a whisk or rotary beater and slowly stir in 4 tablespoons of the stock.

Whisk the egg mixture back into the remaining stock. Place the pan over low heat, and cook gently for a few seconds, until the mixture thickens enough to coat the back of a wooden spoon. Be careful not to let the sauce boil or it will curdle.

Taste the sauce and add more salt and pepper if necessary. Pour the sauce over the meat and sprinkle with parsley.

Aberdeen, or Arbroath, Smokies

A Scottish speciality, these small haddocks are split, gutted, closed again and smoked whole. Golden brown and headless, they need no further cooking and can be eaten cold, with buttered toast or cut up in a salad. They may also be buttered outside and inside and lightly grilled or warmed in the oven. For a tasty first course, smokies can be filleted and served in a light cheese sauce.

A Scottish speciality, Aberdeen, or Arbroath, Smokies are small haddocks which are gutted and smoked whole.

Abbacchio Brodettato is a classic Roman entrée of braised lamb with a delicate egg and lemon sauce.

Absinthe

Distilled from wormwood, anise and aromatic plants, this pale green liqueur with a very high alcoholic content was invented at the end of the eighteenth century and immediately gained great popularity in France. The oils from wormwood, however, can cause delirium, blindness and insanity. Consequently, the sale of absinthe has been prohibited in France, Switzerland and the United States.

Acetic acid

This acid, which forms the basis of vinegar, is produced by the fermentation of ciders and wines and is used in very small quantities in the making of some sweets. A dilute synthetic solution is sometimes used as an inexpensive substitute for white wine vinegar or for pickling.

Acidify

To add acid, such as lemon juice or vinegar, to a culinary preparation.

Acidity

An acid taste which exists naturally in certain vegetables and fruit and can be eliminated or diminished by BLANCHING.

Acidulate

To make a preparation slightly sour, acid or piquant by the addition of such acids as lemon juice or vinegar. Acidulated water, cold water to which vinegar, lemon or lime juice is added, is used to prevent peeled and cut fruit and vegetables from discolouring when they are exposed to the air.

Adam and Eve Pudding is a dessert of apples baked with a sponge topping.

Adam and Eve Pudding
APPLE AND SPONGE PUDDING

A traditional, inexpensive English pudding, this is an appealing dessert for an informal family lunch or dinner. It should be served hot and can be accompanied by cream or custard sauce. It is easy to make, but care must be taken when preparing the sponge topping.

4 SERVINGS
    1 lb. cooking apples
    5 oz. [⅝ cup] sugar
    ½ teaspoon cinnamon
    2 tablespoons cold water
    4 oz. [½ cup] butter or margarine, softened
    4 oz. [1 cup] self-raising flour
    2 medium-sized eggs, lightly beaten

Preheat the oven to moderate 350°F (Gas Mark 4, 180°C).

Peel and core the apples. Cut into thin slices and put them into a medium-sized oval pie dish.

Sprinkle the apple slices with the cinnamon, water and 1 ounce [2 tablespoons] of sugar.

To prepare the sponge mixture, put the butter and the remaining 4 ounces [½ cup] of sugar into a mixing bowl and beat with a wooden spoon until light and creamy. Add the beaten eggs, a little at a time, to the sugar and butter mixture, beating well between each addition. Sift the flour into the bowl and stir it into the mixture.

Pour the sponge mixture over the apples and spread it evenly with a palette knife. Bake in the middle of the oven for 30 minutes or until the sponge mixture has risen and has begun to turn a pale golden brown. Reduce the oven heat to cool 300°F (Gas Mark 2, 150°C) for another 30 minutes. Serve immediately.

Adrak Chutney
GINGER CHUTNEY

An ideal accompaniment for curry, this Indian recipe for Adrak (AH-druk) Chutney is quick and easy to make. If you have a blender the whole operation takes no more than 10 minutes. This chutney must be eaten immediately or, if stored in a closed jar in the refrigerator, within two days.

6 SERVINGS
    juice of 2 lemons
    4 teaspoons sugar
    4 oz. fresh ginger, peeled and chopped
    3 oz. sultanas [½ cup golden raisins]
    1 clove garlic, crushed
    1½ teaspoons salt

Put the juice of 1½ lemons, 2 teaspoons sugar and all the other ingredients into an electric blender. Blend until the mixture is smooth. Taste and if necessary add the juice of the other half lemon and the rest of the sugar. If you are using a hand chopper be sure to chop the ginger thoroughly as it tends to be fibrous. Serve in a small glass bowl.

Advocaat

A yellow, Dutch liqueur made with brandy, thickened with egg yolks and flavoured with vanilla.

Agar-agar

The gelatine-like product of a red seaweed which has strong setting properties, agar-agar is chiefly produced in Japan, China, the Soviet Union and the United States. Sold in sheet or strip form, it is used commercially in canning, in the production of jellies, creams and emulsions, and as a medium for the laboratory culture of bacteria.

Agneau

A young sheep before the age of one year, which is called lamb in England and spring lamb in the United States, is in France known as *agneau* (AHN-yoh). The French *agneau de lait* is milk-fed lamb, a yearling or a baby lamb which has never been weaned or put out to graze.

Agneau à la Bonne Femme

RAGOÛT OF LAMB

A simple and inexpensive brown stew, Agneau à la Bonne Femme (AHN-yoh ah la bon fahm) *is a French ragoût of spring lamb which is cooked on the top of the stove. It can be made early in the day and reheated immediately before serving. It is traditionally served with rice.*

4 SERVINGS

2 lb. shoulder of lamb, boned
3 tablespoons rendered fresh pork fat or cooking oil
2 tablespoons [¼ cup] flour
1 teaspoon salt
½ teaspoon black pepper
1¼ pints [3 cups] water
1 small clove garlic, crushed
1 bouquet garni, consisting of 2 parsley sprigs, 1 bay leaf and ⅛ teaspoon of dried thyme tied in a piece of cheesecloth
8 small potatoes, peeled
12 small onions
12 small carrots
2 oz. sultanas [⅓ cup golden raisins], washed

Cut the lamb into 2-inch cubes and dry them well on kitchen towels. Heat the fat, or cooking oil, in a large, heavy saucepan. Add the meat, a few pieces at a time, and brown on all sides. As the cubes are done, lift them out of the pan with a slotted spoon, place in a dish and keep warm.

When all the pieces have been browned, return them to the pan and sprinkle with the flour, salt and pepper. Toss the pieces of meat with a spoon to coat them with the other ingredients. Cook over a moderate heat, mixing occasionally, until the flour is lightly browned.

Add the water, the garlic and the bouquet garni. Cover the saucepan, bring to the boil. Lower the heat and simmer for 40 minutes.

Add the potatoes, onions, carrots and sultanas. Replace the lid and simmer for another 45 minutes or until the meat is tender when pierced with a table fork and the vegetables are cooked. Taste the stock and add more seasoning if necessary.

To serve, remove the bouquet garni, put the meat and vegetables into a warmed serving dish and pour the stock over.

Agneau en Brochette

LAMB ON SKEWERS

Agneau en Brochette (AHN-yoh on broh-shet), *cubes of lamb marinated for 3 hours in olive oil and white wine and grilled [broiled]*

with vegetables on skewers, makes a splendid main course for a dinner party. On grand occasions the lamb can be doused with warmed brandy, set alight and served on a metal platter.

4 SERVINGS

1½ lb. boned leg of lamb
3 tablespoons olive oil
3 tablespoons white wine
1 clove of garlic, crushed
1 teaspoon dried rosemary
1 teaspoon salt
16 small tomatoes, washed
16 small [pearl] onions, skinned
2 large green peppers, washed, seeded and cut into large pieces freshly ground black pepper

Trim the excess fat from the lamb and cut into 1½-inch cubes. In a bowl mix the oil, wine, garlic, rosemary, 8 grindings of pepper and the salt. Add the cubes of lamb and turn well with a spoon so that all the pieces are coated. Leave to marinate for 3 hours. Mix occasionally.

Line grilling pan with aluminium foil. Thread the lamb pieces on 8 skewers alternating with tomatoes, onions and green pepper. After placing the skewers on the pan, brush with the remaining marinade. Turn the grill to high and, when red hot, grill the kebabs approximately 2 inches away from the heat for 8 to 10 minutes. Serve with rice, a green salad and garlic bread.

A French ragoût of lamb, Agneau à la Bonne Femme is traditionally made with spring vegetables.

An unusual main dish, Agneau à la Hongroise is cooked on top of the stove and flavoured with herbs, paprika, mushrooms and white wine.

Agneau à la Hongroise
LAMB STEW WITH PAPRIKA

An unusual lamb stew, Agneau à la Hongroise (AHN-yoh ah la ON-grwahz) is flavoured with paprika and mushrooms. A good main dish at lunch or dinner, it may be served with buttered noodles and a fresh, green salad.

6 SERVINGS

3 lb. lower ribs or shoulder of
   lamb, boned
5 oz. [⅝ cup] butter
2 medium-sized onions, peeled and
   chopped
½ teaspoon salt
1 level tablespoon paprika
2 tablespoons [¼ cup] flour
6 fl. oz. [¾ cup] white wine
10 fl. oz. [1¼ cups] veal stock, or
   stock made with a veal or
   chicken stock cube
2 tablespoons tomato purée
1 bouquet garni, consisting of 1
   heaped teaspoon of equal
   quantities of crushed, dried
   parsley, thyme and bay leaf,
   tied in a piece of cheesecloth
8 oz. [1 cup] mushrooms, washed,
   stalks trimmed and sliced
10 fl. oz. [1¼ cups heavy] double cream
2 tablespoons chopped fresh parsley

Cut the lamb into small cubes, dry them on kitchen paper towels and brown them in 4 ounces [½ cup] of butter in a deep, heavy saucepan. When the lamb cubes are well coloured, add the onions, the salt and the paprika and mix thoroughly. Sprinkle with the flour and stir it in. Pour on the white wine, bring to the boil and continue to boil briskly for 5 minutes. Stir in the veal or chicken stock, the tomato purée and add the bouquet garni. Cover and simmer for 30 minutes.

Put the remaining 1 ounce of butter into a frying-pan and lightly sauté the mushrooms. Remove the lamb cubes from the saucepan with a slotted spoon and add to the mushrooms. Remove frying-pan from the heat. Set aside.

Increase heat under saucepan to high and boil briskly until the sauce is reduced by half. Add the lamb and mushrooms and mix together. Reduce heat to low. Cover and simmer for 20 minutes. Remove the bouquet garni. Stir in the cream.

To serve, put the lamb, mushrooms and sauce on a warmed serving dish and sprinkle with fresh, chopped parsley.

Agneau aux Tomates
LAMB STEW WITH TOMATOES

A simple lamb dish, Agneau aux Tomates (AHN-yoh oh toh-MAHT), is easy to prepare and is a suitable main dish for an informal lunch or dinner. Serve with a green vegetable and creamed potatoes.

4 SERVINGS

2 lb. boned shoulder of lamb,
   trimmed of excess fat
3 tablespoons vegetable oil
1 garlic clove, crushed
4 fl. oz. [½ cup] white wine
8 fl. oz. [1 cup] veal or chicken stock
½ teaspoon salt
¼ teaspoon black pepper
1 lb. small tomatoes, blanched,
   peeled and seeded
1 tablespoon flour, dissolved in
   2 tablespoons wine
2 tablespoons finely chopped
   parsley

With a sharp knife, cut the lamb into 1½-inch cubes, dry them well on a kitchen towel.

In a large, heavy saucepan, heat 2 tablespoons of the oil, over moderate heat. Add the lamb cubes and fry them, stirring frequently for 6 to 8 minutes or until they are browned all over.

Add the garlic, wine, stock, salt and pepper and stir well. Bring the liquid to the boil. Reduce the heat to low and simmer for 30 minutes or until the lamb is tender when pierced with the point of a sharp knife.

Meanwhile, in a small frying-pan heat the remaining amount of oil over moderate heat. When the foam subsides, add the tomatoes and cook them gently, stirring frequently, for 5 minutes. Remove the pan from the heat. Set aside and keep warm.

Stir the dissolved flour into the lamb mixture in the saucepan. Cook, stirring constantly, for 3 minutes or until the liquid has thickened slightly. Stir in the tomatoes. Remove pan from heat and transfer the stew to a warmed serving dish. Sprinkle over the parsley and serve.

Agurkai su Rukcscia Grietne
CUCUMBER AND SOURED CREAM SALAD

Refreshing, tasty and attractive, this cucumber and soured cream salad (ah-GOOR-ki soo rook-schee-a gree-et-ney) originated in the Baltic States. It is easy to make, does not take very long and could accompany almost any plainly cooked fish or meat dish. If fresh dill is not available parsley can be substituted. It will be equally decorative, but it will not give the same flavour.

4 SERVINGS

3 medium-sized cucumbers,
   peeled
5 teaspoons salt
3 tablespoons white wine vinegar
1 teaspoon French mustard
6 tablespoons soured cream
½ teaspoon sugar
⅛ teaspoon white pepper
3 eggs, hard-boiled
1 tablespoon finely-chopped, fresh
   dill or 2 tablespoons chopped
   parsley

Thinly sliced cucumbers in a vinegar and dill dressing, Agurkesalat can be used as a garnish, or served with meat or poultry dishes.

Aïgo Bouïdo

FRENCH PROVENÇAL GARLIC SOUP

Quick and easy to make, Aïgo Bouïdo (ai-go BWEE-doe), *a French Provençal soup, is inexpensive and unusual. It has the added advantage that most of it can be prepared early in the day on which it is to be served. Because the garlic is boiled, its flavour becomes delicious, aromatic and almost indefinable. Served as a prelude to steak, salad and an elegant chocolate dessert, Aïgo Bouïdo will be a unique beginning to a delightful dinner.*

4 SERVINGS

16 garlic cloves, unpeeled and
   coarsely chopped
1 bay leaf
½ teaspoon dried thyme
1 tablespoon dried sage
1 teaspoon salt
3 cloves
3 parsley sprigs
2 pints [5 cups] water
3 egg yolks
4 tablespoons [¼ cup] olive oil
2 tablespoons chopped fresh
   parsley

Place the garlic, bay leaf, thyme, sage, salt, cloves and parsley sprigs in a large saucepan. Pour the water into the saucepan and bring to the boil. Reduce the heat and simmer the soup, un-covered, for 30 minutes.

Pour the soup through a strainer into a large bowl, and press all the juice from the garlic with a wooden spoon. Wash the saucepan and return the soup to the clean pan.

Place the egg yolks in a bowl and with a wire whisk, or rotary beater, beat them until they are thick and creamy. Add the oil drop by drop, beating continuously, until all the oil is incorporated and the mixture is smooth.

Just before serving, bring the soup back to the boil. Spoon the egg and oil mixture into a warm soup tureen and with a wire whisk beat in about one-quarter of the hot soup. Pour in the rest of the soup and stir.

Sprinkle the chopped parsley over the soup.

The soup may be served with French bread, bread sticks or toast and a bowl of grated Parmesan Cheese which is sprinkled on the soup when it is served.

Cut the cucumbers into ½ inch thick slices. Place the salt and 2 tablespoons of the vinegar into a large mixing bowl and stir until the salt is dissolved. Add the cucumber slices to the salt and vinegar and, using a large spoon, toss them gently until thoroughly mixed.

With a slotted spoon, remove the cucumber slices from the bowl and place them on kitchen paper towels to drain.

In a small mixing bowl mix together the mustard, the remaining 1 tablespoon of vinegar, the soured cream, sugar and white pepper.

Halve the eggs, remove the yolks and put aside. Cut the egg whites into thin strips. Using the back of a wooden spoon, press the egg yolks through a fine sieve, or strainer, on to a plate.

With a wire whisk beat the sieved egg yolks into the soured cream mixture. Continue to beat until the dressing is smooth and creamy. Add the strips of egg white and mix well.

Place the drained cucumber slices in a shallow serving bowl. Pour the dressing over the cucumber and with a wooden spoon toss gently until they are well-coated. Sprinkle with chopped dill or parlsey. Place in the refrigerator to chill for at least 1 hour before serving.

Agurkesalat

DANISH PICKLED CUCUMBER SALAD

*In Denmark, Agurkesalat (ah-*GOOR-*keh-sa-*LAHT) *is often used to garnish* smørre-brød, *the famous Danish open sandwiches of thin slices of rye bread topped with a*

huge variety of appetizingly arranged meats, seafood, eggs and cheese. Agurkesalat can also be served as an accompaniment to meat or poultry dishes. It is inexpensive and simply prepared, but it must be made early in the day on which it is to be used because it takes a total of at least 5 hours for the cucumbers to pickle.

4 SALAD SERVINGS

3 cucumbers, washed
1 tablespoon plus 1 teaspoon salt
1 tablespoon sugar
¼ teaspoon white pepper
4 fl. oz. [½ cup] white vinegar
1 tablespoon lemon juice
3 tablespoons chopped fresh
   dill or 1 tablespoon dried dill

With a table fork score down the skin of the cucumbers to make ridges. Cut the cucumbers into very thin slices. Place the cucumber slices in a shallow dish and sprinkle with 1 tablespoon of the salt. Cover and set aside for 2 hours. (This removes the excess water from the cucumbers.)

Meanwhile, mix the remaining 1 tea-spoon of salt with the sugar, pepper, vinegar and lemon juice. With a fork beat lightly until the sugar is dissolved.

With a slotted spoon remove the cucumber slices and place them on a double piece of kitchen paper towel. Place another piece of paper on top and press to remove the liquid.

Arrange the cucumber slices attrac-tively in a serving dish. Pour the vinegar dressing over the cucumber slices and sprinkle the dill over the top. Place in the refrigerator and leave for at least 3 hours before serving.

Aïgo-Sau

MEDITERRANEAN FISH STEW

A traditional dish in the South of France, Aïgo-Sau (ai-go-saw) is easy to prepare. It can be made with one or more types of fish and is an excellent lunch or informal dinner party dish.

4 SERVINGS

1½ lb. fresh fish, boned
6 medium potatoes, peeled and sliced
1 bay leaf
1 onion, peeled and finely chopped
1 celery stalk, chopped
2 cloves of garlic, peeled and crushed plus 1 whole, peeled garlic clove
1 teaspoon salt
½ teaspoon black pepper
1 teaspoon each of fennel, chopped parsley and grated orange rind
3 fl. oz. [⅜ cup] olive oil
boiling water
8 fl. oz. [1 cup] alioli
4 slices of dry, toasted, French bread

Cut the fish into serving-size pieces and arrange in the bottom of a large saucepan. Cover with the potatoes. Add the bay leaf, onion, celery and crushed garlic.

Sprinkle with salt, pepper, fennel, parsley and grated orange rind. Pour on the olive oil and add boiling water to cover. Boil rapidly for 20 minutes or until the potatoes are tender.

Strain the broth into another saucepan and put the fish and potatoes on a warmed serving dish. Just before serving the broth, remove the saucepan from the heat and, stirring constantly, very slowly add the alioli.

Place rounds of toast, well rubbed with the peeled garlic clove, in individual soup bowls and pour the broth over them. Serve the fish and potatoes separately on a warmed serving dish.

Left: A simple Mediterranean fish stew and broth, Aïgo-Sau can be made with one or more types of fish.

Aiguillette de boeuf

Aiguillette de boeuf (ai-GWEE-yet deh berf) is the French cookery term for the top part or rump of beef which is usually braised or poached.

Aillade

A term which is used in the South of France, aillade (AYE-yahd) is applied to different preparations which are all predominantly flavoured with garlic. Among these are aillade sauce, an oil, vinegar and garlic dressing, which is served with cold meat and fish as well as with potatoes, and bread *à l'aillade*, slices of toasted bread which are well rubbed with garlic and sprinkled with olive oil.

Ajja

SPICY SCRAMBLED EGGS WITH SAUSAGE AND GREEN PEPPERS

A Tunisian dish, Ajja (AJ-ja) is easy to prepare and can be served at lunch or an informal dinner. Although the Tunisians use a great deal of cayenne pepper in this dish, the first time you make it, unless your palate is accustomed to very hot food, it might be wise to use only a few grains.

4 SERVINGS

4 medium-sized, sweet, green peppers
½ teaspoon ground cayenne pepper
¼ teaspoon ground cumin
⅛ teaspoon salt
2 tablespoons olive oil
1 lb. spicy sausage such as hot Italian sausage or Spanish chorizos, cut into 1-inch rounds
1 garlic clove, finely chopped
14 oz. canned Italian, peeled plum tomatoes; or 3 large, ripe firm tomatoes, peeled and quartered
4 tablespoons [¼ cup] cold water freshly ground black pepper
6 eggs, lightly beaten

Cut the peppers into quarters, remove the seeds and trim off the white pith. Cut lengthways into ½-inch wide strips. Set aside.

In a small dish mix the cayenne, cumin and salt together. Set aside.

Right: Scrambled eggs with sausage and green pepper, Ajja is an unusual and spicy Tunisian dish.

Pour the oil into a large heavy frying-pan and place over high heat until the oil is hot. Add the sliced sausage and fry, turning frequently, until the sausage is brown.

Stir in the garlic, the cayenne, cumin and salt mixture, the tomatoes and water and 6 grindings of black pepper. Cook over moderate heat until the mixture is thick. Stir occasionally to prevent the tomatoes sticking to the pan. Add the strips of pepper, cover the pan and cook for another 5 minutes.

Pour the beaten eggs over the sausage mixture. Cook over low heat, stirring constantly until the eggs are just cooked. Do not over cook as the eggs will be too hard and will not blend with the other ingredients.

Albacore

A large, deep-sea, game fish, albacore, a species of tuna fish, has white meat and is used for the best canned tuna fish and for the most delicate dishes.

Albóndigas

MEAT BALLS IN TOMATO SAUCE

A traditional Mexican dish, Albóndigas (al-BON-dee-gas) probably has its origins in Spain. It is also made in Brazil and in Scotland where it is known as Almundigoes. An inexpensive, filling, lunch or dinner dish, it is usually served with plain boiled rice.

4 SERVINGS

1 lb. minced [ground] beef
½ lb. minced [ground] pork
1 thick slice white bread cold water
1 medium-sized egg
1 teaspoon salt
½ teaspoon dried sage
½ teaspoon dried mint
¼ teaspoon black pepper
2 tablespoons cooking oil
2 medium-sized onions, chopped
1½ lb. tomatoes, peeled and chopped
1 clove garlic, crushed
½ teaspoon dried coriander

In a large bowl mix together the beef and pork. Soak the slice of bread in the cold water and squeeze dry. Crumble the bread and mix into the meat. Stir in the egg and the salt, sage, mint and pepper. Mix well.

With your hands, shape the meat into balls the size of walnuts.

Put the cooking oil into a deep, heavy saucepan and fry the meat balls until they are brown. Remove with a slotted spoon and set aside.

Put the onions into the saucepan and fry them until they are golden brown. Add the tomatoes, garlic and coriander. Cover and simmer for 30 minutes.

Add the meat balls and continue to simmer, covered, for another 30 minutes. Taste and add salt and pepper if necessary.

To serve, place the meat balls in the centre of a deep, warmed serving dish, pour the sauce over them and surround with rice.

Albóndigas Soup

Albóndigas is also the name given to a spicy, Mexican tomato soup which includes a few small balls of the albóndigas meat mixture.

6 SERVINGS

1 oz. [2 tablespoons] butter
2 onions, chopped
¼ teaspoon chilli powder
½ teaspoon dried oregano
2 lb. tomatoes, peeled and sieved
water
1 teaspoon salt
MEAT BALLS
½ lb. minced [ground] beef
1 slice white bread, grated into
   breadcrumbs
1 small egg
1 small clove garlic, crushed
   a large pinch of dried sage, mint
   and coriander
   freshly ground black pepper
½ teaspoon salt

In a large saucepan melt the butter over moderate heat. Add the onions and cook gently until they are soft, but not brown. Add the chilli powder and oregano. Stir and cook for 30 seconds before adding the sieved tomatoes which have been made up to 4 pints [2½ quarts] with water. Add the salt and cook uncovered, over moderate heat, for 1 hour, or until the liquid is reduced by half.

Put all the ingredients for the meat balls in a medium-sized mixing bowl and mix well with your hands. Roll the mixture into small balls the size of walnuts. Add these to the soup. Cover and simmer over low heat for 40 minutes.

Albumen

This is the name sometimes used for the whites of eggs. It is frequently confused with ALBUMIN which is the protein part of egg white.

Albumin

A protein which forms part of blood, milk and egg white. Soluble in water and dilute salt solutions, albumin coagulates when heated.

Albumin powder can be substituted for egg whites when making meringues and some cake icings.

Alcohol

Alcohol, a word of Arabic origin, is as old as man. There are a large number of alcohols, a whole chemical series with varying characteristics, each composed of carbon, hydrogen and oxygen combined in a similar pattern.

The alcohol which is the principal active ingredient of wines, spirits and beers is known as ethyl alcohol. It is a colourless liquid with a faint odour.

Alcohol is easily made by yeast fermentation of fruits, grains and vegetables and, as a consequence, was known to early man in the form of mead, ale and wine.

Al Dente

An Italian cooking term, *al dente* (ahl-DEN-tay) literally translated means 'to the tooth'. It is used to describe the point at which food, particularly pasta and rice, is properly cooked, that is, it is firm to the bite, but not soft.

Ale

A word originally used to describe an alcoholic beverage which was brewed from barley malt, ale was the common drink in northern countries where there were few or no vineyards and, therefore, little or no wine.

After the introduction of hops into England from Flanders in the sixteenth century, ale was increasingly flavoured with hops and today the term ale is almost synonymous with beer although it is never applied to black beers or lager.

Alebele

COCONUT FILLED DESSERT PANCAKES

Alebele (al-a-beel) *originates in Goa on the west coast of India where Portuguese influence is evident in the cooking. The original recipe calls for fresh coconut and*

jaggery, a crude, dark, palm sugar. This recipe is an adaptation using desiccated coconut, brown sugar and treacle [molasses].

4 SERVINGS

PANCAKES
4 oz. [1 cup] flour
2 teaspoons castor sugar
1 egg plus 1 egg yolk
6 fl. oz. [¾ cup] milk mixed with
   2 fl. oz. [¼ cup] water
2 tablespoons melted butter
FILLING
4 teaspoons brown sugar
2 teaspoons treacle [molasses]
2 oz. fine desiccated coconut
   soaked in 7 tablespoons milk for
1 hour
1 teaspoon fresh ginger, finely
   grated
½ teaspoon aniseeds

For the pancakes, sift the flour and sugar into a medium-sized mixing bowl. Make a well in the centre of the flour and break the eggs into it. Add a tablespoon of the milk and water to the eggs and stir with a wooden spoon, mixing well. Slowly incorporate the flour and sugar.

Add the milk and water a little at a time. Continue mixing until all the flour and half the milk mixture is blended to make a thick batter. Add 1 tablespoon cooled, melted butter and whisk briskly. Whisk in the rest of the milk and water. Cover and keep in a cool place for 30 minutes.

Meanwhile mix together all the ingredients for the filling in a small bowl and set aside.

Heat a medium-sized frying-pan. Grease lightly with melted butter. Pour one tablespoon of the batter into the pan and tip the pan quickly to spread the batter evenly. Cook over a high heat until the pancake is brown on the underside. Turn over with a palette knife and cook for 30 seconds or until brown. Turn on to a plate and keep warm.

Spread one spoonful of the coconut filling across the lower third of each pancake and roll neatly. Arrange the pancakes on a plate and serve.

Ale Berry

This drink is traditionally drunk in the North of England at bedtime to prevent a cold.

2 PINTS

2 pints [5 cups] brown ale
2 tablespoons rolled oats
1 small piece fresh ginger, grated,
   or ½ teaspoon ground ginger
½ teaspoon grated nutmeg
2 tablespoons brown sugar
   juice of half a lemon

Roll out each half of the pastry between two pieces of floured greaseproof or waxed paper to prevent it sticking.

Fold the edges to make a neat rectangle of pastry and role out again between the sheets of paper.

Remove the top sheet and lift the pastry by the lower sheet onto the buttered baking tray.

Spread the raspberry purée evenly over one half of the baked pastry leaving about $\frac{1}{4}$ inch around the edges.

Carefully slide the other piece of baked pastry off the baking tray onto the raspberry covered piece.

When the torte is iced leave it to cool for at least 4 hours before cutting it into 2 inch by 3 inch pieces.

Put the ale into a large saucepan over moderate heat and stir in the oats, ginger and nutmeg. Bring to the boil and simmer for 15 to 20 minutes. Strain the liquid into a warmed jug through a fine sieve. Stir in the sugar and lemon juice and taste. Add more sugar if necessary.

Serve very hot in glass or pottery mugs.

Ale Posset

An old-fashioned English drink, this is made of equal quantities of hot ale and hot milk mixed together. It is sweetened with sugar, flavoured with grated ginger or nutmeg and drunk very hot.

Alewife

An important food fish, the alewife is a member of the shad family. It is caught off the Atlantic coast of North America and in some lakes and rivers. It exists in great abundance in Lake Ontario.

The alewife grows to about a foot long and resembles the herring. In the St. Lawrence Bay area this fish is known as Gaspereu or Sawbelly and is called Round Pompano in Bermuda.

Fresh alewife is cooked in the same ways as shad or herring. Alewife is generally salt-packed, but it is also sometimes smoked.

Alexander Torte

ICED RASPBERRY-FILLED PASTRY CAKES

Delicately flavoured, crisp and cut into cakes, Alexander Torte was traditionally eaten as a lunch or dinner dessert in Latvia, but it can also be served at tea. It should be made early on the day you plan to serve it, or even the night before, because the icing must be hard before the torte is cut.

ABOUT 24 CAKES

12 oz. [3 cups] flour
$\frac{1}{4}$ teaspoon salt
4 oz. [$\frac{1}{2}$ cup] unsalted butter, cut into pieces
4 oz. [$\frac{1}{2}$ cup] margarine, diced
3 tablespoons sugar
1 egg lightly beaten
12 oz. [1$\frac{1}{2}$ cups] raspberry jam
2 oz. [$\frac{1}{4}$ cup] butter, softened
8 oz. icing [1$\frac{3}{4}$ cups confectioners'] sugar, sifted
3 tablespoons cold water
2 tablespoons lemon juice

Sift the flour and salt into a large mixing bowl. Add the butter and margarine. With your fingertips, rub the butter and margarine into the flour until the mixture resembles fine breadcrumbs. Add the sugar and the egg and mix well. With a knife stir the pastry until it begins to form a ball, then with your hands, gently knead the pastry until it is smooth.

Wrap the pastry in aluminium foil and chill in the refrigerator for 1 hour.

To make purée of the jam, hold a strainer over a small saucepan and, with a wooden spoon, press the jam through. Place the saucepan over low heat, and cook, stirring all the time, until the purée thickens. Set aside to cool.

Preheat the oven to cool 300°F (Gas Mark 2, 150°C).

Halve the pastry. Cut out 4 pieces of greaseproof paper 9 × 16 inches. Dust the paper with flour. Place half of the pastry on a piece of the floured paper and place another on top, flour side down. Roll out the pastry to the shape of the paper, fold over uneven edges and roll again. Repeat with other half.

Grease two baking sheets with the softened butter. Remove the top pieces of paper from the pastry, and lift the other pieces of paper and pastry and place them, paper side up, on to the baking sheets. Remove the paper. Place the baking sheets in the oven and bake the pastry for 45 to 50 minutes, or until it is crisp.

Allow the pastry to cool on the trays for 5 minutes. Spread the raspberry purée over one piece of the pastry and carefully slide the other piece on top.

Mix the icing sugar in a bowl with cold water and lemon juice. Spread the icing evenly over the top of the torte. Leave the icing to set for at least 4 hours.

Algérienne, à l'

Algérienne, (al-JAIR-yen) is the name of a garnish, usually for meat, which consists of small, whole tomatoes braised in oil, and sweet potatoes cooked in butter.

Alicante Wine

A sweet, red, table wine, very popular in Spain, Alicante wine comes, as its name suggests, from the surrounding areas of Alicante. Rarely stocked in Britain today it was quite popular in Victorian England.

Alioli

The name literally means garlic oil and this sauce has been known in many parts of Spain and in Provence for hundreds of years. It was also known and appreciated by the Romans 2,000 years ago.

The basic recipe is garlic pounded in a mortar and mixed with olive oil, salt and lemon juice. There are many variations which include the addition of cream cheese, walnuts, almonds or eggs.

The Spanish claim that alioli was the original recipe from which mayonnaise was developed in France. According to one story, the Duc de Richelieu, while on a visit to Mahon in Minorca in 1756, so enjoyed the alioli and egg sauce that he took the recipe back to France. The French changed it by excluding the garlic and increasing the lemon juice and the result was called *Mahonaise*.

In France the sauce is called aïoli (i-oh-lee) and is usually served with boiled fish, but it also sometimes accompanies cold meat. A popular Provençal dish is aïoli garni, a combination of boiled cod, octopus, fennel, onions, carrots, French beans, artichokes, baked potatoes, hard-boiled eggs, little snails and chick peas, arranged on a platter and served with aïoli sauce.

Alioli Sauce

GARLIC MAYONNAISE

Alioli (A-lee-o-lee) *is a garlic flavoured sauce which is the traditional accompaniment to boiled and grilled [broiled] meat and fish in Spain.*

4 SERVINGS

4 garlic cloves, peeled
$\frac{1}{2}$ teaspoon salt
2 tablespoons lemon juice
2 egg yolks
10 fl. oz. [1$\frac{1}{4}$ cups] olive oil

Crush the garlic in a garlic press, with a pestle in a mortar or with the flat side of a table knife. In a small mixing bowl add the salt and lemon juice to the crushed garlic and mix thoroughly.

Using a table fork beat in the egg yolks one at a time until the mixture thickens. Beating constantly, add the oil a few drops at a time. When about a third of the oil has been absorbed by the egg-yolk mixture the oil can be added in a slow stream, still beating continually.

If the mixture becomes too stiff to beat easily add a teaspoon of cold water. The finished mayonnaise should be the consistency of thick cream.

Alivenci

CHEESE AND SOURED CREAM SOUFFLÉ

Adapted from an old Romanian recipe, Alivenci (ah-lee-VEEN-che) *can be served with a salad as an unusual lunch or light supper dish. Sprinkled lightly with icing [confectioner's] sugar and accompanied by a hot fruit sauce it is a delicious dessert.*

4 SERVINGS

$\frac{1}{2}$ oz. [1 tablespoon] butter, softened
3 teaspoons flour
8 oz. [1 cup] cream cheese
6 tablespoons [$\frac{3}{4}$ cup] soured cream
3 egg yolks
6 tablespoons [$\frac{3}{4}$ cup] milk
$\frac{1}{2}$ teaspoon salt
3 egg whites

Preheat the oven to moderate 350°F (Gas Mark 4, 180°C).

Using your fingertips or a piece of paper, spread the softened butter over the bottom and sides of a 7-inch soufflé dish. Sprinkle 1 teaspoon of flour into the soufflé dish and shake it so the flour evenly coats the bottom and sides. Leave aside until ready to use.

With a wooden spoon beat the cream cheese into a deep bowl until it is soft and creamy. Using a wire whisk beat in the soured cream, a spoonful at a time. Continue to beat until the mixture is smooth.

Add the egg yolks one at a time, beating well after each one is added. Mix in the milk, salt and the remaining 2 teaspoons of flour. Beat well until the mixture is smooth.

In a medium-sized bowl, beat the egg whites with a wire whisk until they form soft peaks when you lift the whisk out. Fold the whites into the egg-yolk and soured-cream mixture.

Pour the mixture into the prepared soufflé dish. Bake in the centre of the oven for about 35 minutes or until the top has risen and is light golden brown.

Serve immediately.

Allemande, à l'

A term which is applied to dishes garnished or accompanied by such German specialities as smoked sausage, sauerkraut, potato dumplings or pickled pork. The term also refers to dishes served with ALLEMANDE SAUCE.

Allemande Sauce

This classic, French, white sauce is also known as Sauce Blonde or Sauce Parisienne. One of the richest and smoothest of sauces it is served with poultry, veal and eggs.

1 PINT

1$\frac{1}{2}$ oz. [3 tablespoons] butter
1$\frac{1}{2}$ oz. [3 tablespoons] flour
15 fl. oz. [2 cups] hot, strong chicken or veal stock, free of fat
$\frac{1}{2}$ teaspoon salt
$\frac{1}{8}$ teaspoon white pepper
2 egg yolks
5 fl. oz. [$\frac{5}{8}$ cup] single [light] cream

Melt the butter in a medium-sized saucepan over moderate heat. Add the flour and stir with a wooden spoon to blend. Lower the heat and cook for a minute or two. The mixture must not change colour.

Remove from the heat and add the hot stock a little at a time, stirring briskly. When all the stock has been added return the pan to the heat and, stirring all the time, bring the sauce to the boil. Boil for 1 minute.

Remove from the heat and add salt and pepper. The sauce should be quite smooth with no lumps. If, however, it does have lumps push the sauce through a fine sieve.

In a medium-sized mixing bowl blend the egg yolks and cream with a wooden spoon or wire whisk. Slowly add the hot sauce, whisking all the time. When all the sauce has been added and well blended return it to the saucepan. Place it over low heat and, stirring all the time with a wooden spoon, cook the sauce gently for 1 minute. Do not allow it to boil or it will curdle.

Taste the sauce and add more salt and pepper if necessary.

Remove the pan from the heat and pour the sauce into a warmed sauceboat.

Serve at once.

Alligator Pear

A name used in some areas of the United States for the AVOCADO.

Alivenci is an unusual soufflé made with cream cheese and soured cream.

Allspice

This spice comes from a tropical tree that is cultivated in the West Indies and Jamaica and is native to Central America. Sometimes called Jamaica pepper or pimento, the small, sun-dried berries are known as allspice because their taste, as well as their aroma, seem to be a combination of nutmeg, cinnamon and cloves.

Ground allspice is used as a flavouring for cakes, soups, meat dishes and vegetables. Tied in a muslin bag, the allspice berries are often used in the preparation of preserves and pickles.

Allspice Veal Roll

This veal roll is an easily prepared main dish that looks very attractive, particularly if it is garnished with sprigs of watercress or parsley and thin orange slices.

4 SERVINGS

2 lb. breast of veal, boned and trimmed of excess fat
2 oz. [1 cup] fresh white breadcrumbs
1 tablespoon raisins or sultanas
grated rind of 1 orange
1 tablespoon finely chopped parsley
¼ teaspoon dried sage
¼ teaspoon dried thyme
1 tablespoon finely chopped onion
¼ teaspoon salt
freshly ground black pepper
1½ oz. butter [3 tablespoons], cut into pieces
1 tablespoon ground allspice creamed with 1 oz. [2 tablespoons] softened butter
2 oz. [¼ cup] butter, melted
3 tablespoons orange juice

The juice and grated rind of orange flavour this Allspice Veal Roll.

1. *Lay the boned breast of veal, fat side down, on your work surface. Spread the prepared breadcrumb mixture evenly over the meat, keeping it away from the edges. Sprinkle on the salt and 4 grindings of pepper.*

2. *Put the small pieces of butter on the breadcrumb mixture and, pressing down, tightly roll up the veal. Just before the roll is complete, tuck in any of the breadcrumb mixture which has been squeezed out.*

3. *With white cotton string, tie up the veal roll at 1-inch intervals. To do this, cut the string into short lengths. Make a loop at the end of each piece. Put a length round the meat, thread one end through the loop, pull it tight and knot it. Continue with the remaining string.*

Preheat oven to moderate 350°F (Gas Mark 4, 180°C).

Mix together the breadcrumbs, raisins, or sultanas, orange rind, parsley, sage, thyme and the onion.

Put the veal flat on your work surface fat side down. Spread the breadcrumb mixture evenly on the meat. Sprinkle with salt and 4 grindings of pepper. Dot with small pieces of butter. Roll the meat up tightly and tie round with string at 1-inch intervals.

Rub the outer surface of the veal roll with the butter and allspice mixture. Put in a baking dish with melted butter. Pour the orange juice over the meat.

Bake in the centre of the oven, basting occasionally, adding more orange juice if the liquid in the pan reduces too much. Allow 25 minutes to the pound and 25 minutes over.

Put the veal roll on a heated serving plate. Remove the string before serving.

Allumettes

The word *allumettes* (AH-loo-met) literally means matchsticks and is a term used to describe a type of hors d'oeuvre. These are usually strips of pastry stuffed with various fillings, such as a purée of chicken livers, anchovies, sausage meat, breast of chicken with truffles or Parmesan cheese.

Allumettes is also used to describe potatoes which have been cut fine to resemble matchsticks, and then deep fried.

Of Swiss origin is a sweet cake called allumettes which consists of puff pastry cut into strips, spread with a royal icing and baked.

Allumettes

MATCHSTICK POTATOES

Tiny, crisp matchsticks, Allumettes (AH-loo met) are a variety of French deep-fried potatoes. For the best results you need a deep, heavy pan, a wire frying-basket and a cooking thermometer.

4 SERVINGS

2 lb. potatoes
  vegetable oil
  salt

Peel the potatoes and trim them into neat rectangles about 2½-inches long. Drop them into a bowl of cold water to prevent them from discolouring.

With a sharp knife, slice the rectangles lengthways into sticks about ⅛-inch wide and ⅛-inch deep. Soak them in a bowl of cold water for 30 minutes.

Drain the water off the potatoes and dry them thoroughly with a tea towel or kitchen paper. Put at least 3 inches of oil in the pan and heat to 350°F (180°C). Place a handful of allumettes into a wire frying-basket and lower into the hot fat. Fry for 3 minutes, shaking the basket occasionaly to ensure even cooking. Lift the basket to drain the oil from the potatoes and empty them on to kitchen paper.

When all the potatoes are fried, raise the temperature of the oil to about 375°F (190°C). Place the allumettes in the basket and fry again, shaking the basket frequently, for 1 or 2 minutes, or until the potatoes are golden brown. Drain on kitchen paper, sprinkle lightly with salt and serve, very hot, in a warm serving dish.

Almejas a la Marinera

CLAMS IN TOMATO AND GARLIC SAUCE

A Spanish dish, Almejas a la Marinera (ahl-MAY-has a la MAR-in-aira) is clams steamed in white wine and covered with a sauce of tomatoes, onions and garlic. If clams are not available small oysters or cockles can be substituted. This dish may be served as a main course with buttered rice, cooked with a bay leaf, and a salad of lettuce and spring onions [scallions]. For a first course halve the quantities and serve with crusty rolls or French bread.

4 SERVINGS

1½ lb. tomatoes
2 hard-boiled eggs
3 tablespoons olive oil
1 large onion, chopped
2 cloves garlic, crushed
1½ oz. [¾ cup] fresh, coarse, white breadcrumbs
½ teaspoon salt
  coarsely ground black pepper
4 dozen fresh, small clams in shells
15 fl. oz. [2 cups] inexpensive, dry, white wine
2 tablespoons finely chopped parsley
2 lemons, cut in wedges

Low Cal

Put the tomatoes into a bowl. Cover with boiling water. Leave for two minutes.

Thin, crisp Allumettes are a variety of French, deep-fried potatoes.

Remove the tomatoes from the water with a slotted spoon. When they are cool enough to be handled nick the skin with a knife and peel. Chop into small pieces and set aside.

Separate the egg whites from the yolks. Chop the whites into small pieces. Press the yolks through a strainer or if you have a garlic crusher use it instead to sieve the yolks. Set aside.

Heat the oil in a medium-sized frying-pan. Add the onion and fry for 3 minutes. Lower heat, add the garlic and sauté until the onions are soft and transparent but not brown. Add the breadcrumbs, tomatoes, egg yolks, salt and 6 grindings of pepper. Stir and mash with a wooden spoon until the mixture becomes a smooth, thick purée. Set aside.

Place the clams in a heavy pot. Pour the wine over them and bring to the boil. Cover, reduce the heat and simmer for 10 minutes or until the clams open. Throw away any clams that have remained closed.

Place the clams in a deep, heated serving dish. Strain the liquid from the pan and add to the purée. Taste and adjust seasoning by adding more salt and pepper if necessary. Pour the sauce over the clams. Sprinkle with parsley and the egg whites and serve immediately. The lemon wedges should be served on a separate dish.

Almond

The kernel of the fruit of the almond tree of which there are sweet and bitter varieties. The trees are widely grown in Jordan, Spain, North Africa, France and the United States. Sweet almonds are used in making cakes, biscuits, sweets and in savoury dishes. They are also roasted, salted, sugared and ground.

Bitter almonds contain a small amount of poisonous prussic acid. When this is removed the almond oil can be used as a flavouring agent.

Almonds contain protein, fat and minerals, but no starch. More than half their weight is oil which is extracted and used in perfumery or the manufacture of soothing emulsions.

Blanched Almonds

Blanched almonds are those from which the skins have been removed. Although almonds which have been commercially blanched are readily available, almonds are very easy to blanch yourself.

Put the almonds in a small bowl. Boil water in a kettle and pour the boiling water over the almonds until they are completely covered. Leave for about 3 minutes. Remove the almonds one at a time with a spoon and press between the thumb and forefinger. The skin should slip off easily. Dry the almonds on a cloth.

If the blanched almonds are not to be used immediately, put them on a rack in a very cool oven, 225°F (Gas Mark $\frac{1}{4}$, 110°C), for 2 hours to dry. Store the nuts in an airtight container.

Chopped Almonds

Blanch the almonds. Using a sharp knife, chop the almonds into pieces before they are dry. The fineness of the pieces depends on the recipe for which they are required.

Devilled Almonds

Blanch the almonds. Heat a very little butter in a small frying-pan. Add the almonds and toss them in the butter. Dust liberally with salt and a pinch of cayenne pepper. Sprinkle lightly with paprika. Serve with cocktails.

Flaked Almonds

Flaked almonds are mainly used for decorating puddings and cakes. They are available in shops already flaked, but are more tasty done at home immediately before using.

With a sharp knife slit the blanched almonds flatways along the grain so that you make a flat, broad flake. Each almond should make a minimum of four flakes.

Ground Almonds

Used in the making of pastries, biscuits and desserts, commercially ground almonds are widely available. They are, however, easily prepared at home and you will find that they taste better.

Blanch the almonds. Mix them with a few drops of water and a little castor sugar and put them through a fine mincer. They can also be pounded in a mortar with a little castor sugar. If you have a liquidizer, put 4 ounces at a time in the machine and grind at top speed.

Ground almonds should be stored in an airtight container, but if they are not used as soon as possible after grinding they will quickly lose their flavour.

Roasted Almonds

Salted and served as an accompaniment to cocktails or an unsalted, crunchy addition to salads and other dishes, roasted almonds are easy to make at home.

Spread whole, blanched almonds in one layer on a baking tin. Place in a pre-heated, moderate oven 350°F (Gas Mark 4, 180°C), for 10 to 15 minutes. Shake the tin or stir the almonds frequently. Watch carefully to see that they do not burn. Remove from the oven when the almonds are an even, golden brown.

Salted Almonds

An excellent accompaniment to cocktails, salted almonds are widely available in jars and cans, but they are easy to make at home.

4 oz. [$\frac{1}{2}$ cup] butter
4 tablespoons [$\frac{1}{4}$ cup] cooking oil
8 oz. [$1\frac{1}{3}$ cup] whole almonds, blanched
salt

Melt the butter with the oil in a large frying-pan. Put in the almonds and sauté them over a moderate heat, turning them frequently with a slotted spoon. When the almonds are golden brown, remove them with the spoon and spread them out on kitchen paper towels. Sprinkle them with salt while they are still warm, making sure they are well coated.

Salted almonds can be stored in an airtight container for several weeks.

Shredded or Slivered Almonds

Shredded or slivered almonds are used frequently in pastry making and also in confectionery. Blanch the almonds and while they are still damp cut them lengthways into about 15 pieces. If the recipe requires roasted slivers, brown the almonds in the oven after they have been shredded.

Sugared Almonds

Almonds with a sugar or honey coating have been known from earliest times and were recorded as having been served in Ancient Rome at family celebrations. Home-made sugared almonds may not look as beautiful as the commercially made variety, but they surpass them in flavour and texture. They can be stored, for about a week, in an airtight jar.

1 lb. [2 cups] granulated sugar
4 fl. oz. [$\frac{1}{2}$ cup] water
1 teaspoon cinnamon
1 lb. [$2\frac{2}{3}$ cups] unbleached almonds

In a saucepan over low heat dissolve the sugar in the water stirring constantly.

Add the cinnamon, stir, raise the heat and briskly boil the syrup until it falls from the spoon in thick drops. Add the almonds and stir until they are well coated.

Remove the pan from the heat and continue stirring until the syrup dries into sugar.

Put the almonds in a sieve and shake to dislodge the excess sugar. Put the excess sugar back in the pan, add a little water and dissolve again over a low heat. Raise heat and boil until the syrup clears. Add the almonds, stir again until the almonds are coated. Leave to cool and dry.

Almonds

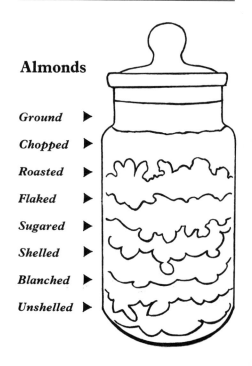

Ground ▶
Chopped ▶
Roasted ▶
Flaked ▶
Sugared ▶
Shelled ▶
Blanched ▶
Unshelled ▶

however, is not always effective. But whether the cherries are well-distributed or sink to the bottom, this cake is delicious.

4 oz. [½ cup] plus 1 teaspoon softened butter
5 oz. [¾ cup] castor sugar
3 large eggs
3½ oz. [⅔ cup] almonds, blanched and ground
1½ oz. plus 2 teaspoons [½ cup] self-raising flour
4 oz. [½ cup] glacé cherries, cut in half
1 teaspoon vanilla essence

Preheat oven to moderate 350°F (Gas Mark 4, 180°C).

Evenly smear 1 teaspoon of butter on the bottom and the sides of a 6¾ × 3¼-inch round cake tin. Sprinkle with 2 teaspoons of flour. Shake the cake tin from side to side to coat the inside surface with a fine film of flour. Tip out excess flour.

In a medium-sized mixing bowl, beat the butter with a wooden spoon until it is very creamy. Add the sugar and beat well until the mixture is light and creamy. Beating continuously, add the eggs one at a time alternating with spoonfuls of ground almonds.

Fold in the flour, cherries and vanilla essence. Turn into the prepared cake tin, gently tapping the tin on the table so that the mixture settles evenly. Bake in the oven for 50 minutes or until a warm, dry skewer comes out clean when inserted in the centre of the cake.

Almond Chicken

An excellent dish for lunch or dinner parties. Almond Chicken can be prepared in advance, reheated in the oven and put under the grill [broiler] just before serving. Serve with buttered broccoli, a tomato salad, crusty rolls and cold, white wine.

4 SERVINGS

1½ oz. [3 tablespoons] butter, plus 1 tablespoon cooking oil
2 chickens each about 2 lb., cut into 6 pieces each
1 small onion, chopped
1 clove garlic, crushed
2 tablespoons flour
12 fl. oz. [1½ cups] chicken stock or a chicken stock cube dissolved in 12 fl. oz. [1½ cups] boiling water
2 tablespoons sherry
2 oz. [⅓ cup] almonds, blanched and shredded
½ teaspoon salt
freshly ground black pepper
1 teaspoon dried tarragon
4 tablespoons [¼ cup heavy] double cream
1 tablespoon Parmesan cheese, grated

Almond Apples

This is an inexpensive and attractive dessert. The apples should be very tart for the best results.

4 SERVINGS

8 oz. [1 cup] granulated sugar
12 fl. oz. [1½ cups] water
4 large, well-shaped, cooking apples, peeled and cored
¼ teaspoon powdered cloves
½ teaspoon powdered cinnamon
½ oz. [1 tablespoon] butter
2 oz. [⅓ cup] almonds, blanched and slivered

In a medium-sized saucepan, over low heat, dissolve the sugar in the water. When the sugar is completely dissolved raise the heat to high and boil the syrup for 5 minutes. Add the apples, lower the heat and simmer covered until the apples are tender.

Preheat the oven to moderate 350°F (Gas Mark 4, 180°C). Remove the apples from the saucepan, place them in an ovenproof dish and set aside. Blend the cloves, cinnamon and butter into the syrup in the saucepan and return it to the heat. Boil the syrup rapidly until it becomes thick.

Pour the syrup into the centres of the apples. Spike the apples all round with the slivered almonds. Bake in the oven for about 15 minutes or until the almonds become brown. Serve very cold with cream.

Almond and Black Cherry Aspic Salad

In the United States sweet aspic salads are often served as an accompaniment to meat and poultry, in the place of the more con-

Almond and Black Cherry Aspic Salad is served with meat or poultry.

___

ventional green or mixed salad. This aspic salad could be served with roast chicken or a roast leg of lamb.

6 SERVINGS

1 tablespoon powdered gelatine
4 fl. oz. [½ cup] cold water
8 fl. oz. [1 cup] orange juice
4 tablespoons sugar
⅛ teaspoon salt
2 fl. oz. [¼ cup] lemon juice
10 oz. [1¼ cups] stoned black cherries, fresh or canned and drained
3 oz. [½ cup] blanched almonds
lettuce

Low Cal

Soak the gelatine in the cold water. Bring the orange juice to the boil. Dissolve the gelatine in it. Add the sugar, salt and lemon juice. Allow to cool to room temperature.

When the mixture begins to set add the cherries and almonds and mix gently. Pour the aspic into a 1½-pint [3¾ cups], wet mould. Chill in the refrigerator until it is firm.

Before serving, dip the mould quickly into a pan of hot water. Unmould the salad on a bed of lettuce leaves.

Almond Cherry Cake

A moist cake which is simple to make, it keeps well and retains its freshness for at least 10 days if it is stored in a tightly-covered cake tin. With this cake, as with all cherry cakes, there is always the problem that the cherries tend to sink to the bottom of the cake. Some cooks recommend rolling the cherries lightly in flour before adding them to the cake batter. This method,

In a large, heavy frying-pan heat the butter and oil until the butter is melted and the mixture is hot but not burning. Put in the chicken pieces a few at a time and brown all over. Remove with a slotted spoon or kitchen tongs and set aside on a plate.

Add the onion and garlic to the pan and sauté for 5 minutes, stirring constantly with a wooden spoon. Sprinkle the flour on the onion mixture and stir well. Add the chicken stock and sherry a little at a time stirring constantly until the sauce is smooth. Raise the heat and bring the mixture to the boil. Add the almonds, salt, 4 grindings of pepper and the tarragon. Return the chicken pieces to the pan and cover. Lower the heat and simmer very gently for 35 to 40 minutes, or until the chicken is tender when pierced with a table fork.

Remove the chicken pieces and arrange in a heated, shallow, fireproof serving dish. Stir the cream into the sauce and heat but do not boil. Pour the sauce over the chicken pieces and sprinkle with grated Parmesan cheese.

Place the dish under the grill [broiler] and brown at high heat, but be careful not to let the cheese burn.

If the dish has been prepared in advance, reheat by covering the serving dish tightly with aluminium foil and placing in a warm oven, 325°F (Gas Mark 3, 170°C) for 45 minutes. Remove and place under the grill and brown.

Almond Cookies

This American cookie recipe is unusual in that no flour is used. Crisp on the outside but chewy inside these cookies are very easy to make.

24 COOKIES

8 oz. [2 cups] almonds, blanched and ground
8 oz. [1⅓ cups] soft brown sugar
1 large egg white
1½ teaspoons butter, melted
cornflour [cornstarch]

Preheat the oven to warm 325°F (Gas Mark 3, 170°C). Prepare a baking sheet by lining it with non-stick silicone paper.

Combine all the ingredients, except the cornflour, in a large mixing bowl and stir until blended. With your hands, mix the ingredients together to form a smooth paste. Shape first into small balls, then flatten into circles. If the mixture is too sticky to handle, first dip your fingers into cornflour and then shape the balls.

Place the circles on the baking sheet and bake for 20 to 25 minutes, or until the cookies are golden brown. Cool the cookies on the baking sheet.

Almond Crunchies

These crunchy biscuits are easy to make and can be served with ice cream, fruit desserts, and with tea.

ABOUT 50 SMALL BISCUITS

6 oz. [¾ cup] sugar
8 oz. [1 cup] softened butter
1 egg yolk
8 oz. [2 cups] flour, sifted
8 oz. [1⅓ cup] almonds, blanched and chopped
¼ teaspoon almond essence

Preheat the oven to moderate 350°F (Gas Mark 4, 180°C).

Line baking sheets with greaseproof paper. In a medium-sized mixing bowl, beat the sugar and butter with a wooden spoon until they are light and creamy. Beat in the egg yolk. Mix in the flour, chopped almonds and almond essence.

Put flour on your hands and pat the dough into a ball. Cover it and chill in the refrigerator for one hour.

Shape the chilled dough into small balls and flatten into rounds. Place on baking sheets and bake for 15 to 20 minutes.

Almond Cherry Cake, which is made with a large proportion of ground almonds and little flour, will keep moist for several days.

Almond and Cucumber Salad Dressing

This is an unusual and delicate dressing for a salad which includes fruit or even for a plain lettuce salad. This recipe makes about 16 fluid ounces [2 cups] of dressing, enough for a salad which serves 8 people. It will keep for several days in the refrigerator in a tightly covered container.

16 FLUID OUNCES

2 egg yolks
2 teaspoons sugar
1 tablespoon melted butter
5 fl. oz. [⅝ cup] milk
2 fl. oz. [¼ cup] vinegar
2 teaspoons salt
 a few grains cayenne pepper
1 teaspoon dry mustard
2 teaspoons cornflour [cornstarch]
2 egg whites
4 oz. [½ cup] cucumber, peeled and sliced
2 oz. [⅓ cup] almonds, blanched and shredded

In the top of a double boiler, or in a bowl over hot water, beat together the egg yolks, sugar, melted butter, 3½ fluid ounces [½ cup] of the milk, vinegar, salt, cayenne and dry mustard. Dissolve the cornflour in 1½ fluid ounces [3 tablespoons] of milk and add it to the other ingredients.

Cook and stir the dressing over boiling water until it is thick. Remove from the heat and set aside. In a mixing bowl beat the egg whites until they form stiff peaks when the whisk is raised. When the dressing is at room temperature fold it into the egg whites. Add the cucumber and almonds and mix lightly. Chill in the refrigerator until ready to serve.

Almond Curry Sauce

A spicy sauce to serve with pot-roasted chicken and browned rice. The recipe calls for a green chilli, but if you are not accustomed to eating pungent food remove the seeds before mincing the chilli. Garam

masala is a prepared, ground spice mixture of cinnamon, cardamom, cloves, cumin seeds, coriander seeds and black pepper. All the ingredients in this recipe are widely available at grocery stores or at Indian, Bangladeshi or Pakistani grocers.

4 SERVINGS

2 tablespoons cooking oil
2 medium-sized onions, minced
¾-inch piece of fresh ginger, peeled and minced or grated
1 green chilli [chili], minced
1 oz. [¼ cup] almonds, blanched and ground
2 teaspoons ground turmeric
1 teaspoon ground coriander
1 teaspoon garam masala
1 x 8 oz. can, Italian tomatoes, sieved
1 oz. [2 tablespoons] creamed coconut
 juice of ½ lemon
1 teaspoon sugar
½ teaspoon salt

Heat the oil in a medium-sized saucepan, add the onions and stir well. Lower the heat to moderate and fry for 8 minutes or until the onions are golden. Add the

Left: Almondine Sauce is a classic almond and butter sauce for fish. Centre left: Almond Custard Sauce is served with puddings, pies and fruit. Above: This Almond and Cucumber Salad Dressing is rich and unusual. Right: Almond Curry Sauce is served with pot-roasted chicken and rice.

ginger and chilli and fry for another minute. Add the almonds, turmeric, coriander and garam masala. Fry for 7 minutes, stirring continuously. If the mixture gets too dry or sticks to the bottom of the pan add a spoonful or two of water.

Add the sieved tomatoes and creamed coconut. Stir until the coconut has dissolved. Add lemon juice, sugar and salt. Stir, raise the heat and bring to the boil. As soon as the sauce is bubbling reduce the heat as low as possible, cover and simmer for 30 minutes. If the sauce is too thick add a little water. Taste and add more salt, sugar or lemon juice if necessary. Serve hot in a separate bowl.

Almond Custard Sauce

The addition of almonds and brandy to a boiled custard makes a delicious sauce for sponge puddings, pies and stewed fruit.

4 SERVINGS

2 egg yolks
1 tablespoon castor sugar
  a pinch of salt
10 fl. oz. [1¼ cups] milk
1 oz. [¼ cup] almonds, blanched and ground
2 teaspoons brandy or 1 teaspoon vanilla essence

In a mixing bowl beat the egg yolks lightly. Beat in the sugar and salt. Put the milk into a saucepan and bring slowly to the boil. Remove from the heat, wait for the milk to go off the boil and pour on to the eggs slowly, stirring all the time.

Return the custard to the pan and cook over a low heat or, preferably, over simmering water until it begins to thicken. Do not let it boil. Stir in the almonds.

Strain the custard. Add the brandy a few drops at a time. Serve warm.

Almond Essence

This flavouring comes from bitter almonds after the oil has been extracted. Today, however, the almond essence used to flavour cakes, puddings and biscuits is generally synthetic.

Almondine Sauce

Simple to make and with a delicate flavour, this classic almond sauce for fish transforms grilled [broiled] or poached fish into a special dish.

4 SERVINGS

2 oz. [¼ cup] unsalted butter
3 oz. [½ cup] almonds, blanched and shredded
½ teaspoon salt

Melt the butter in a small saucepan or frying-pan. Add the almonds and sauté, stirring continuously, until they just begin to brown. Add the salt. Pour over the hot, cooked fish and serve immediately.

23

Alouettes sans Têtes
STUFFED BEEF ROLLS

An interesting and unusual way to serve inexpensive steak, Alouettes sans Têtes (AH-loo-wet sawn tet) makes a good dish for a dinner party. It can be prepared early in the day and warmed in a low oven before serving. Good accompaniments are creamed or sautéed potatoes and a purée of fresh French beans.

4 SERVINGS

- 8 slices of lean beef, each about 5-inches square and ¼-inch thick
- 2 tablespoons cooking oil
- 2 onions, diced
- 2 carrots, diced
- 10 fl. oz. [1¼ cups] beef stock, fresh or made with a stock cube
- ½ lb. tomatoes, peeled, seeded and sliced
- 1 clove garlic, crushed
- 1 bay leaf
- 2 tablespoons chopped parsley

STUFFING
- 6 oz. [¾ cup ground] minced pork or veal
- 1 small onion, finely chopped
- 1 oz. [2 tablespoons] butter softened
- 1 oz.[½ cup]fresh, white breadcrumbs
- 1 tablespoon finely chopped parsley
- 1 teaspoon rubbed sage
- grated rind of 1 lemon
- 1 egg, lightly beaten
- 6 green olives, stoned and coarsely chopped
- ½ teaspoon salt
- black pepper, freshly ground

Preheat the oven to moderate 350°F (Gas Mark 4, 180°C).

To prepare the stuffing, mix the minced pork or veal, the onion, butter, breadcrumbs, parsley, sage, lemon rind and olives together in a bowl. Stir in the egg. Season with the salt and 3 grindings of black pepper. Spread an eighth of stuffing on each piece of steak, roll up carefully and tie with fine thread.

To braise the beef rolls, heat the oil in a large saucepan and brown them a few at a time. Remove them with a slotted spoon and keep them warm.

Add the onions and carrots and, stirring occasionally, cook until brown. Add the stock, tomatoes, garlic and the bay leaf and bring to the boil.

Pour the contents of the saucepan into a casserole dish. Place the beef rolls on

Alouettes sans Têtes is a traditional French dish of stuffed beef rolls in a seasoned tomato sauce.

top. Cover with a well-fitting lid and cook in the oven for 1½ hours.

Remove the beef rolls from the casserole with a slotted spoon. Carefully unwind the thread and place the rolls on a serving dish and keep hot. Holding a sieve over a small saucepan, press the stock and vegetables from the casserole through the sieve with the back of a wooden spoon.

Taste the gravy, add salt and pepper if necessary. Pour over the beef rolls. Sprinkle with chopped parsley just before serving.

Alsacienne, à l'
A great number of preparations are called *à l'alsacienne* (ah-lahl-SAH-see-en). The predominant ingredients in these dishes are sauerkraut, ham and Strasbourg sausage. Certain dishes which are based on *foie gras* are also described by this name.

Alsatian Wines
Alsace, a northeastern province of France, bordering on Germany, is one of the principal wine-producing regions of the country. Alsatian wines are distinguishable by their fruity flavour and fine bouquet. As such, they differ greatly

from those of the rest of France, being far closer to wines of German origin.

Among the best-known wines of the Alsace regions are the Riesling, a fresh white wine with a particularly fragrant bouquet; Sylvaner, a lighter wine than the Riesling with a less sweet fragrance; Gewurztraminer, a dry white wine with a German name and a spicy taste; Muscat, with its characteristic muskiness; Traminer, smooth, fragrant and white, with a sweet flavour; Gentil, white, but remarkably like a rich, red Burgundy in taste.

Aluminium Foil

A wide variety of foods cooked in aluminium foil retain more flavour and food value and remain more moist than when cooked in other ways. Aluminium foil keeps ovens, meat tins and grill [broiler] pans cleaner. It can also be used to shape and mould cake tins and other utensils and to replace lost or broken pan and casserole lids.

When food is cooked in foil, it should always be wrapped loosely to enclose as much air as possible. The enclosed air, when heated, helps to cook the food. Consequently, such foods as vegetables, fish, chops and chicken portions should be wrapped in a large sheet of foil and the edges sealed with double folds or by gathering the edges together to make a bag shape.

For roasting, the foil should not be sealed because a constant supply of the oxygen in the air is needed to brown the meat. To prepare the food for roasting, tear off a piece of foil about three times the length of the meat or poultry. Place the meat in the centre of the foil, lift the two long edges up at right angles, bring the other ends over the top and press firmly together to prevent the parcel from opening during cooking. The foil will contain the fat and juices and prevent the oven from being splashed. It will also allow the meat to brown. If the meat is not as brown or crisp as desired at the end of cooking, open the foil, pour off the fat and juices and return the meat in the open foil to the oven for 10 to 15 minutes.

Individual portions of chicken, chops and steaks are prepared by frying the meat until browned and then wrapping them in a loose foil parcel with sealed edges. Herbs, chopped vegetables and sauces can be added to give extra flavour. Cook at 350°F (Gas Mark 4, 180°C) for 45 minutes to 1½ hours according to thickness.

Vegetables wrapped in loose foil parcels can be cooked in the oven with the meat, or boiled. Add seasonings,

Roasting in Aluminium Foil			
Times given can only be an approximate guide because the shape of the roast and the proportion of bone affects the required cooking time.		Minutes per lb. At 400°F Gas Mark 6, 200°C	Minutes per lb. At 325°F Gas Mark 3, 170°C
Boneless beef:	Rare	20	27
	Medium	25	33
	Well-done	30	40
Beef with bone		Allow 5 minutes less per lb.	
Mutton and lamb		25	33
Pork, veal and stuffed meat		30	40
Gammon and ham		25 to 30	33 to 40
Chicken		15 to 20	20 to 27
Turkey		12 to 15	16 to 20
		At 375°F Gas Mark 5, 190°C	
Fillets and steaks of fish		20 to 30 minutes	according to
Whole fish		30 to 40 minutes	thickness

butter and, if baked, 1 to 2 tablespoons stock or water. If the vegetables are sliced or cut into small pieces, they will cook more quickly than if they are left whole. Allow 1½ to 2 times the normal boiling time.

Ambrosia
ORANGE DESSERT

A favourite dessert in the Southern States of America, in its simplest form Ambrosia consists of thinly sliced oranges sprinkled with shredded coconut and sugar. The

A favourite dessert in the Southern States of America, Ambrosia is made of oranges, pineapple and coconut.

following recipe includes pineapple, but other fruits can be substituted.

4 SERVINGS

3 large oranges
1 small pineapple
1 oz. [⅛ cup superfine] castor sugar
3 oz. [⅜ cup] fresh coconut, coarsely grated, or coarse, desiccated coconut soaked in 4 fl. oz. [½ cup] of water for 30 minutes and then drained

Peel the oranges, carefully removing all the white pith, and cut into thin slices. Peel, slice and core the pineapple and cut each slice into 8 pieces. Combine the sugar and coconut.

In a serving bowl or individual glasses, arrange the orange slices in alternate layers with the pineapple. Sprinkle each layer with a little of the coconut and sugar mixture, keeping enough aside to sprinkle on the top. Chill in the refrigerator for at least 2 hours before serving.

Américaine, à l'

À l'Américaine (ah-lah-MAY-ree-cane) is the name given to various methods of preparing meat, fish, eggs and vegetables. The most famous of these preparations is HOMARD À L'AMÉRICAINE. According to the renowned nineteenth-century chef, Escoffier, this dish originated in Le Restaurant Français in Nice. Made from crayfish and prepared with tomatoes and white wine, it was originally called Langouste de la Méditeranée. Its present name was given it by a Provençal chef who emigrated to the United States in the nineteenth century. Using lobsters instead of crayfish, he first served Homard à l'Américaine in New York in 1860. Since then it has been famous and the classic recipe is given in Escoffier's book, *Ma Cuisine*.

American Apple Pie

Traditional American Apple Pie differs from other apple pies in several ways. First, the pastry is made with a greater proportion of fat to flour than are other pie crusts. In the filling, the apples are cut in rather thick slices. The filling is spiced with cinnamon, allspice and nutmeg and thickened with cornflour [cornstarch]. In the United States, apple pie is frequently served warm with a dollop of vanilla ice cream atop each wedge.

6 TO 8 SERVINGS

PASTRY
12 oz. [3 cups] flour
¼ teaspoon salt
6 oz. [¾ cup] white vegetable fat [shortening]
5-6 tablespoons ice water
1 tablespoon milk or thin cream for glazing
castor [superfine] sugar for dusting

FILLING
2¼ lb. large tart cooking apples
1 tablespoon lemon juice
6 oz. [¾ cup] sugar

1 oz. [2 tablespoons] cornflour [cornstarch]
1 teaspoon finely grated lemon rind
1 teaspoon ground cinnamon
½ teaspoon ground allspice
½ teaspoon freshly grated nutmeg
1 oz. [2 tablespoons] butter, in small pieces plus extra

For the pastry, sift the flour and salt into a large bowl. Cut the fat into the flour until the mixture resembles coarse breadcrumbs. Sprinkle with water, 1 tablespoon at a time, tossing lightly with a fork until the mixture begins to cling together and forms a soft dough.

Gather the mixture into a ball with your fingers. Divide into 2 pieces, making 1 piece larger than the other. Wrap separately in cling film and chill in the refrigerator.

Preheat the oven to 425°F (Gas Mark 7, 220°C).

For the filling, peel, quarter, core and thickly slice the apples, then sprinkle with lemon juice to prevent discoloration.

A traditional American Apple Pie has a double crust and spiced filling.

For the American Apple Pie, line the dish with half the pastry and trim off the excess with a knife.

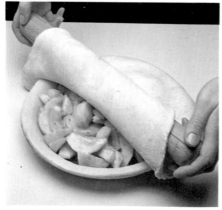

Put the apple filling in the lined dish and, lifting the pastry on the rolling pin, lay it over the top.

Trim the pastry to within ¼-inch of the dish. Tuck the overhanging pastry under the edge of the bottom crust.

Press the two edges of the pastry together to seal them and to make a crimped pattern on the crust.

Mix the sugar with the cornflour [cornstarch], lemon rind and spice; sprinkle over the apples and toss.

Roll out the larger piece of pastry $1\frac{1}{2}$ inches larger all round than the top of a $2\frac{1}{4}$-pint pie dish. Lift the pastry on a rolling pin and unroll over the dish. Press gently in place with your fingers.

Spoon the apples into the dish, mounding them. Dot with butter. Brush the pastry edge lightly with water.

Roll out the remaining pastry $\frac{1}{2}$ inch larger all round than the top of the dish. Lift the pastry on the rolling pin and unroll over the filling. Trim the pastry to within $\frac{1}{2}$ inch of the dish. Tuck the overhang under to build up the edge, pressing the edge and crimp.

Brush the top crust with milk or cream and sprinkle with castor sugar. Cut 3 or 4 small slits in the top or prick in several places with a fork, to make small vents, to allow the steam to escape during cooking.

To prevent overbrowning, cover the pastry edges with foil before baking.

These cocktail snacks, Amuse-Gueules au Fromage, are made with blue cheese.

Remove the foil for the last 10-15 minutes.

Place the dish on a baking sheet and bake for 15 minutes. Lower the heat to 375°F (Gas Mark 5, 190°C) and bake for 30-35 minutes more, until the pastry is crisp. This pie can be served warm or cold.

If you intend to freeze it, set aside to cool completely then freeze in a rigid container for up to 8 months. Defrost for 30 minutes then reheat at 350°F (Gas Mark 4, 180°C).

Amuse-Gueules au Fromage

CHEESE COCKTAIL SNACKS

Amuse-Gueules au Fromage (AH-mooz-gerl oh froh-MAJ) are good cold hors d'oeuvre to serve with pre-dinner drinks or at a cocktail party. They are best served on cocktail sticks. Very simple and quick to make, the cheese balls look elegant and can be prepared well before the time you will need them. Although traditionally prepared with Roquefort cheese they can more economically be made with any blue cheese.

3 oz. [$\frac{3}{8}$ cup] butter, softened
$\frac{1}{2}$ lb. Roquefort or other blue cheese
1 tablespoon finely chopped onion
1 tablespoon finely chopped celery
$\frac{1}{4}$ teaspoon freshly ground black pepper
$\frac{1}{2}$ teaspoon Worcestershire sauce
1 teaspoon brandy
2 tablespoons chopped parsley
$\frac{1}{2}$ teaspoon paprika
5 tablespoons fine white breadcrumbs

Place the butter in a mixing bowl. Cut the cheese into pieces and add to the butter. Using a wooden spoon, cream the butter and cheese until they are blended. Beat in the onion, celery, black pepper, Worcestershire sauce and brandy.

If the mixture is very firm, beat in more butter, a little at a time. Divide into small pieces and roll into small balls.

Mix the parsley, paprika and breadcrumbs together in a bowl.

Dip the cheese balls into the breadcrumb mixture and press them gently so the cheese balls are well coated.

Arrange on a serving dish and put into the refrigerator for at least 45 minutes.

Anchovy

A small member of the same family as the herring, which it resembles in colour and shape, the anchovy is usually not more than 3 inches long. The fresh anchovy has a very delicate flavour but, as the flesh quickly deteriorates, it is eaten fresh only on the Mediterranean coasts and the Atlantic coasts of Portugal and Spain where it is caught.

Anchovies are preserved in salt and this develops their special flavour and colour. They are widely available canned or bottled in oil, or preserved in brine. Because of their very strong, distinctive flavour, preserved anchovies are used only in small quantities as an ingredient of sauces for cold meat and poultry, and for flavouring meat and fish dishes. Fillets of anchovies are often included in French hors d'oeuvre and Italian antipasto, and are a garnish for many dishes.

Dry, salted anchovies should be soaked in cold water for several hours before use to remove some of the salt. The skins can be removed by rubbing on a cloth or by gentle scraping with a knife. The tails should be cut off and the bone removed after splitting the fish open with the index finger and thumb.

Salted anchovies will keep well if they are covered by the brine. Those preserved in oil will also keep well, after the can or bottle is opened, if they are covered by oil.

Anchovy Butter

This quickly prepared savoury spread may be used for hors d'oeuvre, canapes, or as an unusual topping for grilled fish.

4 OUNCES

4 oz. [½ cup] butter
8 anchovy fillets, finely chopped
2 teaspoons lemon juice
2 teaspoons chopped parsley

Cream the butter until it is soft. Add the anchovy fillets and, with a wooden spoon, beat until smooth. Mix in the lemon juice and chopped parsley. Chill.

Anchovy Essence

Commercially made for flavouring sauces and stuffings, anchovy essence is a mixture of anchovies, cayenne pepper, capers and various herbs.

Anchovy fillets, which have a strong distinctive flavour, are used as a garnish and are the main ingredient of many savoury dishes.

Anchovy Rolls

These small savoury rolls can be served as canapés at cocktail parties or as an accompaniment to drinks before a dinner party.

thinly sliced, 1-day-old, white
bread
butter for spreading
prepared mustard
salt and pepper
hard cheese, grated
anchovy fillets
melted butter

Preheat oven to hot 425°F (Gas Mark 7, 220°C).

Remove the crusts from the bread. Spread each slice with butter and mustard. Sprinkle with salt, pepper and cheese. Put an anchovy fillet on each slice and roll up, securing with a wooden cocktail stick.

Prepare as many rolls as you require. Place them on a baking sheet, brush with melted butter and bake in the oven until the rolls are golden brown, about 7 to 8 minutes.

Cut each roll in half, so that they are easy to handle. Serve immediately.

Anchoyade
ANCHOVY HORS D'OEUVRE

In Provence, from where this recipe comes, Anchoyade (on-show-yahd), is served with a glass of wine or with drinks. There are many variations of Anchoyade. Minced, raw onion and chopped, hard-boiled egg can be sprinkled on the top. A few drops of

brandy can be added to the paste, and after spreading the toast, it can be browned in the oven. This is a simple recipe.

4 SERVINGS

2 oz. canned anchovies
1 clove garlic
1 tablespoon olive oil
½ teaspoon vinegar
several grindings of black pepper
4 slices brown bread

Put the anchovies and garlic in a mortar and, with a pestle, pound to a coarse paste. Add the olive oil, vinegar and pepper and mix well. Meanwhile, toast the bread on one side only. Cut each slice into 4 pieces. Spread the anchovy paste on to the untoasted side. Serve with drinks.

Anchoyade à la Niçoise

Another variation of Anchoyade, Anchoyade à la Niçoise (on-show-yahd ah lah nee-SWAHZ) may be made with fried bread instead of toast.

2 SERVINGS

2 oz. canned anchovies
1 tablespoon plus one teaspoon olive oil
½ teaspoon vinegar
black pepper
8 shallots, or small onions, chopped
5 sprigs parsley, chopped
4 slices brown bread, toasted on one side only
2 tomatoes, sliced
2 tablespoons breadcrumbs
1 clove garlic, crushed

Pound the anchovies in a mortar to a paste. Add 1 tablespoon of oil, vinegar and pepper and mix well. Add the shallots and parsley, less 1 teaspoon, and spread on the toast. Place the sliced tomatoes on top. Mix the breadcrumbs, crushed garlic, 1 teaspoon of parsley and 1 teaspoon of olive oil together and sprinkle on top. Brown under a hot grill for a few minutes.

Ancienne, à l'

A l'Ancienne (ah l'on-SEE-en) literally means 'in the old style'. It is usually applied to preparations with a mixed garnish. It is most commonly used to describe braised dishes, ragoûts in pastry shells and for some veal and chicken BLANQUETTES and FRICASSEES.

Andalouse, à l'

A l'Andalouse (ah l'ON-dah-looze) is the name given to preparations which are characterized mainly by tomatoes, sweet pimientoes, rice and, sometimes, small sausages.

Andalousian Beefsteaks

This Spanish recipe for minced steak is enlivened by the addition of sherry to the gravy. Served with a simple pilaff and sautéed tomatoes, it is a delicious variation of the inexpensive and ordinary hamburger.

Andalousian Beefsteaks are a variation of the inexpensive hamburger.

4 SERVINGS

PILAFF
8 oz. [1 cup] long-grain rice
19 fl. oz. [2⅜ cups] water
2 bay leaves
1 teaspoon salt
1 onion, chopped
2 tablespoons butter
4 cloves
STEAKS
2 oz. [¼ cup] butter
1½ lb. minced [ground] steak
1 medium-sized onion, chopped
1 small clove garlic, crushed
1 teaspoon salt
freshly ground pepper
4 tablespoons flour
3 tablespoons cooking oil
4 tomatoes, cut in halves
3 fl. oz. [⅜ cup] sherry

Wash and soak the rice in cold water for 30 minutes. Drain the rice and put in a medium-sized saucepan with the water, the bay leaves and salt. Bring it to the boil over high heat. When the water is boiling vigorously, cover the pan and turn the heat to very low. After 10 minutes, the rice should be cooked and the water completely absorbed. If the rice is still damp, leave covered for another 5 minutes.

In a small frying-pan over moderate heat, sauté the onion and cloves in the butter until the onion is soft. Discard the cloves and mix the onion into the boiled rice. Set aside and keep hot.

To prepare the steaks, melt half the butter in a small frying-pan over moderate heat and lightly fry the onion and garlic. Put the minced beef in a mixing bowl. Add the cooked onion and garlic, salt and 7 grindings of pepper. Mix well, using your hands, and shape into 8 flat, round patties. Dip each patty into the flour and fry in oil in a large frying-pan. While the meat is cooking, melt remaining butter in a small frying-pan and sauté the tomato halves.

When the steaks are cooked, about 15 minutes, pile the pilaff in the centre of a serving dish and place the patties around it. Place a half tomato on each steak. Raise the heat under the large frying-pan and add the sherry to the meat juices. Boil quickly for 2 minutes. Pour over the steaks and serve.

Andalousian Chicken

Chicken stuffed with ham and rice and colourfully garnished, this adaptation of a Spanish dish is inexpensive and impressive, but it does take time to prepare.

1 chicken, about 4 lb.
2 oz. [¼ cup] butter
1 tablespoon olive oil
1 large onion
1 bouquet garni (consisting of 3
  sprigs of parsley, 1 small bay leaf
  and 1 spray of thyme tied together)
  or ½ teaspoon dried bouquet garni
1 teaspoon salt
  freshly ground pepper
1 scant tablespoon flour
2 tablespoons tomato purée
4 fl. oz. [½ cup] white wine
STUFFING
4 oz. [2 cups] cooked rice
4 oz. [½ cup] cooked ham, diced
2 teaspoons paprika
1 teaspoon salt
GARNISH
2 tablespoons oil
1 large onion, sliced in rings
2 large sweet peppers, sliced in
  rings, seeded and with the white
  pith removed

Stuffed with ham and rice, Andalousian Chicken is a delicious and attractive way to serve pot-roasted chicken.

1 lb. tomatoes, peeled and chopped
1 teaspoon salt
  freshly ground pepper

Wash the chicken inside and out and dry it using kitchen paper towels. Mix the rice, ham, paprika and salt together and stuff the chicken with the mixture. Pin the neck flap neatly over the back with a small skewer.

Heat the butter and oil in a heavy stewing pan. Lightly brown the chicken on all sides. Add the onion and the bouquet garni. Lower the heat, cover and cook for about 1 hour, or until the chicken is tender.

While the chicken is cooking, make the garnish. Heat the oil in a frying-pan over moderate heat. Sauté the onions for 2 to 3 minutes. Add the peppers, tomatoes,

salt and 5 grindings of pepper and cook gently until the vegetables are soft. Set aside and keep hot.

Remove the chicken from the pan. Place on a heated serving dish. Remove the skewer. Surround with the garnish.

Discard the onion and bouquet garni from the stew pan. Place the pan on a high heat. Sprinkle in the flour, stirring constantly with a wooden spoon. Stir in the tomato purée and the wine. Still stirring, bring to the boil. Pour over the chicken. Serve immediately.

Andouille

A very large pork sausage, which is popular in Normandy in France, Andouille (ON-dwee) is made from the large intestines and stomach of the pig. It is usually eaten cold, cut in thin slices, as an hors d'oeuvre. Also sold uncooked, Andouille may be served hot, after being poached and grilled, with a garnish of mashed potatoes.

Andouillettes

Similar to ANDOUILLE, Andouillettes (ON-dwee-yet) are made from the small intestines of the pig. In France, Andouillettes are usually sold already poached. They are then grilled and served with mashed potatoes.

Angelica

This herb, which grows wild in the Alps, in the Pyrenees and in northern Europe, has always been highly valued because every part of the plant has some use. Oil distilled from the seeds and roots is used in flavouring liqueurs and wines. The leaves are used for flavouring stewed fruit. The fresh stalks and leaf stems, candied in sugar, are used to garnish desserts and as a flavouring.

Angelica Tart

This pleasant dessert is a rich, shortcrust pastry filled with a bland cream cheese filling and flavoured with candied angelica.

ONE 8-INCH TART

PASTRY
4 oz. [1 cup] flour
$\frac{1}{8}$ teaspoon salt
2 oz. [$\frac{1}{4}$ cup] butter
2 teaspoons sugar
1 egg yolk
2 to 3 tablespoons cold water

FILLING
8 oz. cream cheese
3 oz. [$\frac{3}{8}$ cup] sugar
2 tablespoons double [heavy] cream
2 eggs, lightly beaten
2 oz. [$\frac{1}{3}$ cup] crystallized angelica, chopped into very small pieces

Sift the flour and salt into a large mixing bowl. Add the butter and using your fingertips rub it into the flour until the mixture resembles fine breadcrumbs. Stir in the sugar.

Beat the egg yolk with 2 tablespoons of the water. Stir this into the flour-and-butter mixture. Add the extra water if necessary to make a firm dough. Lightly knead the pastry and chill in the refrigerator for 15 minutes. Preheat the oven to moderate 350°F (Gas Mark 4, 180°C).

For the filling, press the cream cheese through a strainer into a bowl. Add the sugar and beat until well blended. Stir in the cream and eggs. Beat well to mix, then fold in the angelica.

On a floured board, roll out the pastry and line an 8-inch pie dish. Ease the pastry into the dish and trim the edges with a knife. Prick the bottom of the pastry with a fork. Spoon in the filling and bake for about 45 minutes until the filling is firm. Cool before serving.

Angélique Confite

CANDIED ANGELICA

If you grow your own angelica or can buy it fresh, it is worthwhile making your own Angélique Confite (on-JAY-leek con-feet). Although it takes over a week to prepare —most of which time it is drying on a rack—it is easy to do. Once made it must be kept in a well-stoppered jar. Use it for cakes, trifles and tarts.

12 x 4-inch lengths of tender, young angelica stems
1 pint [2$\frac{1}{2}$ cups] boiling water
1 lb. [2 cups] granulated sugar
1 pint [2$\frac{1}{2}$ cups] water
extra sugar

Place the angelica in a mixing bowl. Pour the boiling water over it and leave to soak for 24 hours.

Remove the angelica. Peel and wash in cold, running water. Put remaining water and the sugar in a saucepan.

Over a low heat, dissolve the sugar. When it is completely dissolved raise the heat and bring to the boil. Boil for 10 minutes. Add the angelica and continue to boil for 20 minutes.

Remove the angelica from the pan and place on a rack. Cover the syrup and set aside. Leave the angelica to dry for 3 days.

After 3 days, bring the syrup to the boil, add the angelica and boil for 20 minutes. Remove the angelica and leave on a rack for 4 days. Sprinkle with sugar and store in an airtight bottle.

Angel Cake

A truly North American cake, Angel Cake has an incredibly light and airy texture.

8 SERVINGS

7 oz. [$\frac{7}{8}$ cup] castor sugar
3 oz. [$\frac{3}{4}$ cup] flour
1 oz. [2 tablespoons] cornflour [cornstarch]
$\frac{1}{4}$ teaspoon salt
10 egg whites
1 tablespoon lemon juice
1 tablespoon hot water
1 teaspoon cream of tartar
1 teaspoon vanilla essence

Preheat oven to moderate 350°F (Gas Mark 4, 180°C), with a shelf placed just below centre of oven. Select a 9-inch American angel cake pan or spring-form cake tin with a tube centre (ungreased).

Sift the flours with the salt, add one third of the sugar and sift together 3 times.

Put the egg whites into a bowl with the lemon juice and hot water, whisk until foamy. Add the cream of tartar and 1 tablespoon of sugar and whisk until soft peaks form. Gradually whisk in the remaining sugar, 1 tablespoon at a time.

Add the vanilla. Sift $\frac{1}{4}$ flour mixture over the egg whites and fold in until incorporated. Repeat with the remaining flour.

Turn the mixture into the tin and level the surface, then cut through the mixture with a palette knife to burst air pockets.

Bake the cake for 45 minutes or until dry and firm.

Invert the tin over the neck of a bottle and leave until cold.

Run a palette knife around the sides, then turn out.

Angels on Horseback

An English savoury, this unusual hot hors d'oeuvre may be served as an accompaniment to before-dinner drinks or as a first course.

4 SERVINGS

8 oysters without shells
8 strips of bacon
8 wooden cocktail sticks
8 buttered slices of toast
salt
pepper
parsley, chopped

Preheat grill [broiler] to high.

Roll each oyster in a strip of bacon, sprinkle with salt and pepper, fasten with

An American favourite, Angel Cake is a very light, impressive dessert.

Anguilla Marinate

MARINATED EEL

  ①

A favourite Venetian dish, Anguilla Marinate (ahn-GWEE-lah mah-ree-NAH-tay) can be prepared a day in advance and kept covered in the refrigerator. The flavour of the eels improves with several hours of marinating.

6 SERVINGS

```
  6 tablespoons oil
  1 lb. onions, finely sliced
  2 cloves garlic, finely chopped
  2 bay leaves
  1 teaspoon dried rosemary
  8 peppercorns
  6 fl. oz. [¾ cup] wine vinegar
  6 fl. oz. [¾ cup] water
2½ lb. eels, skinned and cleaned
  4 oz. [1 cup] flour
  ½ teaspoon salt
  ½ teaspoon pepper
```

In a saucepan, heat half the oil and sauté the onions and garlic for 5 minutes over moderate heat. Add the bay leaves, rosemary and peppercorns and continue cooking for another 4 minutes. Pour in the vinegar and water. Season with the salt and pepper and simmer uncovered over a low heat for 15 minutes.

Meanwhile, cut the eels into 3-inch pieces. Season the flour with salt and pepper and roll the pieces of eel in the mixture. Fry the eel in remaining oil in a large frying-pan for about 10 minutes. Place the fried eels in a deep dish and pour the hot marinade over them. Cool, then refrigerate. Leave for several hours before serving.

To serve, arrange the eel pieces on a serving dish and spoon a little of the marinade over them.

Anguilles au Vert

EELS IN GREEN SAUCE

  ①

A Flemish dish, Anguilles au Vert (on-GWEE-yeh oh vair) are eels simmered with wine, butter and green herbs. Occasionally eaten hot, it is preferable to serve this dish when it is cold. Fresh herbs should be used whenever possible, but if they are not available, half quantities of dried herbs can be substituted. Such herbs as sorrel and chervil can be included when available. Tender nettles can be substituted for the spinach. Anguilles au Vert can be served as

---

a cocktail stick and grill, turning frequently, until the bacon is cooked. Remove cocktail sticks and place on hot, buttered slices of toast. Garnish with parsley and serve very hot.

Anglaise, à l'

A l'Anglaise (ah LON-glaze) is the name given to preparations which are most often cooked in water or in white stock. The term also applies to fish poached in court bouillon, fish rolled in breadcrumbs and then grilled or fried, and potatoes which are steamed or boiled in water.

Angler Fish

Also known as Frogfish and Sea Devil, this large and ugly fish has a flat, spiky head with an enormous mouth. Three filaments grow out of its forward dorsal fin, the longest one acting as a bait to attract prey. Angler fish is a bottom-living fish and is found on the Atlantic seaboard of Europe and North America. It has no scales and is flabby and sticky to

touch. Gastronomically, it is rather tasteless and is used mainly as an ingredient of fish soups.

Angostura

The bark of a small South American tree, angostura is aromatic and bitter and is used in medicines and beverages. It is also the patent name of a brand of bitters which has a basis of rum and is flavoured with aromatic herbs. Although originally intended to be used for medicinal purposes, angostura is now used in the preparation of pink gin and other cocktails and as a flavouring for some fruit dishes.

Animelle

A culinary term for the testicles of animals, in particular those of rams. In the past, *animelle* (a-nee-mehl) were eaten in France, Italy and Spain, but they are less popular today. They can, however, still be found in meat markets in many Middle Eastern countries.

a main dish or, if the quantities are halved, as a first course.

4 SERVINGS

3 oz. [⅜ cup] butter
½ lb. spinach, washed and chopped
1 teaspoon chopped, fresh tarragon
3 tablespoons chopped, parsley
1 teaspoon chopped, fresh sage
2 eels, about 1 lb. each, skinned,
  cleaned and cut into 3-inch pieces
  freshly ground pepper
1 teaspoon salt
10 fl. oz. [1¼ cups] white wine
3 egg yolks
1 tablespoon lemon juice

In a large, heavy frying-pan, melt the butter and lightly sauté the spinach, tarragon, parsley and sage. Add the eel pieces and stir with a wooden spoon to mix all the ingredients. Season with the salt and 8 grindings of pepper. Add the wine and bring to the boil. Lower the heat, cover and simmer for 10 to 15 minutes or until the eel pieces are tender. Remove from the heat.

In a bowl, lightly beat the egg yolks until mixed. Stir in, a spoonful at a time, 4 tablespoons of the hot liquid from the pan in which the eels cooked. Pour the egg mixture very slowly into the pan, stirring continuously. Add the lemon juice, taste and add more salt and pepper if necessary. Pour into a serving dish and refrigerate. Serve very cold.

Anise

Anise, which is also known as sweet cumin, is one of the sweetest smelling of

herbs. It produces aniseed which are small, light brown and have a liquorice flavour. The plant is a member of the carrot family and has feathery leaves. Found mainly in Egypt, Greece and Asia Minor, anise is a popular flavouring throughout Europe.

Anise has certain medicinal uses, although its main use is in the manufacture of liquors. It is also used as a flavouring in many culinary preparations.

Anise Fork Biscuits [Cookies]

Aniseed makes a change of flavouring for fork biscuits which are traditionally flavoured with lemon or chocolate.

ABOUT 28 BISCUITS

4 oz. [½ cup] butter, softened
2 oz. castor [¼ cup fine] sugar
1 heaped teaspoon aniseed
1 large egg
5 oz. [1¼ cups] self-raising flour
  a pinch of salt

Preheat the oven to moderate 350°F (Gas Mark 4, 180°C). Line a baking sheet with non-stick silicone paper.

Beat the butter with a wooden spoon until it is soft. Add the sugar and continue beating until the mixture is light. Mix in the aniseed. Add the egg and beat until it is well mixed. Add the flour gradually with the salt and stir in well.

Shape the dough into small balls. Place them on the baking sheet leaving space between them. Using a fork dipped in water, flatten out each ball. Bake in a moderate oven for 15 minutes.

Aniseed-flavoured carrots make an unusual and interesting vegetable dish.

Aniseed Carrots

This is an unusual combination of flavours and makes a most interesting vegetable dish to serve with roasted or grilled meat, chicken or fish.

4 SERVINGS

1½ lb. carrots
1 tablespoon soft brown sugar
2 oz. [¼ cup] butter
1 heaped teaspoon aniseed
1 teaspoon salt
¼ teaspoon pepper

Wash and scrape the carrots and cut off the tops. If you are using small carrots leave them whole. Large carrots should be cut in quarters lengthways.

Put the sugar, butter, aniseed, salt and pepper into a saucepan. When the mixture begins to bubble add the carrots. Stir well, cover, lower the heat and simmer for about 15 minutes or until the carrots are tender when pierced with a table fork. Serve hot.

Aniseed Sugar

Aniseed sugar is used for flavouring cakes, sponges, biscuits [cookies] and creams. The proportion of aniseed to sugar varies according to the strength of flavour required. For instance, for a cake, 2 tablespoons aniseed are added to 1 pound of castor sugar. For creams and custards, however, the proportion can go

Ani

up to 4 ounces [½ cup] of aniseed to 1 pound of castor sugar.

To make aniseed sugar, clean the aniseed by rubbing the seeds on a sieve to remove the stalks. Dry them in a very cool oven for about 6 hours and then pound in a mortar with the sugar until it is very fine. Push through a fine sieve and use.

Anisette

A liqueur the flavour of which is obtained principally from aniseed. The best French Anisette is made at Bordeaux.

Antipasto

In Italy, dinner begins with antipasto, the appetizer. There are no rules about the combinations of food included in an antipasto but the preparation of an attractive antipasto plate requires ingenuity. Its taste and colour appeal depend on the variety of foods as well as on their arrangement.

Lettuce and sliced fennel, for example, used as a green and white border will improve the appearance of even a simple selection of celery, radishes, small pickled beets, salami and anchovies. To this platter a few large green and/or black olives and strips of brilliant pimiento can be added.

Another typical Italian antipasto would include pickled mushrooms, halved or sliced hard-boiled eggs, tuna fish roe, lettuce, and very thin slices of prosciutto, Italian ham.

Small pickled green peppers, artichoke hearts, pimiento strips, slices of fennel, sliced dry pork sausage and anchovy fillets would be another delicious combination.

When the choice of foods has been made and the serving plate arranged, it is customary to pour a little olive oil and a very small quantity of wine vinegar over the food.

Apéritif

Apéritif (ah-PAY-ree-teef) is the French name for a drink which is taken before meals and considered an appetite stimulant. *Apéritifs* differ in alcoholic content and flavour and are often bitter. They are drunk alone or diluted with water. One of the most popular *apéritifs* is VERMOUTH.

Antipasto, the colourful Italian first course of meat, eggs, fish and raw and cooked vegetables, arranged for two, four and six servings.

Apfelbettelmann

GERMAN APPLE PUDDING

An apple pudding which comes from the south of Germany, Apfelbettelman (AHP-fehl-bet-tel-mun) is very easy to make.

6 SERVINGS

3 oz. [½ cup] raisins
3 fl. oz. [⅜ cup] orange juice
    grated rind of 1 small lemon
2 oz. [¼ cup] butter, softened
8 oz. [2½ cups] breadcrumbs, made
    from pumpernickel bread
6 oz. [¾ cup] brown sugar
4 oz. [⅔ cup] almonds, chopped
1 teaspoon ground mixed spice
4 tablespoons melted butter
1½ lb. cooking apples

Soak the raisins in a mixing bowl with the orange juice and lemon rind for at least 30 minutes.

Preheat the oven to moderate 350°F (Gas Mark 4, 180°C). Grease a 3-pint ovenproof dish with 1 tablespoon butter.

Add the breadcrumbs, sugar, almonds, mixed spice and melted butter to the raisins.

Peel, core and thinly slice the apples. Put one-third of the breadcrumb mixture into the dish and place half the apple slices on top. Add another third of the breadcrumbs and then the remaining apples. Finish with the remaining bread-crumbs. Dot with the rest of the softened butter and bake for 35 minutes.

Apfelkuchen

GERMAN APPLE AND CUSTARD TART

An unusual apple tart from Bavaria, Apfelkuchen (AHP-fehl-KOO-khen) is a combination of apples, rum, eggs and cream.

6 SERVINGS

PASTRY
6 oz. [1½ cups] flour
3 oz. [⅜ cup] unsalted butter
1 tablespoon castor sugar
    grated rind of 1 lemon
2 egg yolks
FILLING
1 oz. [⅓ cup] breadcrumbs mixed
    with 2 tablespoons melted butter
1 lb. cooking apples, peeled, cored
    and sliced thinly
2 tablespoons currants soaked in
    2 tablespoons rum
CUSTARD
1 whole egg plus 1 yolk
2 tablespoons castor [fine] sugar
10 fl. oz. double cream [1¼ cups heavy
    cream]

1 tablespoon sugar

Preheat the oven to moderate 350°F (Gas Mark 4, 180°C).

For the pastry, sift the flour into a mixing bowl. With a knife, cut in the chilled butter until it forms small pieces. Using your fingertips, rub the butter into the flour until the mixture looks like fine breadcrumbs. Add the sugar and lemon rind. With a spoon, mix in the egg yolks one at a time. Then, using your hands, work the pastry until it is smooth.

Line a cake tin which is about 7½-inches in diameter, 2-inches deep and has a removable bottom, with the pastry, using your fingers to press it evenly into the bottom and sides.

To fill the tart crust, first spread the breadcrumb and melted butter mixture on the bottom. Place the apples on top. Remove the currants from the rum and put the rum aside. Sprinkle the currants over the apples. Bake in the oven for 25 minutes.

Reset the oven to warm 300°F (Gas Mark 1, 150°C).

To make the custard, beat the eggs and sugar with a whisk until thick. Beat in the rum and cream. Pour half the mixture evenly over the apples. Return to the oven and bake for 20 minutes or until the custard is set. Pour the remaining custard over the top and bake for 30 minutes more.

Remove the tart from the oven and reset to moderate 350°F (Gas Mark 4, 180°C). Sprinkle the top of the tart with the sugar. Place the tart on the topmost rack of the oven and brown lightly for about 10 minutes. Let the tart cool. Carefully remove from the cake tin before serving.

Apfelstrudel

Apfelstrudel (AHP-fehl-SHTROO-d'l) is delicious, inexpensive and time-consuming. If you have never made it before, give yourself plenty of time—possibly a whole afternoon. It requires a great deal of practise to make a perfect strudel and the more often you make it, the better it will be. The quantity given in this recipe should make enough dough for a 6-foot strudel. But beginners may wish to start by making a 3- or 4-foot strudel. Because the dough must be very smooth and thin it is important that it is kneaded very thoroughly. Otherwise the texture will be heavy instead of light and flaky and as it is important to use a large surface, you may have to use your dining room table.

Serve Apfelstrudel as a hot or cold dessert with cream.

PASTRY
10 oz. [2½ cups] flour
½ teaspoon salt
1 egg, lightly beaten
7 fl. oz. [⅞ cup] tepid water
2 tablespoons melted butter
FILLING
3 lb. cooking apples, peeled, cored
    and cut into thin slices
4 oz. [½ cup] sugar
1 teaspoon ground cinnamon
3 oz. [½ cup] raisins
3 oz. [½ cup] almonds or walnuts,
    chopped
    grated rind of 1 lemon
4 oz. [½ cup] melted butter
2 oz. [⅔ cup] white breadcrumbs

Sift the flour and salt into a large mixing bowl. In a small bowl mix together the egg, water and butter. With a wooden spoon, stir the egg-and-water mixture into the flour and mix well. Then knead until a firm dough is formed.

Place the dough on a floured board and continue kneading until it is smooth and elastic. This will take about 10 minutes. Place the dough in a warm, large mixing bowl. Cover the bowl with a cloth and set it aside in a warm draught-free place for 30 minutes.

Meanwhile prepare the filling. In a medium-sized mixing bowl mix together the apples, sugar, cinnamon, raisins, almonds or walnuts and lemon rind.

Spread out a large, clean cloth (a sheet is ideal) on a table. Sprinkle the cloth with flour. Place the dough on the cloth and, with a floured rolling pin, roll the dough out as thinly as possible.

With the back of your hands, lift and stretch the dough, pulling the dough until it is wafer thin. This should be done as carefully as possible. Do not worry if a few small holes appear in the dough. With scissors, trim the outer edges of the dough so that the sides are straight.

Preheat the oven to very hot 450°F (Gas Mark 8, 230°C). Grease two baking sheets with 1 tablespoon melted butter.

Brush the dough with half of the melted butter and sprinkle it with nearly all of the breadcrumbs. Spoon the apple mixture in a long strip on to the dough, 3 inches away from the edges of the pastry nearest to you, and within 2 inches of each end.

Using the cloth, lift the dough over the filling and roll it up like a Swiss [jelly] roll. Tuck in the ends. Brush the top of the dough with the remaining melted butter and cover with the rest of the breadcrumbs.

With a sharp knife, divide the strudel into pieces long enough to fit the baking sheets. Place the strudel on the baking

For the Apfelstrudel, on a large clean cloth sprinkled with flour, roll out the dough as thinly as possible.

With the backs of your hands pull the dough until it stretches over the table and is wafer thin.

Brush the stretched dough with the melted butter and then cover it with almost all of the breadcrumbs.

Place the apple filling on the edge nearest to you 3 inches from the edge and to within 2 inches of the ends.

Lift the cloth and use it to roll the dough over the filling. Continue rolling until all the pastry is rolled.

Brush the top of the roll with melted butter and sprinkle it with breadcrumbs before cutting.

Bacon, apples and onions are fried to make Appel-Fläsk, a Swedish dish.

Preheat the oven to moderate 350°F (Gas Mark 4, 180°C). Grease 12 patty tins with a little butter.

In a medium-sized mixing bowl, cream the butter with the sugar using a wooden spoon, or electric mixer, until the mixture is light and fluffy. Beat in the egg and then fold in the flour. With your hands, lightly knead the dough until it is smooth. Chill it in the refrigerator for 15 minutes.

For the filling, melt the butter in a small saucepan over low heat. Add the apples to the pan and cook them gently for about 15 minutes or until they are beginning to soften. Stir in the sugar.

Set aside one-third of the dough. Divide the remaining two-thirds into 12 and roll each piece into a ball. Flatten each ball with the heel of your hand and press it into a patty tin.

Spoon the apple filling into the pastry cases and put a teaspoonful of apricot jam on top. Sprinkle each one with a few slivered almonds.

Roll out the reserved dough and, using a pastry cutter a little larger than the patty tins, cut out 12 rounds. Dampen the edges of each pastry case and press the pastry rounds on top. Press the edges together with a fork to seal.

Bake the pies in the centre of the oven for 35 to 45 minutes or until firm and golden brown. Allow to cool slightly, then remove from the tins. Sprinkle with icing [confectioners'] sugar.

sheets with the seams underneath.

Bake the strudels in the centre of the oven for 10 minutes, then reduce the oven temperature to fairly hot 400°F (Gas Mark 6, 200°C), and continue to bake for a further 20 minutes or until the apfelstrudel is crisp and golden brown.

Appareil

Appareil (ah-PAH-ray) is a french cooking term which is synonymous with the word 'mixture'. It is used to describe the preparations necessary for the making of a dish.

Äppel-Fläsk

BACON COOKED WITH APPLES AND ONIONS

A very simple and tasty dish from Sweden, Äppel-Fläsk (EHP-pel flesk) *is inexpensive and easy for a busy housewife to make for lunch or supper.*

4 SERVINGS

2 tablespoons oil
1 lb. onions, sliced
1 lb. cooking apples, cored and
    sliced
    freshly ground black pepper
½ teaspoon dried dill (optional)
¾ lb. bacon slices
1 tablespoon chopped parsley

In a large frying-pan, heat the oil over moderate heat. Add the onions to the pan and fry them until they are transparent.

Stir in the apples. Cover the pan and cook for about 10 to 15 minutes or until the apples are soft. Stir occasionally. Add pepper to taste and the dill, if you are using it. Transfer the apple mixture to a warmed serving dish and keep warm.

With a sharp knife remove the rind from the bacon and discard it. Wash out the frying-pan and in it fry the bacon until it is crisp. Remove the bacon from the pan and drain it on kitchen paper towels.

Mix the bacon into the apple mixture and sprinkle with the parsley.

Äppelformar

SMALL APPLE PIES

Small pies filled with apple, apricot jam and slivered almonds, Äppelformar (EHP-pel-FOR-mar) *is a Scandinavian recipe. Usually served with coffee they are equally delicious for tea or a picnic.*

12 SMALL PIES

PASTRY
3 oz. [⅜ cup] butter
4 oz. [½ cup] sugar
1 large egg
6 oz. [1½ cups] self-raising flour
FILLING
2 tablespoons butter
2 large cooking apples, peeled,
    cored and thinly sliced
2 oz. [¼ cup] sugar
4 tablespoons apricot jam
1 oz. [¼ cup] almonds, slivered
icing [confectioners'] sugar

Appenzell

This full fat cheese derives its name from the eastern Swiss canton of Appenzell. It has a delicate flavour and is similar in appearance to the Swiss cheeses Emmenthal and Gruyère.

Apple

The most important and widely grown fruit in the temperate climates of the world, the apple has been cultivated for over 3,000 years. Apples were always particularly valued for their keeping qualities and, until refrigeration, gas and other storage methods were introduced in the twentieth century, they were almost the only fresh fruit available during the winter.

Apples were probably introduced into Britain from Europe. From there they were taken by settlers to America and Australia and, later, seedlings of new varieties were sent back to Britain.

During the nineteenth century, amateur and professional growers developed many new varieties of apples. The most famous English dessert apple is probably Cox's Orange Pippin. In about 1850, a Mr. Cox, a retired brewer, raised a seedling from Ribston, another popular variety. The resulting fruit was of exceptional quality with a sweet, crisp flesh and a strong, aromatic skin. From this apple many other dessert varieties have been developed.

Apples have a low vitamin C content and, do not have great food value, but they are one of the most popular and versatile fruits. In addition to their decorative value in a fruit bowl and, served raw, as an enjoyable sweet, apples can be cooked in many different ways to produce a huge variety of desserts. They can be prepared to accompany certain meat and cheese dishes and they can be baked, stewed, fried, puréed, cooked in pastry or used as a garnish. They can be preserved as jelly, jam, pickles, chutney and dried apple rings. Certain varieties are used to make CIDER and apple wine.

Cooking apples are rich in pectin and are useful in making jam because they can be combined with fruits that have little pectin.

Apple Amber

A delicious and good-looking dessert, Apple Amber can be served hot or cold.

4 SERVINGS

SHORTCRUST PASTRY
4 oz. [1 cup] flour
¼ teaspoon salt
2 oz. [¼ cup] vegetable shortening
  cold water, to mix

FILLING
1 lb. cooking apples
2 oz. [¼ cup] butter
  sugar
  grated rind of 1 lemon
  juice of 1 lemon
2 egg yolks, lightly beaten

MERINGUE
2 egg whites
3 oz. castor [⅜ cup fine] sugar

To make the pastry, sift together the flour and salt. With your fingertips, rub the fat very lightly into the flour mixture until it resembles fine breadcrumbs. Mix to a stiff paste with very little cold water.

An apple-filled pastry shell, Apple Amber is topped with meringue.

The dough should bind together into a ball, leaving the sides of the bowl clean.

Turn out on to a floured board and knead very lightly. Roll out, handling the dough as little as possible. Line an 8-inch pie dish with the pastry.

Preheat oven to very hot 450°F (Gas Mark 8, 230°C).

For the filling, peel, core and slice the apples. Put 2 tablespoons of cold water into a saucepan, add the apples and the butter and cook until tender, about 10 minutes. Add sugar to taste.

Rub the mixture through a sieve or beat until smooth. Add the lemon rind, the lemon juice and the egg yolks to the apple mixture. Mix together and pour into the pie dish. Bake for about 30 minutes or until the pastry is browned and the filling is set.

For the meringue, whisk the egg whites until they are very stiff. Fold in 2 ounces [¼ cup] of sugar.

When the pastry and apple filling are done, reset the oven temperature to very cool 250°F (Gas Mark ½, 130°C). Pile the meringue lightly on top of the apple filling. Dredge with the remaining sugar. Bake for 30 to 40 minutes or until the meringue is crisp and lightly golden brown on top.

Apples, Baked

This recipe for Baked Apples, is inexpensive, easy to cook and a pleasant dessert. It can be varied by adding cinnamon, nutmeg, ground cloves or mace to the sugar. Dried fruit may be substituted for the sugar or the apples may be basted with dry sherry during the baking and served with sherry-flavoured custard sauce.

4 SERVINGS

4 cooking apples
2 oz. [¼ cup] light brown sugar
   water
1 oz. [2 tablespoons] butter

Preheat the oven to moderate 350°F (Gas Mark 4, 180°C).

Wash the apples and with an apple corer remove the cores. Peel off about 1 inch of skin from the tops of the apples.

Arrange the apples in a baking dish and fill the centres with sugar. Top each apple with a little butter and pour enough water into the baking dish to a depth of ½-inch.

Bake the apples for about 30 minutes or until they are soft, basting frequently with the syrup in the baking dish. Serve hot or cold.

Apple Brandy

A colourless spirit distilled from cider, apple brandy is widely made in the apple-growing regions of France and in some parts of North America. CALVADOS, the famous apple brandy, is made in Normandy.

A simple dish, Baked Apples may be flavoured with spices or sherry.

Apple Bread Pudding

A pleasant dessert for Sunday lunch, Apple Bread Pudding can be prepared in advance and served cold with a hot sauce or baked at the last minute and served with cream.

4 TO 6 SERVINGS

8 fl. oz. [1 cup] milk
5 oz. [2½ cups] fresh breadcrumbs
2 egg yolks
1 oz. [2 tablespoons] butter
2 tablespoons brandy or 1 teaspoon vanilla essence
2 oz. [⅓ cup] almonds, slivered
2 oz. [⅓ cup] raisins
2 oz. [⅓ cup] currants
4 oz. [½ cup] sugar
½ teaspoon ground cinnamon
½ teaspoon ground cloves
1½ lb. apples, peeled, cored and thinly sliced
2 egg whites

Preheat the oven to moderately hot 375°F (Gas Mark 5, 190°C).

In a small saucepan, heat the milk over moderate heat. Add the breadcrumbs and cook for 2 minutes. Cool slightly before beating in the egg yolks, butter, brandy or vanilla essence, almonds, raisins, currants, 6 tablespoons sugar, cinnamon and cloves. Add the sliced apples and mix well.

With a whisk or rotary beater, beat the egg whites until they are stiff and form peaks. Gradually add the remaining sugar and continue beating until the egg whites and sugar are well mixed. Fold into the apple mixture.

Grease a medium-sized baking dish and fill it with the pudding mixture. Bake for 40 minutes.

Apples Bristol

An unusual apple and orange dessert, Apples Bristol are best made with Cox's Orange Pippin apples, but other dessert apples can be used. This dish should be served very cold and can be accompanied by whipped cream.

4 SERVINGS

15 fl. oz. [1⅞ cups] water
4 oz. [½ cup] sugar
6 dessert apples
2 large oranges
CARAMEL
3 oz. [⅜ cup fine] castor sugar
4 fl. oz. [½ cup] water

Put the water and granulated sugar in a medium-sized saucepan over a low heat.

An apple and orange dessert, Apples Bristol is sprinkled with caramel.

Stir until the sugar has dissolved and then boil rapidly for 5 minutes.

Peel and core the apples and cut them into quarters. Add all the apples to the syrup in the saucepan, cover and simmer gently for 10 minutes, or until the apples are tender when pierced with a table fork. Remove from the heat, replace the lid and leave to cool.

With a sharp knife, score around the centre of one orange and pull off one-half of the rind. Cut the rind into fine strips. To remove the bitter taste, put the strips into a small pan of boiling water and simmer for 5 minutes. Drain the orange strips, rinse them in cold water and drain again. Set aside.

With a very sharp knife, cut the peel and white pith from the oranges. Slice the oranges into thin rounds and set aside.

To make the caramel, put the water and sugar in a small saucepan over moderate heat and stir until the sugar has dissolved. Bring to the boil and continue boiling until the syrup turns a dark golden brown. Pour on to a lightly greased baking sheet and leave to harden.

To serve, remove the apples from the saucepan with a slotted spoon and put them into a serving bowl. Arrange the orange slices on top of the apples and add 4 tablespoons of syrup from the saucepan. Scatter the orange strips over the orange slices. Crush the caramel into small pieces and sprinkle over the top.

Put the serving bowl into the refrigerator for at least 2 hours before serving.

Apple Brown Betty

This dessert is a form of charlotte. It can also be made with other fruits, such as apricots, gooseberries or a mixture of apples and blackberries.

4 SERVINGS
- 2 oz. [¼ cup] plus 1 teaspoon butter
- 6 oz. [3 cups] fresh breadcrumbs
- 2 lb. apples, cored, peeled and thinly sliced
- 4 oz. [⅔ cup] brown sugar
- ¼ teaspoon grated nutmeg
- grated rind of ½ lemon
- 2 tablespoons lemon juice
- 4 oz. [⅔ cup] raisins
- 3 fl. oz. [⅜ cup] sherry

Preheat the oven to fairly hot 375°F (Gas Mark 5, 190°C). Grease a medium-sized, ovenproof dish with 1 teaspoon butter.

Place a layer of one third of breadcrumbs on the bottom of the ovenproof dish. Dot with some butter. Place half the apples next, sprinkled with half the sugar, nutmeg, grated lemon rind and raisins. Sprinkle with 1 tablespoon of lemon juice. Lay another third of breadcrumbs on top. Dot with butter and place the rest of the apples on top, sprinkled with the remainder of the sugar, nutmeg, lemon rind, raisins and lemon juice. Cover with the remaining breadcrumbs, dot with butter and bake in the oven for about 40 minutes or until the apples are tender and the top is golden brown.

Pour the sherry over the pudding and bake for 5 minutes more. Serve hot with cream or custard sauce.

Apple Butter

Apple butter, or apple marmalade as it is sometimes called, is a useful and tasty addition to your store cupboard. Not only can apple butter be used as a spread, but it is also an excellent base for a mousse or as a filling for tarts and cakes.

ABOUT 5½ PINTS
- 4 lb. well-flavoured apples
- 16 fl. oz. [2 cups] cider
- granulated sugar
- 2 teaspoons powdered cinnamon
- 1 teaspoon ground cloves
- ½ teaspoon ground allspice
- juice and grated rind of 1 lemon

Wash and quarter the apples, but do not peel them or remove the seeds. Put the apple quarters and the cider in a large preserving pan or saucepan. Bring to the boil over high heat. Lower the heat and simmer uncovered until the apples are very soft.

Rub the fruit and cider mixture through a fine sieve. To every 8 fluid ounces, add 4 ounces [½ cup] of sugar. Return the apple and sugar mixture to the saucepan and add the cinnamon, cloves, allspice, lemon juice and rind. Stir constantly, over low heat, until the sugar is dissolved.

Raise the heat and boil rapidly until the apple butter thickens. To test, place a spoonful of the butter on a cold plate. When no rim of liquid separates around the edge, the apple butter is ready.

Pour the butter into hot, clean, dry jars and seal with waxed paper and cellophane covers.

Apple Charlotte

This delicious hot pudding is said to have been named after the heroine in Goethe's novel Werther.

4 TO 6 SERVINGS

FILLING
  2 lb. cooking apples, peeled, cored and cut into quarters
  4 oz. [½ cup] sugar
    the rind of 1 lemon
  2 oz. [¼ cup] plus 1 teaspoon butter
  1 loaf of white bread a day or two old, crusts removed and cut into as many thin slices as required
  4 tablespoons melted butter
    castor sugar

SAUCE
  5 tablespoons apricot jam
  3 tablespoons water
  2 tablespoons sherry

Preheat the oven to moderate 350°F (Gas Mark 4, 180°C). Grease a charlotte mould or ovenproof dish with 1 teaspoon butter.

Put the apples, sugar, lemon rind and butter in a medium-sized saucepan and, stirring occasionally with a wooden spoon, simmer gently until the apples are very soft. They should neither be completely whole nor completely mashed. Discard the lemon rind.

Cut the bread slices in halves. Dip the halved slices in the melted butter and line the bottom and sides of the mould or pudding bowl, overlapping the slices slightly. Fill with the apple mixture and cover with a layer of bread slices dipped in melted butter. Sprinkle the pudding with castor sugar and bake in the oven for 40 minutes, or until the top is golden brown.

While the charlotte is baking, put the jam and water in a small saucepan. Stir and bring to the boil. Lower the heat and simmer for 3 minutes. Remove from the heat and stir in the sherry.

After taking the apple charlotte from the oven, let it stand for a minute or two before turning it out on to a warmed serving dish. Pour the warm, but not hot, jam sauce over it and serve immediately.

Apple Corer

This useful tool for removing complete apple cores neatly is sometimes combined with apple peelers or with gadgets which simultaneously cut an apple into quarters. Apple corers can also be used to take a neat plug out of some fruits and vegetables before stuffing them.

An Apple Dumpling is a whole, cored apple wrapped in pastry and baked.

Apple and Cucumber Salad

A simple, fresh salad, this is a good accompaniment to cold fowl, fish or meat.

4 SERVINGS

1 lb. crisp dessert apples
　juice of 1 lemon
1 small cucumber
½ teaspoon salt
2 grindings black pepper
2 fl. oz. double cream [¼ cup heavy
　cream], whipped
　lettuce leaves, washed and dried

Peel, core and cut the apples into thin slices. Put the apple slices in a dish and sprinkle with the lemon juice to prevent them from discolouring.

Wash the cucumber and cut it into thin slices. Add the slices to the apple in the bowl. Sprinkle with salt and pepper. With a spoon, gently toss the apple and cucumber slices so they are evenly mixed. Stir in the whipped cream.

To serve, line a salad bowl with lettuce leaves. Pile the apple and cucumber mixture in the centre.

Apple Dumplings

This is an attractive, traditional English pudding which is usually eaten in the winter.

6 SERVINGS

PASTRY
11 oz. [2¾ cups] flour
½ teaspoon salt
3 oz. [6 tablespoons] butter, diced
3 oz. [⅜ cup] white vegetable fat
　[shortening], diced
3 tablespoons cold water
FILLING
6 large dessert apples, cored
4 oz. [½ cup] soft brown sugar
　grated rind of 1 lemon
½ teaspoon cinnamon
2 oz. sultanas [⅓ cup golden raisins]
6 cloves
　milk, to glaze
　castor sugar

Preheat the oven to hot 400°F (Gas Mark 6, 200°C).

For the pastry, sift the flour and salt into a large mixing bowl. Add the diced fats and cut them into the flour with a pastry cutter or a knife. With your fingertips, rub the fats into the flour until the mixture resembles fine breadcrumbs.

Make a well in the centre of the flour mixture and add the water. With your hands, mix and knead until smooth. If the pastry is too dry add more water, a little at

a time. Chill for 30 minutes.

Roll out the pastry fairly thinly and trim to a rectangle 21 × 14 inches, reserving the trimmings. Cut into 6 squares. Centre an apple on each square.

Mix together the brown sugar, lemon rind, cinnamon and sultanas [golden raisins] and use to fill the centre of each apple, inserting 1 clove in the middle.

Lift the edges of the pastry squares to enclose each apple completely. Moisten the edges with water and seal.

Place the dumplings on a greased baking sheet. Cut 24 leaves from the reserved pastry. Moisten and attach 4 leaves to each apple. Brush the dumpling with milk and dust with castor sugar.

Bake for 30 minutes then reduce the oven temperature to 275°F (Gas Mark 1, 140°C) and bake for a further 10 minutes, cover with foil to stop overbrowning. Serve hot or cold with ice cream.

Apple-Filled Pancakes

This unusual and inexpensive dessert is known in Germany, where it originated, as Apfelfannkuchen (AHP-fehl-fahn-KOO-khen). *The pancakes could also be served for tea or at a late Sunday breakfast.*

4 SERVINGS

PANCAKES
4 oz. [1 cup] flour
2 teaspoons sugar
1 egg plus 1 egg yolk
10 fl. oz. [1¼ cups] milk
1 tablespoon melted butter
FILLING
2 oz. [¼ cup] butter
2 lb. cooking apples, peeled, cored
　and cut into thin slices
2 tablespoons brown sugar
1 teaspoon ground cinnamon
　a little castor sugar and cinnamon

Sift the flour and sugar into a large mixing bowl. Make a well in the centre of the flour mixture and put the eggs into it. Add a tablespoon of milk to the eggs. Stir the eggs and milk with a wooden spoon until they are mixed. Slowly incorporate the flour and sugar, adding the milk a little at a time.

Continue mixing until all the flour and half the milk are blended to make a thick batter. Change to a whisk or rotary beater and briskly whisk the batter, adding the remaining milk. Cover and keep in a cool place for 30 minutes.

For the filling, melt all the butter in a frying-pan over moderate heat. Put in the apples, sugar and cinammon. Sauté gently, stirring occasionally, until the apples are soft. Set aside, but keep hot.

Heat a medium-sized frying-pan. Grease lightly with melted butter. Pour two tablespoons of the batter into the pan and tip the pan quickly to spread the batter evenly. Cook over a high heat until the pancake is brown on the underside. Turn over with a palette knife and cook for 30 seconds or until brown. Turn on to a plate and keep warm. Make all the pancakes.

Spread a large spoonful of the apple filling on the lower half of each pancake and roll neatly. Arrange the pancakes on a plate, sprinkle with castor sugar and cinnamon and serve.

For Apple-Filled Pancakes, put a spoonful of apple mixture on each pancake.

Starting from the side with the apple mixture, neatly roll up each pancake.

Arrange the pancakes on a plate and sprinkle with sugar and cinnamon.

Apple Florentine

A classic recipe, this English single-crust apple pie is traditionally made with flaky pastry. It should be served very hot with plenty of thick cream.

6 SERVINGS

FILLING

2 lb. cooking apples
2 oz. [¼ cup] butter
4 oz. [⅔ cup] brown sugar
¼ teaspoon ground cinnamon
½ teaspoon grated lemon rind
5 fl. oz. [⅝ cup] sweet cider
¼ teaspoon grated nutmeg
¼ teaspoon lemon juice
½ teaspoon ground cinnamon
2 teaspoons sugar
  icing [confectioners'] sugar

PASTRY

6 oz. [1½ cups] flour
½ teaspoon salt
2 oz. [¼ cup] butter
2 oz. [¼ cup] lard
3 to 4 tablespoons cold water

Peel and core the apples and cut them into quarters. Melt the butter in a medium-sized frying-pan over a moderate heat and add the apples. Sauté gently, stirring occasionally until the apples are soft and light brown. Drain off any remaining butter.

Sprinkle the apples with the brown sugar, ¼ teaspoon of the cinnamon and the grated lemon rind and mix thoroughly. Put into a shallow 8-inch earthenware or glass pie dish. Set aside.

Preheat the oven to hot 425°F (Gas Mark 7, 220°C).

To make the pastry, sift the flour into a mixing bowl and add the salt. Divide the butter into two pieces and add one piece to the flour. With your fingertips, rub the fat into the flour until it resembles fine breadcrumbs. With a knife, mix in the water to form a firm dough.

Put the dough on a floured board and with your hands shape it into a square. Roll out the dough into an oblong and dot two-thirds of it with small pieces of half the lard. Fold over one-third of the pastry and then the other third to make a neat, square parcel. Press the edges with the rolling-pin to seal.

Turn the pastry round so that the

A classic recipe, Apple Florentine is flavoured with spiced cider.

sealed ends are facing you and roll out again into an oblong. Dot with pieces of the remaining lard, fold in three, seal the edges, turn the pastry and roll out again. Repeat this process with the remaining butter. Wrap dough in waxed paper and chill in the refrigerator for 10 minutes.

Roll out the pastry, fold again in three, and, with your hands, shape quickly into a round. Roll out into a circle slightly larger than the pie dish and, using the rolling pin, lay the pastry on the pie dish. Trim the excess pastry with a sharp knife. Crimp the edge of the pastry with your thumb and forefinger to make a pattern.

From the surplus pastry make a rose to decorate the centre of the pie. Bake this separately. Bake the pie in the oven for 30 minutes, or until the pastry is golden brown.

While the pie is baking, prepare the spiced cider. Put the cider into a small saucepan over low heat with the nutmeg, lemon juice and remaining cinnamon. Heat gently, add the sugar and stir until it is dissolved. Taste the cider, adding more sugar if necessary.

When the pie is baked, remove it from the oven. Cut a small hole in the

centre of the pie and pour in the spiced cider. Fill the hole with the pastry rose. Dust the pastry with icing sugar and serve very hot.

Apple Flambé

Apple Flambé (flom-bay) is an elegant and more expensive version of the simple baked apple. The slow method of cooking ensures that the apples stay white and whole. The amount of sugar needed may vary according to the tartness of the apples used. This is an ideal hot dessert for a winter lunch or dinner party and is delicious served with whipped cream or hot custard sauce.

4 SERVINGS

4 large, juicy, crisp, dessert apples
4 oz. [⅔ cup] raisins and candied peel, mixed
4 oz. [⅔ cup] hazelnuts, chopped, or almonds, blanched and chopped
a pinch of grated nutmeg
2 tablespoons castor [fine] sugar
2 fl. oz. [¼ cup] water
1 tablespoon butter
4 tablespoons brandy or Grand Marnier

Apple rings dipped in batter and fried, Apple Fritters make a good dessert.

Preheat the oven to 300°F (Gas Mark 2, 150°C).

Wash, core and peel the apples. Put them in an ovenproof serving dish.

Put the raisins, candied peel, chopped nuts, nutmeg and sugar in a bowl and mix well. Stuff the centres of the apples with the mixture. Put the water and the butter in the bottom of the dish and place in the centre of the oven. Cook for 2 hours or until the apples are tender. Baste the apples with the liquid every half hour.

When the apples are cooked, remove them from the oven. Just before serving, pour a tablespoon of warmed brandy or Grand Marnier over each apple and ignite it. Bring to the table flaming.

Apple Fritters

This is a simple and inexpensive dessert. Make the batter and prepare the fruit ahead of your meal, then dip the fritters in batter and cook just before serving.

4 SERVINGS

4 oz. [1 cup] flour
¼ teaspoon salt
1 egg
1 tablespoon vegetable oil
5 fl. oz. [⅝ cup] milk
1 lb. firm dessert apples
2 tablespoons lemon juice
castor sugar for dredging
oil for frying

Sift the flour and salt into a medium-sized mixing bowl. Make a well in the centre of the flour, break in the egg and add the oil.

With a wooden spoon, mix the egg and oil, slowly incorporating the flour and gradually adding the milk. Mix to a smooth batter, then beat well. Cover and keep in a cool place for 30 minutes.

Peel and core the apples and slice into rings ¼ inch thick. Lay the apple rings on a plate sprinkle with lemon juice and sugar.

Heat the oil in a deep-fat fryer with the basket in place to 350°F (Gas Mark 4, 180°C). Cook the apple rings in two batches. Using a skewer dip them into the batter then place in the basket and lower into the hot oil. Cook the rings on both sides until they are golden.

Drain well on absorbent paper. Arrange on a plate, dredge with sugar and serve.

Apple Hat

Apple Hat is a traditional, steamed, English pudding. Very filling and satisfying, it is good served as the dessert for a winter luncheon.

4 SERVINGS

    butter for greasing
5 oz. [1¼ cups] self-raising flour
½ teaspoon salt
3 oz. [⅜ cup] coarsely shredded beef
    suet
    about 4 fl. oz. [½ cup] milk
3 cooking apples, peeled, cored
    and sliced
2 oz. [¼ cup] soft brown sugar
    grated rind of 1 lemon
1 oz. [2 tablespoons] raisins
1 oz. [2 tablespoons] currants
1 tablespoon water

Generously grease a 1½-pint pudding basin.

Sift the flour and salt into a mixing bowl and stir in the suet. Add enough milk to make a soft dough. Knead until smooth.

Roll out the pastry on a lightly floured surface to a 10-inch circle. Cut out a quarter wedge from the circle and set aside. Use the remaining pastry to line the basin.

Fill with layers of apples, sugar, lemon rind, raisins and currants. Sprinkle with water.

Roll out the reserved pastry to a circle large enough to fit the top of the basin. Brush the edges with water and place on top of the filling. Press the edges down firmly to seal.

Grease a large circle of greaseproof [waxed] paper and make a pleat in the centre. Cover the pudding basin with the paper, greased side down and secure with string.

Place the basin in a saucepan and pour in boiling water to come two-thirds of the way up the side. Cover and steam over low heat for 3 hours, adding more boiling water if necessary.

Turn the pudding out on to a serving plate and serve with hot custard sauce or cream.

Apple Mousse à la Chantilly

The basis of this dessert, Apple Mousse à la Chantilly (ah lah SHON-tee-yee), is apple 'marmalade' or 'butter' flavoured with vanilla essence rather than with the usual cinnamon, cloves and lemon. The apples should be of a well-flavoured dessert variety.

4 SERVINGS
2 lb. apples
16 fl. oz. [2 cups] cider
    granulated sugar
1 teaspoon vanilla essence
10 fl. oz. double cream [1¼ cups
    heavy cream]

Wash the apples, cut them in quarters, but do not core them. Place the apples in a medium-sized saucepan with the cider and simmer over low heat until soft.

With the back of a wooden spoon, push the apple and cider mixture through a sieve. Measure the pulp in a jug and add 4 ounces [½ cup] of granulated sugar to every 8 fluid ounces [1 cup].

Return the apple pulp to the pan. Over low heat, stirring all the time with a wooden spoon, dissolve the sugar. When the sugar is dissolved raise the heat to high and boil the mixture rapidly until it is very thick and a small drop will not fall from the spoon.

Put the apple mixture in a bowl. When it is cool place the bowl in a basin with ice in it and whisk the apple mixture.

In a small mixing bowl, beat half the cream until it is thick but not stiff. Fold it into the apple mixture with the vanilla essence. Pile the mixture into individual glass dishes. Top with the rest of the cream, stiffly whipped.

Apple Pie

This single-crust, English apple pie is traditionally served with custard sauce.

4 SERVINGS
PASTRY
6 oz. [1½ cups] plain flour
2 teaspoons castor sugar
    a pinch of salt
1½ oz. [3 tablespoons] butter
1½ oz. [3 tablespoons] vegetable fat
1 to 2 tablespoons iced water
    castor sugar
FILLING
1½ lb. apples
¼ teaspoon freshly grated nutmeg
    or ½ teaspoon ground nutmeg
6 oz. [¾ cup] brown sugar
2 cloves
1 tablespoon butter

Preheat the oven to hot 400°F (Gas Mark 6, 200°C).

Sift the flour, sugar and salt into a medium-sized mixing bowl. Put in the butter and vegetable fat and cut them into small pieces with a table knife. With your fingertips, rub the fat into the flour until the mixture looks like fine breadcrumbs.

Add 1 tablespoon of iced water and, using the knife, mix it into the flour mixture. With your hands, mix and knead the dough until it is smooth. Add more water if the dough is too dry. Chill the dough in the refrigerator for 10 minutes.

Peel, core and cut the apples into thin slices. Arrange the apple slices in a medium-sized pie dish, sprinkle with nutmeg and with all of the sugar if the apples are very tart, less if they are not. Add the cloves and dot the top with butter. Cover with foil and bake for 20 minutes. Remove from the oven and cool.

Roll out the pastry ¼-inch thick. Lift the pastry on your rolling pin and lay it over the pie. Press down the edge and trim the pastry with a sharp knife. Mark the edge with the knife or the back of a fork. Brush the top of the pie with water and dredge with castor sugar. Return the pie to the oven and bake for 30 minutes. Serve hot.

Apple and Pork Casserole

A simple pork dish, served in the casserole in which it is cooked, this is a good family lunch or informal dinner-party dish which can be made with inexpensive cuts of pork. It can be served with a green or root vegetable.

4 SERVINGS
2 lb. lean pork, boned
1 oz. [2 tablespoons] butter, softened
2 medium-sized onions, chopped
½ teaspoon dried sage
½ teaspoon salt
2 grindings black pepper
2 medium-sized cooking apples,
    peeled, cored and thinly sliced
3 tablespoons water
1½ lb. potatoes, peeled
2 tablespoons hot milk
1 tablespoon butter, cut into pieces

Preheat the oven to warm 325°F (Gas Mark 3, 170°C).

Remove any excess fat from the pork, then cut it into cubes. Grease a large oven-proof casserole with teaspoon of butter.

Put the onions, sage, salt and pepper in a mixing bowl and stir to mix.

Into the casserole place about one-third of the pork cubes. Cover them with one-half of the onion mixture and then with half of the sliced apples. Continue to fill the casserole with the remaining pork, onions and apples finishing with a layer of pork. Add the water.

Cover the casserole with a lid or piece of aluminium foil. Cook in the oven for 2 to 2½ hours or until the pork is tender. About 30 minutes before the pork is cooked, boil the potatoes in lightly salted water in a covered saucepan. When tender, drain thoroughly, return to the saucepan and shake over a low heat to dry them. Press the potatoes through a coarse sieve or mash them thoroughly. Return them to the pan and beat in the hot milk and softened butter until the potato is light and fluffy.

When the pork is cooked, spread the potato over it. Using a fork, roughen the surface of the potato layer into small peaks. Dot with small pieces of butter and return the casserole to the oven for 15 minutes, or until the potato topping is golden brown. Serve immediately.

Apple and Potato Stuffing

This is an excellent stuffing for goose. It should be well seasoned, so taste it before using and add more salt and pepper if necessary. This quantity is sufficient for one goose.

1 oz. [2 tablespoons] butter
1 lb. onions, peeled and sliced
1 lb. apples, peeled, cored and finely sliced
   juice of 1 orange
3 parsley sprigs
6 leaves fresh sage or 1½ teaspoons dried sage
1 teaspoon salt
   freshly ground black pepper
1 lb. potatoes, boiled and mashed
   grated rind of 1 orange

Melt the butter in a medium-sized saucepan over moderate heat. Add the onions and sauté until they are soft but not brown. Add the apples, orange juice, parsley, sage, salt and 7 grindings of pepper. Cook until the apples are soft.

Press the apple and onion mixture through a sieve and mix well with the

mashed potatoes and grated orange rind to make a fairly firm stuffing. Taste and correct seasoning if necessary.

Apple and Rice Pudding

An inexpensive dessert, Apple and Rice Pudding looks attractive and has a pleasant sour-sweet taste. The quantity of sugar needed depends very much on the tartness of the apples.

6 SERVINGS

4 oz [⅔ cup] long-grain rice
10 fl. oz. [1¼ cups] milk or milk mixed with single [light] cream
   grated rind of 1 lemon
4 oz. [½ cup] plus 2 tablespoons sugar
   a pinch of salt
2 egg yolks, plus 2 egg whites
1½ lb. apples, peeled and thinly sliced
2 oz. sultanas [⅓ cup golden raisins]
1 oz. [2 tablespoons] butter
4 fl. oz. [½ cup] cider or apple juice

Flavoured with sage and onions and topped with mashed potatoes, Apple and Pork Casserole is easy to make.

Preheat the oven to moderate 350°F (Gas Mark 4, 180°C).

Wash the rice thoroughly, soak for 30 minutes in cold water and drain. Put the milk, lemon rind, 2 ounces [¼ cup] of sugar and the salt in a medium-sized saucepan. Bring to the boil over moderate heat. Add the rice and, when the mixture comes to the boil again, reduce the heat to very low. Cover and simmer for 10 minutes, until the rice is cooked and the milk absorbed. Remove from the heat. With a fork, thoroughly mix in the egg yolks.

Put half the rice mixture in a deep baking dish, then half the apples and sultanas. Sprinkle with 2 tablespoons of sugar and dot with half the butter. Put the remaining rice on the apples and top with the remaining apples, sultanas and 2 tablespoons of sugar. Dot with the remaining butter. Pour the cider or apple juice over the apples and bake for 45 minutes. Reset the oven to cool 300°F (Gas Mark 2, 150°C).

In a small bowl beat the whites of the eggs until stiff. Fold in the 2 tablespoons of sugar. Spread the meringue over the apples. Return the pudding to the oven and bake for about 20 minutes or until the meringue is golden. Serve immediately.

Apple Sauce

Tart Apple Sauce is a delicate accompaniment to goose, duck or pork dishes. Apple Sauce and horseradish is excellent served with pork dishes. Just add horseradish to taste and blend into the Apple Sauce. A somewhat sweeter Apple Sauce, served with cream, is a simple and tasty dessert.

ABOUT 9 FLUID OUNCES

1 lb. cooking apples, peeled, cored and sliced
finely grated rind of 1 lemon
2 tablespoons lemon juice
2 tablespoons sugar, or to taste
2 tablespoons water
1 oz. [2 tablespoons] butter, cut into small pieces

Place the apples in a large saucepan with the lemon rind and juice, sugar and water.

Place the pan over high heat and bring to the boil. Reduce the heat to low, cover and simmer for 20 minutes or until the apples are soft.

Either rub the apples through a sieve or purée in a blender or food processor. Beat in the butter. Serve hot as an accompaniment to roast pork, or cold as a dessert with custard or whipped cream.

Spoon the apple sauce into a rigid container or polythene bag or yoghurt carton and freeze for up to 9 months. Defrost at room temperature for 4 hours.

Apple Sauce Cake

This moist, spicy cake has a pleasant cinnamon flavour. It can be served plain or covered with a caramel icing.

6 SERVINGS

7 oz. [1¾ cups] self-raising flour
¼ teaspoon salt
1 teaspoon baking powder
1 teaspoon cinnamon
½ teaspoon ground cloves
4 oz. [½ cup] butter, softened
5 oz. [⅝ cup] soft brown sugar
3 eggs
4 oz. [⅔ cup] raisins
4 oz. [1 cup] walnuts, chopped
9 fl. oz. [1⅛ cups] apple sauce
sifted icing [confectioners'] sugar

Preheat the oven to moderate 350°F (Gas Mark 4, 180°C). Grease an 8-inch cake tin, line the base with greaseproof [waxed] paper and grease the paper.

Sift the flour, salt, baking powder, cinnamon and cloves into a bowl.

Cream the butter and sugar in another bowl. Beat in the eggs, one at a time, adding a little flour with each one.

Fold in the remaining flour. Stir in the raisins, walnuts and apple sauce.

Pour into the cake tin. Bake in the centre of the oven for 50 minutes or until a fine warmed skewer inserted into the centre comes out clean.

Leave for 5 minutes before turning out on to a wire rack to cool completely.

Dust with the icing [confectioners'] sugar before serving.

Apple Snow

Apple Snow is a light, frothy dessert which can be served with sponge fingers or biscuits. It is inexpensive and easy to make.

4 SERVINGS

1 lb. cooking apples
rind of ½ lemon
2 tablespoons water
4 oz. castor [½ cup fine] sugar
2 egg whites

Preheat the oven to fairly hot 375°F (Gas Mark 5, 190°C).

Core the apples and, with a sharp knife, slit the skin round the centre. Place the apples in a fireproof dish with the lemon rind and 2 tablespoons of

water. Bake until the apples are soft. This will take about 1 hour.

Discard the lemon peel. Allow the apples to cool, remove the skins and rub through a sieve.

Whisk the egg whites until they are frothy. Add the sugar a little at a time and beat until the mixture stands up in peaks when the whisk is removed. Gradually add the apple pulp, beating until it is thoroughly mixed with the egg white. Taste and add more sugar if necessary. Serve cold.

Apple Sonning

This delicious dessert can be eaten hot served with a hot sabayon sauce, or cold with the same sauce chilled and made with an additional egg yolk.

6 SERVINGS

4 oz. [½ cup] butter
1½ lb. apples peeled, cored and sliced
½ teaspoon powdered cinnamon
1 oz. cornflour [¼ cup cornstarch]
6 oz. [¾ cup] sugar
2 eggs plus 1 egg yolk
SABAYON SAUCE
3 egg yolks
3 oz. castor [⅜ cup fine] sugar
½ teaspoon arrowroot
4 fl. oz. [½ cup] sherry

Preheat the oven to warm 325°F (Gas Mark 3, 170°C). Grease a soufflé dish or pudding basin with a little butter and dust lightly with flour.

Melt the butter in a medium-sized saucepan over moderate heat. Add the apples and cinnamon. Cover and simmer until the apples are soft.

Rub the apples through a sieve. Put the pulp back in the saucepan and add the cornflour and sugar. Stir with a wooden spoon over low heat until the mixture thickens. Remove from the heat and turn into a mixing bowl to cool.

In a large bowl, using a whisk or rotary beater, whisk the eggs and yolk until they are very pale. Fold the beaten eggs into the apple mixture and mix well. Pour into the soufflé dish and bake for 1 hour.

Just before the dessert is ready, make the sauce. In a medium-sized bowl, whisk the egg yolks with the sugar and arrowroot until they are almost white. Stand the bowl in a pan of hot water over a low heat and whisk until the sauce becomes thick. Add the sherry and raise the heat until the water boils. Whisk for a minute or two more. Pour the sauce into a sauce boat or bowl and, if serving the dessert hot, serve immediately.

Apple Turnovers

These apple-filled pastry triangles make a delicious and decorative luncheon dessert. They are also suitable to serve with tea.

12 TURNOVERS

PASTRY

$\frac{1}{2}$ oz. [1 tablespoon] butter or margarine
3 large cooking apples, cored and sliced
2 oz. sultanas [$\frac{1}{3}$ cup golden raisins]
2 oz. [$\frac{1}{3}$ cup] currants
    grated rind of 1 lemon
2 oz. [$\frac{1}{4}$ cup] soft light brown sugar
7 oz. made-weight puff pastry, defrosted if frozen

GLAZE

1 large egg white, lightly beaten castor sugar

Preheat the oven to fairly hot 400°F (Gas Mark 6, 200°C).

Melt the butter or margarine in a heavy-based saucepan. Add the cooking apples, sultanas, currants, lemon rind and

Crisp apple-filled triangles of puff pastry, Apple Turnovers are delicious hot or cold.

soft brown sugar, simmer for about 10 minutes, stirring occasionally, until the apples are soft.

Roll out the pastry on a lightly floured board to a 16- × 12-inch rectangle. Cut into 12 squares.

Place a little of the apple mixture on each square. Brush the edges with water and fold over to make triangles. Press the edges together to seal, knock up by tapping the edges horizontally with a knife blade.

Place the triangles on a baking sheet and pierce each one with a skewer or the top of a knife, to allow the steam to escape and prevent the filling from boiling over. Lightly brush the top of each turnover with the beaten egg white and generously sprinkle with sugar.

Bake for 10 minutes. Reduce the oven temperature to moderate 350°F (Gas Mark 4, 180°C) and bake for a further 20

minutes.

Sprinkle with extra castor sugar, if wished. A mixture of castor sugar and ground cinnamon adds extra flavour. Serve hot for dessert with custard sauce or whipped cream, or cold for picnics or packed lunches.

Apricot

The fruit of a tree which is native to North China, the apricot was brought from Armenia to Italy, where it was cultivated over 2,000 years ago. Apricots are now widely grown in the warmer temperate countries. They are exported in fresh, canned and dried form from Spain, South Africa, the United States and Australia.

Like the peach, the apricot must be really ripe to be sweet and juicy. It is popular as a dessert fruit, in fruit dishes and in salads. It is one of the fruits most used in pastry making and confectionery. Apricots have a low sugar content and, when dried, are rich in iron.

To peel apricots easily, put them in boiling water for a minute or two.

Lightly brush with the reduced syrup and sprinkle the top with the flaked almonds.

Serve immediately.

Apricot Brandy

This alcoholic liqueur has a sweetened spirit or brandy base flavoured with dried apricots. Made in Britain, Holland and France, it is usually sold as a liqueur. In Southern Hungary, where apricots are very plentiful, a superb apricot brandy is distilled from fresh, crushed apricots and apricot kernels.

Apricots in Brandy

Elegant and expensive, this dessert is easily made and can be prepared a week or even two weeks in advance of a special dinner party. Apricots in Brandy can be served alone or as a sauce for ice cream.

6 SERVINGS

1 lb. dried apricots
4 oz. [½ cup] sugar
  brandy

Place the apricots and sugar in a mixing bowl. Pour over enough brandy to completely cover the fruit. Cover and leave in a cool place for at least 36 hours. The longer the apricots are soaked the more the flavour improves. Serve chilled.

Apricot Condé

A classic French dessert, Apricot Condé is easy to prepare and makes an elegant end to a special dinner.

6 SERVINGS

1 teaspoon vegetable oil
4 oz. [⅔ cup] round-grain rice
1½ pints [3¾ cups] milk
12 oz. [1½ cups] sugar
1 oz. [2 tablespoons] butter
⅛ teaspoon salt
1 teaspoon vanilla essence
6 egg yolks, lightly beaten
2 lb. apricots, peeled, halved and
  stoned
8 fl. oz. [1 cup] water
2 tablespoons kirsch
1 oz. [¼ cup] flaked almonds

Preheat the oven to cool 300°F (Gas Mark 2, 150°C). Lightly grease an 8-inch soufflé dish with the oil. Set aside.

Apricot Condé, a classic French dessert of apricots, rice and eggs, is ideal for a dinner party.

Apricot Bourdaloue Tart

A pretty apricot tart which has an orange-flavoured crème filling. The sharp taste of the apricots contrasts pleasantly with the sweet crème. This classic French dessert is guaranteed to impress your guests.

6 SERVINGS

6 oz. made-weight shortcrust
  [pie crust] pastry, defrosted if
  frozen
FILLING
4 oz. [½ cup] sugar
9 fl. oz. [1⅛ cups] water
1 tablespoon lemon juice
1 lb. large apricots, halved and
  stoned or 16 oz. [1 lb.] apricot
  halves canned in natural syrup,
  drained
2 egg yolks
2 oz. [¼ cup] castor [superfine] sugar
  grated rind of 1 orange
1½ oz. [3 tablespoons] flour
1½ oz. [3 tablespoons] cornflour
  [cornstarch]
9 fl. oz. [1¼ cups] milk
1 egg white
1 oz. [2 tablespoons] flaked toasted
  almonds

Preheat the oven to hot 425°F (Gas Mark 7, 220°C). Carefully roll out the pastry on a lightly floured surface and use to line an 8-inch loose-bottomed fluted flan tin or pie dish.

Line the pastry with foil and baking beans and bake for 15 minutes. Remove the foil and beans, reduce the oven temperature to 375°F (Gas Mark 5,

A flan filled with orange-flavoured cream, Apricot Bourdaloue may be made with fresh or canned apricots.

190°C) and bake for a further 10 minutes until the pastry is crisp, then set aside and leave until cold.

Meanwhile, to make the filling, dissolve the sugar in the water and lemon juice in a saucepan over moderate heat. Bring the mixture to the boil. Add the apricots and simmer for 10 minutes, without stirring, or until the apricots are just tender but still firm to the touch.

Drain the apricots. Boil the syrup until reduced and thick; then set aside until completely cold.

Whisk the egg yolks with half the castor sugar in a bowl. Add the orange rind, flour and cornflour [cornstarch] and beat until the mixture becomes smooth and glossy.

Bring the milk just to boiling point in a small saucepan over moderate heat. Slowly pour it into the egg mixture, stirring until smooth.

Return the mixture to the saucepan and cook over moderate heat, stirring occasionally, until thick and smooth. Set aside until cold.

When everything is cold, place the pastry case on a serving plate. Whisk the egg white with the remaining castor sugar and fold into the cream with a large metal spoon or spatula. Spoon the chilled custard into the case and smooth the surface.

Decoratively arrange the poached apricots on top of the custard filling.

In a large flameproof casserole, bring the rice, milk, 4 ounces [½ cup] of the sugar, the butter, salt and vanilla essence to the boil over moderate heat, stirring constantly.

Cover the casserole and transfer it to the oven. Bake for 1 hour, or until all the liquid has been absorbed.

Remove the casserole from the oven. Stir in the egg yolks and place the casserole over low heat. Cook, stirring constantly, for 3 minutes. Remove the casserole from the heat and set it aside to cool.

Slice half a pound of the apricots. Set aside.

When the rice mixture is cool, spoon one-third of it into the soufflé dish. Place half the apricot slices on top. Continue making layers, ending with the rice mixture. Cover the dish and place it in the refrigerator to chill for 2 hours or until the rice mixture is firm.

Meanwhile, to make the sauce, in a medium-sized saucepan, dissolve the remaining sugar in the water over moderate heat, stirring constantly. Add the remaining apricot halves. Reduce the heat to low and simmer for 10 minutes or until the apricots are tender but still firm. Remove the pan from the heat.

With a slotted spoon, remove 12 apricot halves from the pan and set them aside.

Purée the remaining apricot halves with the syrup in a strainer or blender and return the purée to the saucepan. Return the pan to high heat. Boil for 3 minutes. Remove the pan from the heat.

Stir in the kirsch and almonds. Pour the sauce into a bowl and set it aside to cool.

Then place it in the refrigerator to chill.

Unmould the pudding on to a serving dish. Arrange the reserved apricot halves on the top and around the sides. Spoon over the sauce and serve immediately.

Apricot Glaze

Jam glazes are used to give a glossy surface to fruit flans and tarts. In classic recipes, apricot jam forms the basis of the glaze for yellow fruits.

4 FLUID OUNCES

4 tablespoons apricot jam
3 fl. oz. [⅜ cup] water
1 teaspoon lemon juice

Combine the jam and water in a small saucepan. Stirring, cook over moderate heat for 5 minutes. Add the lemon juice and stir well. Remove from the heat and strain.

Apricots Granville

The brandy in this recipe may be omitted but it does make a dish of poached apricots into a more delicious dessert.

4 SERVINGS

1½ lb. firm apricots
2½ pints [6¼ cups] water
1 lb. [2 cups] granulated sugar
½ vanilla pod
4 fl. oz. [½ cup] brandy

Blanch and peel the apricots and cut them in halves. Crack the stones with a hammer or nutcracker and remove the kernels.

Put the water, sugar and the vanilla pod in a medium-sized saucepan over moderate heat. Stir to dissolve the sugar, raise the heat and bring the syrup to a boil. Add the apricots and kernels to the syrup. Lower the heat and simmer for 5 minutes.

Remove the pan from the heat and allow the apricots to cool in the syrup for about 20 minutes. Remove the fruit and the kernels with a slotted spoon and place in a bowl.

Take out the vanilla pod. Return the pan to the stove and boil rapidly until the syrup is thick. Remove from the heat. Add the brandy. Pour this sauce over the apricots. Chill in the refrigerator and serve with cream.

Apricot Jam

This jam, which is excellent for making apricot sauce and apricot glaze, is made with fresh apricots. Only firm, flavourful fruit should be used. Over-ripe fruit will prevent the jam from setting.

MAKES ABOUT 5 POUNDS

3 lb. fresh apricots, halved and
   stoned
1 large lemon, quartered
9 fl. oz. [1⅛ cups] water
3 lb. [6 cups] sugar
1 tablespoon orange-flower water

Put the apricots, lemon quarters and the water in a large, heavy-based saucepan. Bring to the boil, then simmer for 15 minutes or until the fruit is tender and the water reduced slightly.

Meanwhile heat the oven to 225°F (Gas mark ¼, 110°C). Spread the sugar on a baking tray and warm it in the oven. Warm the clean jars.

Apricot Jam may be made with fresh fruit, or dried fruit and almonds.

Add the orange-flower water and sugar to the fruit and stir until dissolved. Boil rapidly for about 15 minutes, or until the jam has reached setting point. To test for setting, place a spoonful of jam on a cold plate; if set, the surface of the jam will wrinkle when pushed with a finger. If it has not reached this point; boil for a few minutes more, then repeat the test.

Skim the surface of the jam with a slotted spoon to remove any scum, remove the lemon quarters and allow jam to cool slightly.

Pour the jam into warm jars, cover immediately and allow to cool, then label and store.

To give a lovely almondy flavour to the jam, crack open a few of the apricot stones, soak the kernels in boiling water, then remove the skins and put the kernels in a muslin bag. Place the bag in the preserving pan with the apricots; remove it before bottling.

Apricot Jam with Almonds

Made with dried apricots, this jam can be prepared at any time of the year.

ABOUT 5 POUNDS

1 lb. dried apricots
3 pints [7½ cups] water
  juice of 1 lemon
3 lb. sugar
2 oz. [⅓ cup] almonds, blanched

Wash the apricots and put them in a large bowl with the water, making sure that they are completely covered. Leave them to soak for 24 hours.

Transfer the apricots and the water to a preserving-pan or a very large saucepan. Over moderate heat, stirring occasionally with a wooden spoon, simmer for 30 minutes, or until the fruit is very tender.

Add the lemon juice and sugar. Stir until the sugar is dissolved. Put in the almonds, bring the jam to the boil and continue to boil rapidly for 15 minutes.

To test the jam for setting, remove pan from the heat and put a spoonful of jam on a cold plate or saucer and allow it to cool. Setting point has been reached when the surface of the jam sets and wrinkles when you push it with your finger. If the setting point has not been reached, return the pan to the heat and continue boiling, testing every few minutes.

When the setting point is reached, skim the scum off the surface of the jam with a slotted spoon.

Using a jug or ladle, fill clean, warm, dry jars to within ½-inch of the tops.

This Apricot Salad has a dressing of soured cream with fresh tarragon.

Wipe the outside and the inside rim of the jars with a warm, damp cloth to remove any drops of jam.

While the jam is still hot, put a small round of wax paper in each jar. Then put on a vegetable parchment or cellophane cover and fasten with string or an elastic band. Label the jars and, when cold, store them in a cool, dry cupboard.

Apricot Pudding

This delicious pudding, made with dried apricots, is firm on top but soft and creamy underneath. It is inexpensive and very easy to make.

6 SERVINGS

6 oz. [1 cup] dried apricots
10 fl. oz. [1¼ cups] water
4 eggs
  grated rind and juice of 1 lemon
5 tablespoons flour
2 tablespoons melted butter
6 oz. [¾ cup] sugar
  a pinch of salt
10 fl. oz. [1¼ cups] milk

Preheat the oven to moderate 350°F (Gas Mark 4, 180°C). Lightly grease an ovenproof soufflé dish.

Put the apricots in a medium-sized saucepan with the water. Bring to the boil, lower the heat and then simmer for 10 minutes, or until the apricots are tender. Put the apricots and the liquid into an electric blender and blend, or push through a sieve to make a purée.

Separate the whites of the eggs from the yolks. Set the egg whites aside. In a medium-sized mixing bowl, beat the yolks thoroughly with a whisk or a rotary beater, adding the grated lemon rind and the juice, the flour, melted butter, sugar, salt, milk and the apricot purée. Beat until well mixed.

Whisk the egg whites until they stand up in peaks when the whisk is removed. Fold the egg whites into the apricot mixture. Pour into the soufflé dish.

Put 1 inch of water into a baking pan and place the soufflé dish in it. Place in the centre of the oven and bake for 40 minutes or until the top of the pudding is firm to the touch. Eat warm or cold.

Apricot Salad

This salad, made with fresh apricots and served with a tarragon cream dressing, is a good accompaniment to hot or cold ham.

4 SERVINGS

2 lb. ripe apricots
DRESSING
4 tablespoons thick sour
  cream
3 tablespoons tarragon vinegar
1 tablespoon sugar
½ teaspoon salt
4 grindings black pepper
  a few tarragon leaves,
  chopped

Blanch and peel the apricots. Cut each apricot in half and remove the stone. Arrange the apricot halves in a glass serving bowl. Crack the stones with a nutcracker or hammer. Take out the kernels, chop them and set aside.

To make the dressing, put the sour cream into a bowl and stir in the vinegar, sugar, salt and pepper. When it is thoroughly mixed taste the dressing and adjust the seasoning if necessary.

Just before serving, pour the dressing over the apricots. Sprinkle with the tarragon leaves and chopped kernels.

Apricots and Gammon or Ham

An easy-to-make and satisfying hot supper dish, this can be served with mashed potatoes and a green vegetable. If fresh apricots are not available, drained, canned apricots may be substituted. They should be put on the gammon slices without additional cooking and the syrup in which they are packed can be used in the baking.

4 SERVINGS

  6 oz. [¾ cup] sugar
10 fl. oz. [1¼ cups] water
  1 lb. fresh apricots, blanched, peeled, halved and stoned
  4 thick slices gammon or ham, 6 to 8 oz. each
  8 cloves
  4 teaspoons soft brown sugar
  1 oz. [2 tablespoons] butter

Preheat the oven to fairly hot 375°F (Gas Mark 5, 190°C).

In a medium-sized saucepan, dissolve the sugar in the water over moderate heat. Bring to the boil. Add the apricot halves, lower the heat and simmer for about 10 minutes or until the apricots are tender but still firm. Remove from the heat.

Place the gammon or ham in a large baking dish. Insert the cloves into the fat and sprinkle the slices with the brown sugar.

Drain the apricots and arrange them on top of the gammon, adding a tablespoon of the syrup around each slice. Dot with butter and bake uncovered for 40 minutes, basting occasionally.

Apricot Tart

Inexpensive and easy to prepare, this is a summer dessert to be made when apricots are in season. Use half bananas and half apricots as a variation.

4 SERVINGS

PASTRY
  5 oz. [1¼ cups] flour
  1 tablespoon sugar
  1 oz. [2 tablespoons] butter
1½ oz. [3 tablespoons] vegetable fat
  1 egg yolk, lightly beaten
  1 to 2 tablespoons iced water
GLAZE
  3 large tablespoons apricot jam
  1 tablespoon water
    a squeeze of lemon juice
FILLING
  1 lb. apricots, blanched, peeled, halved and stoned
  4 oz. [½ cup] sugar
  1 oz. [2 tablespoons] butter
  1 oz. [¼ cup] almonds, blanched and shredded

Sift the flour and sugar into a medium-sized mixing bowl. Add the butter and vegetable fat and cut them into small pieces with a table knife. With your fingertips, rub the fat into the flour until the mixture resembles very fine breadcrumbs.

Add the egg yolk and ½ tablespoon of iced water and, using the knife, mix it into the flour mixture. With your hands, mix and knead the dough until it is smooth. Add more water if the pastry is dry. Make a ball of the pastry. Cover it with greaseproof paper and chill in the refrigerator for 20 minutes.

Preheat oven to fairly hot 375°F (Gas Mark 5, 190°C).

Roll out the pastry and with it line an 8-inch or 9-inch flan tin with a removable bottom. Cover the pastry with aluminium foil. Weigh it down with dried beans or peas and bake for 10 minutes. Remove the beans and the foil, prick the bottom of the pastry with a fork and return it to the oven for 5 minutes.

To prepare the glaze, boil the jam and water in a small saucepan for 5 minutes. Sieve the mixture and add the lemon juice.

Brush a little of the glaze on the bottom of the pastry. Place the apricots, cut sides down, in the pastry case. Sprinkle with the sugar and dot with the butter. Place the tart in the oven and

---

Fresh or canned apricots and ham or gammon baked together is an easy-to-prepare lunch or dinner dish.

bake for 35 minutes, or until the fruit has coloured slightly.

Remove the tart from the tin and place on a rack. Sprinkle with the shredded almonds and brush over with the glaze. Serve warm or cold with cream.

Aquavit

A Scandinavian liquor distilled from potatoes or grain and flavoured with caraway seeds, there are many varieties of aquavit. They range from colourless to light orange, and some are flavoured with other herbs and spices. In Scandinavia, aquavit is usually served before or at the beginning of a meal and is tossed down in one gulp.

Arabian Stewed Lamb

  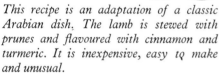

This recipe is an adaptation of a classic Arabian dish. The lamb is stewed with prunes and flavoured with cinnamon and turmeric. It is inexpensive, easy to make and unusual.

4 SERVINGS

2 tablespoons cooking oil
2 lb. lamb leg or shoulder, boned and cut into 1½-inch cubes
1 large onion, sliced
1 clove garlic, crushed
1 teaspoon powdered turmeric
2-inch cinnamon stick
1 teaspoon salt
    freshly ground black pepper
1 tablespoon flour
12 fl. oz. [1½ cups] beef stock
1 tablespoon brown sugar
16 prunes, stoned and soaked in water for 2 hours

Heat the oil in a large saucepan over moderate heat. Add the lamb cubes and sauté, stirring occasionally, until the cubes are brown on all sides. Using a slotted spoon, remove the pieces of lamb and set aside on a plate.

Add the onion to the pan and fry until it is golden brown, stirring occasionally. Add the garlic, turmeric, cinnamon, salt and 7 grindings of pepper. Stir and sauté for 5 minutes. Add the flour, stir and cook for a few seconds before gradually adding the stock.

Raise the heat and continue stirring until the mixture comes to the boil. Return the meat to the pan, lower the heat and simmer for 40 minutes or until

Left. Arabian Stewed Lamb, flavoured with prunes, cinnamon and turmeric, is an adaptation of an Eastern recipe.

the lamb is tender. Ten minutes before the lamb is cooked, add the sugar and the prunes. Serve hot with rice which has been boiled with a bay leaf.

Aragosta Fra Diavolo

LOBSTER WITH DEVILLED SAUCE

Aragosta Fra Diavolo (ah-rah-GO-stah frah dee-AH-voh-loh) is a spicy, Italian lobster dish. Serve it as a main course with a green salad and crusty bread.

4 SERVINGS

2 large lobsters, cooked
1 oz. [2 tablespoons] butter
1 tablespoon oil
4 shallots, finely chopped
2 cloves garlic, crushed
14 oz. canned tomatoes, drained
½ teaspoon dried thyme
½ teaspoon powdered bay leaf
1 tablespoon chopped parsley
1 teaspoon Tabasco sauce
2 teaspoons vinegar
1 teaspoon salt
¼ teaspoon black pepper
1 teaspoon sugar
5 fl. oz. [⅝ cup] red wine

Halve the lobsters and crack the large claws. Place the lobsters in a casserole.

Melt the butter in a saucepan over moderate heat. Add the oil. When hot, add the shallots and garlic and fry until they are soft. Add the tomatoes, thyme, bay leaf, parsley, Tabasco sauce, vinegar, salt, pepper and sugar. Stir, cover the pan and cook over low heat for 5 minutes.

Preheat the oven to moderate 350°F (Gas Mark 4, 180°C).

Light buns topped with brown sugar, almonds and raisins, Aranygaluska are traditionally eaten hot in Hungary.

Add the wine to the sauce, raise the heat and cook briskly, stirring occasionally, until the sauce is fairly thick.

Pour the sauce over the lobsters. Cover the casserole and bake in the oven for 20 minutes.

Aranygaluska

HUNGARIAN BUNS

Light, golden buns with a sugary filling and topping, Aranygaluska (AH-rahn-y'-GAH-loosh-kah) are traditionally served with morning or afternoon coffee. They are best eaten fresh from the oven, but they can be reheated.

ABOUT 14 BUNS

5 fl. oz. [⅝ cup] milk
1 tablespoon butter
3 tablespoons sugar
1 large egg, lightly beaten
2 fl. oz. [¼ cup] tepid water
1 tablespoon dried yeast
14 oz. [3½ cups] sifted flour
    pinch of salt
4 tablespoons melted butter

FILLING

2 oz. [⅓ cup] soft brown sugar
3 oz. [½ cup] raisins
2 oz. [⅓ cup] blanched almonds, finely chopped
¼ teaspoon ground cinnamon

Put milk, 2 tablespoons sugar, and 1 tablespoon butter in a small saucepan

over low heat, stir until the butter has melted and the sugar dissolved. Remove from the heat. When the mixture has cooled, beat in the egg.

Pour the tepid water into a bowl, stir in the remaining amount of sugar and sprinkle the yeast over the top. Set aside and leave for 20 minutes or until the mixture is frothy. Stir the yeast mixture into the milk, butter and egg liquid.

Put the flour and salt into a mixing bowl and make a well in the centre. Pour in the mixture from the saucepan, and, with a wooden spoon, mix it into the flour to form a stiff dough. Cover the bowl with a clean cloth and put it in a warm place until the dough has doubled in size.

For the filling, mix together the sugar, almonds, raisins and cinnamon.

When the dough has risen, put it on a floured surface. Knead it thoroughly with your hands for about 10 minutes, or until the dough is elastic and smooth. Then divide the dough into small pieces the size of a walnut and roll into balls.

Grease a 10-inch loose based cake tin with a little of the melted butter. Coat half of the dough balls in butter and place together in the bottom of the cake tin. Sprinkle half of the filling on top. Coat the remaining dough balls in butter and place on top of the filling. Spoon the remaining filling over the top.

Preheat the oven to cool 300°F (Gas Mark 2, 150°C).

Cover the cake tin with a piece of oiled plastic wrap and leave in a warm place

Sweet pepper salad with black olives and cheese, Ardei cu Untdelemn is an adaptation of a Romanian recipe.

for 30 to 40 minutes until the buns have risen.

Bake in the oven, on the middle shelf, for 30 minutes. Then raise the heat to fairly hot 400°F (Gas Mark 6, 200°C) and cook for 15 to 20 minutes, or until the buns are brown and firm.

Allow to cool in the tin for 5 minutes then turn the cake tin onto a wire rack and press the base of the tin to loosen the buns. Remove the base and reverse the buns back onto the wire rack. Leave to cool. Separate the buns.

Archbishop

A hot sherry or wine punch, this is an excellent drink for cold evenings or for a winter party.

4 TO 6 SERVINGS

1 Seville orange
20 cloves
1 tablespoon brown sugar
1 bottle medium-dry sherry, dry Bordeaux or dry, white wine

Preheat the oven to moderate 350°F (Gas Mark 4, 180°C).

Press the cloves into the skin of the orange. Place the orange on the middle shelf of the oven and cook for about 30 minutes, or until the orange is brown.

Cut the orange in half and sprinkle

the flesh with the sugar. Put the halves in the bottom of a punch bowl, or a large glass or china bowl.

Pour the sherry, or wine, into a stainless-steel or enamelled saucepan and heat until it is hot but not boiling. If you are using a glass bowl, put a metal spoon in it to prevent the bowl from cracking and pour in the wine. Serve immediately in punch cups or warmed wine glasses, putting a spoon in each glass.

Archiduc, à l'

A French cooking term, *à l'archiduc* (ah LAHR-chee-dook) is applied to a large number of dishes and usually indicates preparations seasoned with paprika and blended with cream.

Ardei cu Untdelemn

MARINATED PEPPER SALAD

A Romanian sweet pepper salad, Ardei cu Untdelemn (ahr-DAY koo oon-deh-LEM) can be served as an hors d'oeuvre, as a salad course or as an accompaniment to a meat dish. The peppers in the marinade, without the cheese and olives, can be kept in a jar with a tight fitting lid and stored in the refrigerator for a few days.

4 SERVINGS

4 green peppers
4 red peppers
6 tablespoons white vinegar
2 tablespoons medium dry sherry
1 tablespoon Worcestershire sauce
6 tablespoons olive oil
1 teaspoon salt
 freshly ground black pepper
2 teaspoons sugar
1 teaspoon paprika
12 black olives, stoned
8 oz. cream cheese cut into cubes

Wash and dry the peppers. Halve and remove the seeds and white pith. Cut the peppers into quarters. Half fill a saucepan with water and bring to the boil. Add the peppers and blanch for 3 minutes. Drain and dry on kitchen paper towels. Cool.

In a large mixing bowl, put the vinegar, sherry, Worcestershire sauce, oil, salt, 8 grindings of pepper, sugar and paprika. Stir well to mix. Taste and add more seasoning if necessary.

Put the peppers into the marinade and turn and mix until they are coated with the dressing. Cover and marinate for 24 hours in the refrigerator.

To serve, place the peppers in a shallow bowl or dish. Spoon a little of the marinade over them. Place the olives and cheese over the top and serve.

Ardei Umplutzi cu Orez

STUFFED GREEN PEPPERS AND TOMATO SAUCE

An unusual way of cooking peppers which comes from Romania, Ardei Umplutzi cu Orez (ar-DAY- oom-plootz koo oh-rayz) makes an excellent accompaniment to any braised meat.

4 SERVINGS

Low Cal

4 large green peppers
5 fl. oz. [⅝ cup] yoghurt
    chopped parsley
FILLING
1 tablespoon oil
2 onions, finely chopped
2 stalks celery, finely chopped
6 oz. [3 cups] cooked long-grain
    rice
2 tablespoons chopped parsley
¼ teaspoon mixed herbs
1 teaspoon salt
    freshly ground black pepper
1 egg
SAUCE
1 oz. [2 tablespoons] butter
1 onion, finely chopped
1 tablespoon flour
8 fl. oz. [1 cup] chicken stock
¾ lb. tomatoes, peeled and chopped
½ teaspoon salt
½ teaspoon sugar
2 teaspoons tomato purée

Cut the tops off the peppers and scoop out the seeds and white pith.

For the filling, heat the oil in a saucepan over medium heat. Add the onions and celery and stirring occasionally, fry for 3 to 4 minutes until soft but not brown. Stir in the rice, parsley, mixed herbs, salt, 6 grindings of pepper. Remove the pan from the heat and leave to cool slightly. Stir in the egg and mix well. Stuff the peppers pressing the filling down with the back of a spoon.

Preheat the oven to moderate 350°F (Gas Mark 4, 180°C).

For the sauce, place the butter in a flameproof casserole and melt over moderate heat. Add the onion and fry gently for 2 to 3 minutes until they are soft but not brown. Stir in the flour and cook for 1 minute. Pour the chicken stock slowly into the onion mixture stirring all the time with a wooden spoon. Continue stirring and cook until the sauce is thick and boiling. Add the tomatoes, salt, sugar and tomato purée.

Remove the casserole from the heat. Place the green peppers in the sauce, cover the casserole and cook in the oven for 35 to 40 minutes until the peppers are cooked. Remove the lid and spoon the yogurt over each pepper, sprinkle with parsley and serve immediately.

A Romanian dish, Ardei Umplutzi cu Orez is stuffed peppers in a tomato sauce topped with yogurt.

Areca Nut

The areca nut, or betel nut, is the fruit of the areca palm tree, which is indigenous to Malaysia but is also grown in Sri Lanka, India, Thailand and the Phillipines. The betel nut has a red or orange outer skin and the actual nut is a light brown colour with white flesh. The people of South Asia chew this nut which is considered to aid the digestion and is a mild narcotic. The nut is often chopped into small pieces, wrapped in a betel leaf with lime and aromatic flavouring and chewed. Chewing the betel nut produces a flow of red saliva which temporarily stains the mouth and teeth.

Arlésienne, à l'

A French cooking term, à l'Arlésienne (ah lahr-LAYZ-yen) is used to indicate dishes garnished in three different ways. One consists of sautéed aubergines, [eggplants] tomatoes, onion rings, and another is applied to a garnish of small, whole tomatoes fried in butter, and pickled chicory hearts sautéed in oil. Small tomatoes filled with a rice mixture, olives stuffed with a chicken and anchovy mixture, and new potatoes form the third garnish.

Armagnac

Famous brandies distilled in the Gers Department of France, armagnacs are considered to be equal to the best cognacs. The sandy soil of the vineyards produces a special wine from which the brandies are distilled in one operation. The resulting liquid is aged in barrels made of black Gascony oak which imparts a distinctive flavour to the armagnacs.

Armoricaine

Armorica is the Latin name for the region in northwestern France which includes the Gaul coast between the Seine and the Loire Rivers. The name derives from two Celtic words: *ar* which means on and *mor* which means sea. This region is more commonly known as Brittany. The culinary term *à l'Armoricaine* (ah lahr-MOH-ree-ken) applies to the many French dishes originating from this region and should not be confused with the term *à l'Americaine*.

Armoricaine also refers to a particularly delicious variety of Brittany oyster.

Arnavut Cigeri

LAMB'S LIVER WITH PEPPERS

A Turkish dish, Arnavut Cigeri (ahr-na-VOOT gee-ayr-ay) is spicy sautéed liver accompanied by an onion and pepper salad. It is quickly and simply prepared and is served as a first course. Larger quantities may be served as a main course.

4 SERVINGS

1 lb. lamb's liver, cut into cubes
3 fl. oz. [⅜ cup] anisette
3 onions, sliced
2 tablespoons chopped parsley
2 red peppers, seeds and white pith removed and sliced
½ teaspoon salt
freshly ground black pepper
1 teaspoon garlic salt
1 teaspoon sugar
2 teaspoons lemon juice
3 tablespoons flour
5 fl. oz. [⅝ cup] vegetable oil

Put the lamb cubes and anisette into a mixing bowl. Mix well and set aside. Blanch the onion rings in boiling water for 4 minutes. Drain and place in a bowl with the parsley, pepper slices, ½ teaspoon salt, 7 grindings of black pepper, ½ teaspoon garlic salt, sugar, and lemon juice. Toss well together and set aside.

On a large plate mix the flour and the remaining ½ teaspoon of garlic salt. With a slotted spoon, remove the liver cubes from the anisette and coat in the flour mixture.

Heat the oil in a frying-pan until it is very hot. Shake off the excess flour from the liver and fry for 2 to 3 minutes or until the cubes are lightly brown. Drain the fried liver on kitchen paper towels.

Place the liver on a heated serving dish and arrange the onion and red pepper salad around the dish.

If liked the salad may be served separately in a bowl.

Arni Psito

ROAST LEG OF LAMB

Arni Psito (ahr-nee psee-toh) is considered a great delicacy in Greece and is traditionally eaten at Easter.

6 SERVINGS

5 lb. leg of lamb
1 garlic clove, crushed
1 teaspoon grated lemon rind
1 teaspoon salt
freshly ground black pepper
1 oz. [2 tablespoons] butter
2 tablespoons oil
2 tablespoons lemon juice
4 fl. oz. [½ cup] stock or water
2 onions, chopped
2 tablespoons chopped parsley
6 oz. mushrooms, sliced

Preheat the oven to very hot 475°F (Gas Mark 9, 240°C).

In a mixing bowl, put the garlic, lemon rind, salt and 6 grindings of black pepper. Mix well. Spread the garlic mixture over the lamb. Place the lamb, skin side up into a roasting tin.

Place the butter and oil in a small saucepan and melt over low heat. Add the lemon juice and the stock, or water. Bring to the boil and pour into the roasting tin. Cook in the oven for 20 minutes.

Reduce the heat to moderate 350°F (Gas Mark 4, 180°C). Add the onions, parsley and mushrooms and continue cooking for about 2 hours.

Place the meat on a serving dish and arrange the onion mixture around it with cooked rice sautéed in butter.

Aroma

This word, when applied to a food or a wine, indicates its characteristic smell. Aroma is an important aspect of all foods as it contributes greatly to the appetizing quality of a dish. It can tell the cook much about the food being prepared, its freshness and the balance of seasoning. A particular method of cooking brings out an aroma or may impart one.

Aromatic

The term aromatic is used to describe the many fragrant herbs, spices, fruits, flowers and vegetables which are used to add aroma in cooking, pastry-making and confectionery.

A delicious Greek way of roasting leg of lamb, Arni Psito is served with a savoury mushroom and onion sauce and rice.

Aromatic Bitters

Aromatic bitters are alcoholic drinks flavoured with roots, barks, herbs or fruits. They are drunk either as aperitifs to whet the appetite, as liqueurs after a meal, or are used in small quantities in mixed drinks.

Some aromatic bitters, for example Orange Bitters, are sold under the name which gives them their predominant flavour. But, more commonly, they have commercial brand names. The best known

are Abbots Aged Bitters, which are made in the United States, Amer Picon in France, Angostura in Trinidad, Boonekamp in Holland, Campari in Italy and Underberg in Germany.

The preparation of aromatic liqueurs originated in France in the sixteenth century, although early Hebrew literature records that sweet or bitter herbs were sometimes added to wine to improve its flavour.

Some bitters are said to be digestive aids. In the United States during prohibition in the 1920s, Dr. Seigert's Angostura Bitters were considered to have medicinal properties and so were exempt from prohibition.

Arrack

Derived from the Arabic *araq*, meaning sweat and juice, arrack is the name for a wide range of strong, rough spirits which are distilled from whatever ingredients are widely and cheaply available. In Asia these ingredients include fermented rice, dates, palm sap, molasses, grapes or grain.

In the Middle East and the Balkans, arrack is known under many names—*raki* in Turkey, *ouzo* in Greece, *mastika* in Bulgaria, *zibib* in Egypt and *arrack* in the Lebanon, Syria, Iran, Iraq and Jordan. In these regions the drink is flavoured with aniseed and is superior to the fiery brews of the Far East.

Arrosto Perugina

ITALIAN ROAST PORK

This roast loin of pork, flavoured with fennel, cloves and garlic and basted with dry white wine, can be served hot or cold. An Italian dish, Arrosto Perugina (ah-ROH-sto per-roo-JEE-neh) is roasted in a slow oven so that the meat remains moist and juicy. Serve it with a green salad and white wine.

4 TO 6 SERVINGS

3½ to 4 lb. pork loin, boned and rolled
4 garlic cloves
4 cloves
½ tablespoon finely chopped fennel leaves or ½ teaspoon dried fennel
1½ teaspoons salt
freshly ground black pepper
10 fl. oz. [1¼ cups] dry white wine
10 fl. oz. [1¼ cups] water

Preheat the oven to cool 300°F (Gas Mark 2, 150°C).

Peel the garlic cloves and slit them into four lengthways. Moisten the garlic slivers with water and roll them in the fennel. With a sharp, pointed kitchen knife, make incisions in the pork large enough to insert 1 sliver of garlic and 1 whole clove. Insert all the garlic, fennel and cloves and rub the meat with the salt and 5 grindings of pepper.

Lay the meat in a deep baking dish and pour in the wine and water. Place the baking dish in the middle of the oven. Basting occasionally, allow 45 minutes cooking time per pound of meat. When cooked, the meat should be quite moist.

If the pork is to be served hot, remove it from the baking dish and place on a warmed serving dish. If the pork is to be served cold, allow it to cool in the juices in the baking dish before removing it.

Arrowroot

Arrowroot is a pure starch which is obtained from the root of a tropical plant. Dried in the sun, the root is ground to a fine, white powder. Very nutritious, arrowroot is easily digested and was once a popular ingredient in foods for children and invalids.

Used for thickening sauces, soups and puddings in place of flour or cornflour, only half as much arrowroot is required to produce the same result as with flour. For making milk puddings, arrowroot is used in the same way and in the same

proportions as cornflour. As a thickening agent for clear liquids, arrowroot is particularly good because it does not cause clouding.

The name arrowroot is said to come from its American Indian name, *aranuta*, which means 'flour-root'. Most arrowroot is imported from the West Indies.

Arroz con Pollo

CHICKEN WITH RICE

A chicken and rice dish from Spain, Arroz con Pollo (ah-ROHS kohn poh-loh) is flavoured with garlic and spices. Cooked in a casserole it makes a delicious main course.

4 SERVINGS

3 tablespoons vegetable oil
6 slices streaky bacon, chopped
1 x 5lb. chicken, cut into serving pieces.
2 tablespoons seasoned flour
2 onions, chopped
1 garlic clove, crushed
14 oz. canned tomatoes, drained
3 oz. [½ cup] canned pimientos, drained
2 teaspoons paprika
¼ teaspoon saffron
8 oz. [1⅓ cup] long grain rice
1 teaspoon salt
1 pint [2½ cups] water
6 oz. frozen peas
2 tablespoons chopped parsley

Heat the oil in a flameproof casserole over medium heat. Add the bacon and fry for about 5 minutes until crisp. Remove the bacon with a slotted spoon and drain on kitchen paper towels. Set aside.

Coat the chicken pieces in the seasoned flour, and add to the fat in the casserole. Place over moderate heat and fry the chicken on all sides until a light golden brown. Remove the chicken pieces from the casserole and set aside.

Preheat the oven to moderate 350°F (Gas Mark 4, 180°C).

Drain off most of the oil from the casserole. Put the onions and garlic in to the casserole and fry over moderate heat, stirring occasionally for 2 to 3 minutes until the onions are soft.

Place the chicken on top of the onions and add the tomatoes, pimientos, paprika, saffron, salt and water. Raise the heat and bring to the boil. Add the rice and bacon and stir well to mix the ingredients.

Cover the casserole with a lid or piece of aluminium foil and place in the oven, cook for about 30 minutes.

Add the peas and cook for a further 10 minutes or until the chicken is tender. Sprinkle with the chopped parsley.

A chicken and rice casserole with peas, Arroz con Pollo is flavoured with parsley, saffron and garlic.

To prepare an artichoke, cut off the stalk with a sharp knife and pull off any tough or bruised outer leaves.

Lay it on its side and slice off the top third. Rub all the cut edges and the base with a piece of lemon.

With kitchen scissors, trim ¼-inch off the points of the remaining leaves and rub the cut edges with lemon.

Artichoke

This is the name given to three quite different vegetables, the globe artichoke, the JERUSALEM ARTICHOKE, and the JAPANESE, or Chinese ARTICHOKE.

The globe, or leafy artichoke, which looks like a large thistle, is indigenous to Europe and North Africa, but is now grown in almost every part of the world. There are many varieties which are cultivated for the bud of the flower. The part of the artichoke where the bud joins the stem is called the heart, or *fond*, and has a delicate flavour. Growing from this are the fleshy leaves. At the base of each leaf is a small edible section. Inside the leaves is the inedible choke, a fine, hair-like growth which develops into the flower.

Globe artichokes are rich in iron, mineral salts and iodine and contain some vitamin C. They can be boiled whole, fried, baked stuffed, used to make soup, or the hearts served in a salad. Very small, young artichokes can be eaten whole, raw or fried in batter. In Italy these are bottled in olive oil and are served as an hors d'oeuvre.

Artichokes should never be cooked in aluminium or iron saucepans, as the flesh will turn grey. The best tasting artichokes are heavy, with compact, fleshy, green or purple-green leaves and firm, green stems.

To eat an artichoke, pull off a leaf with your fingers and dip the bottom part of it in melted butter or sauce. Now scrape off this tender flesh between your teeth. Only the tender flesh at the bottom of the leaf is edible. When you have removed all the leaves, you will come to the heart. Scrape off and discard the hairy choke surrounding it. The heart is eaten with a knife and fork.

Artichokes, Boiled

Boiled artichokes may be served hot with melted butter, Hollandaise sauce, or various

Artichokes are cooked in boiling, salted water until the bases are tender.

cream sauces. They may also be chilled and served with vinaigrette sauce or mayonnaise. They make a delicious first course, but they can also be served instead of a salad or as the vegetable accompaniment to a meat dish. The dechoking of the artichokes may be done before or after cooking.

6 SERVINGS

6 medium-sized artichokes
1 lemon, cut in quarters
8 pints water
3 tablespoons salt

With a sharp knife, cut the stalks off the artichokes. Pull off any bruised or tough outer leaves. Lay each artichoke on its side and slice off the top third of it. With kitchen scissors, trim ¼-inch off the points of the rest of the leaves. Wash the artichoke under cold running water. Rub the cut edges with a piece of the lemon to prevent them discolouring.

If you wish to remove the chokes before cooking, spread the top leaves apart and pull out the prickly leaves surrounding the hairy choke. With a teaspoon, scrape out the choke. Squeeze a little lemon juice into the centre and press the leaves back together again.

Put the water into a large saucepan and bring to a boil over medium heat. Add the salt. Drop in the artichokes, base down, and bring the water to a boil again. Boil briskly, uncovered, turning the artichokes occasionally. If you have removed the chokes, cook for about 15 minutes. If the chokes have not been removed, cook for about 30 minutes. The artichokes are cooked when their bases are tender when pierced with a sharp knife and the leaves pull out easily.

With a slotted spoon, remove the artichokes from the saucepan and drain them upside down in a colander.

To remove the choke, spread the top leaves apart and pull out the prickly leaves surrounding the hairy choke.

With a teaspoon, scrape out the choke. Squeeze lemon juice into the centre and press the leaves back together.

Rub all the cut edges with lemon to prevent the artichoke from discolouring. It is now ready to cook.

To prepare artichoke hearts, bend back the lower leaves of each artichoke until they snap off.

Remove all outer leaves until you reach those bending inwards. With a sharp knife, slice off the stalk.

Place the artichoke on its side and cut off the remaining leaves just above the white heart.

Rotating the base of the artichoke against the knife blade, trim off all the green leaf bases.

Artichoke Hearts

Artichoke hearts are the tender, fleshy bases of artichokes. They make a delicious but rather expensive hors d'oeuvre. They may be stuffed with mushrooms, spinach, pâté or sausage meat mixed with chopped onions. As a vegetable course for a dinner or lunch party, they may be braised with butter or served with a Mornay or Hollandaise sauce.

To prevent discolouring, drop each trimmed heart into a bowl of acidulated water in a proportion of 1 tablespoon of lemon juice or vinegar to 1½ pints of water.

4 SERVINGS

12 large artichokes
 2 pints [5 cups] water containing
    3 tablespoons lemon juice
 ½ lemon
 2 oz. [½ cup] flour
 3 pints [7½ cups] cold water
 4 tablespoons lemon juice
 2 teaspoons salt

Hold each artichoke and bend the leaves back until they snap off. Continue until you reach the inside leaves which have begun to fold inwards.

With a sharp knife, cut off the stalks of the artichokes.

Place each artichoke on its side and slice off the remaining leaves just above the heart. Rub the cut parts of the artichoke well with lemon juice. Rotating the base of the artichoke against the knife blade, trim the base of all pieces of green to expose the whitish surface of the heart. As each heart is trimmed, drop it into the bowl of acidulated water.

Put the flour in a medium-sized saucepan and stir in 2 tablespoons of water to make a smooth paste. Stir in the rest of the water, the lemon juice and the salt. Bring it to a boil and simmer for 5 minutes.

Add the artichoke hearts. Bring the liquid to the boil, then simmer for 30 to 40 minutes, or until the hearts are tender when pierced with a knife. Make sure that the liquid covers the artichoke hearts all the time they are cooking, adding water if necessary.

Drain the hearts and serve with melted butter, or use any of the following recipes for artichoke hearts.

Artichoke Heart Soufflé

Serve this unusual soufflé as a first course or as the main course for lunch or supper. It may be accompanied by allumette potatoes and a salad of cold, cooked French

Unusual and delicately flavoured, Artichoke Heart Soufflé may be served as a first course or as a light main course for lunch or supper.

beans with a vinaigrette sauce, or a tossed green salad. A well-chilled, light, dry, white Italian or French wine would go well with this soufflé.

4 SERVINGS

 2 oz. [¼ cup] plus 1 teaspoon butter
 2 oz. [½ cup] flour, sifted
 ¼ teaspoon salt
 5 grindings black pepper
 ¼ teaspoon grated nutmeg
10 fl. oz. [1¼ cups] milk
 2 tablespoons single [light] cream
 2 oz. [½ cup] Gruyère cheese, grated
 6 artichoke hearts, cooked fresh, or
    canned
 4 egg yolks
 5 egg whites

Preheat the oven to 400°F (Gas Mark 6, 200°C). Grease a 3-pint soufflé dish with 1 teaspoon butter. Tie a strip of greaseproof paper around the rim of the soufflé dish so it projects 2 inches above the top.

Melt the remaining amount of butter in a large, heavy saucepan over low heat. Remove from the heat and, with a wooden spoon, stir in the flour. Replace the saucepan on the heat and, stirring constantly, cook for 2 minutes. Add the salt, pepper and nutmeg. Mix well. Add the milk, a little at a time, and, stirring continously, bring to the boil. Boil for 2 minutes, still stirring, until the sauce thickens. Remove from the heat and stir in the cream and the grated cheese.

Place the artichoke hearts in a bowl and, with a table fork, mash them well. Add to the cheese mixture. Add the egg yolks to the mixture and stir well.

Beat the egg whites in a medium-sized mixing bowl with a whisk until they form stiff peaks. Be careful not to over-beat the whites or they will begin to collapse.

Fold a large tablespoon of beaten egg white into the sauce. With a rubber spatula, scoop the rest of the egg whites on top of the mixture and fold in very gently. Pour the mixture into the soufflé dish. It should fill two-thirds of the dish.

Place the dish on the middle shelf of the oven and reduce the heat to 375°F (Gas Mark 5, 190°C). Bake for 35 minutes. When the soufflé is ready, the top should be brown and it should have risen 2 or 3 inches above the top of the dish. To be sure the soufflé is cooked, plunge a thin knife into the centre. If the soufflé is ready the knife will come out clean.

Serve immediately.

Artichokes Braised with Mixed Vegetables

This tasty artichoke casserole with the addition of other vegetables makes a nourishing and tasty dish. For a complete meal, sausages or bacon may be added to this vegetable and artichoke casserole. It can be prepared in advance and reheated just before serving.

4 SERVINGS

4 large artichokes
4 pints [5 pints] water
1 tablespoon plus 1 teaspoon salt
4 oz. [½ cup] butter
4 onions, sliced
1 large garlic clove, chopped
6 stalks celery, sliced
2 large potatoes cut into quarters
4 carrots scraped and sliced
2 turnips, peeled and cubed
   freshly ground black pepper
3 fl. oz. [⅜ cup] white wine
15 fl. oz. [1⅞ cups] beef stock
1 bouquet garni, consisting of 4
   sprigs of parsley, 1 spray of
   thyme and 1 small bay
   leaf, tied together
2 oz. mushrooms, washed
   and sliced
2 tablespoons chopped parsley

Prepare the artichokes for cooking. Cut off the tops of the leaves so that the artichokes are about 2½ inches high. Slice them lengthways into quarters and cut out the chokes.

In a large saucepan, bring the water to a boil and add 1 tablespoon of salt. Drop the artichoke quarters into the boiling water. Boil for 10 minutes and drain well on kitchen paper towels.

Preheat the oven to moderate 350°F (Gas Mark 4, 180°C).

In a large casserole, which is big enough to hold the artichokes in one layer, melt most of the butter. Fry the onions over low heat for 5 minutes, or until they are golden, but not brown. Stir in the garlic.

Place the artichoke hearts in the casserole. Add the celery, potatoes, carrots, turnips, 4 grindings of pepper and remaining salt. Cook over low heat for 10 minutes.

Pour the wine into the casserole and bring to the boil over high heat. Add the beef stock and the bouquet garni.

Cover the casserole, transfer it to the oven and cook gently for 1 to 1¼ hours, or until the liquid has almost evaporated and the vegetables are tender.

Ten minutes before the vegetables have finished cooking, put the remaining butter in a small saucepan and sauté the mushrooms for 5 minutes. Add them to the casserole.

Before serving, discard the bouquet garni and sprinkle the vegetables with chopped parlsey.

Artichokes with Dill Sauce

Artichokes with Dill Sauce is a way artichokes are served as a first course in Greece. The dill sauce gives the artichokes an unusual flavour.

6 SERVINGS

6 tablespoons lemon juice
4 tablespoons flour
8 fl. oz. [1 cup] water
6 medium-sized artichokes
8 fl. oz. [1 cup] olive oil
1 medium-sized onion, chopped
3 tablespoons finely chopped fresh
   dill or 2½ teaspoons dried dill
1½ teaspoons salt

Pour the lemon juice into a large mixing bowl. Add the flour and, using a whisk, beat the mixture until it is smooth. Add the water and continue beating until the liquid is a thin, smooth paste.

Prepare and trim the artichokes, removing the chokes. Put them into the lemon-and-flour mixture and turn them until they are evenly coated. Leave them to soak.

Heat the olive oil, over moderate heat, in a large casserole. Add the onions, reduce the heat and sauté them gently for 5 minutes. Do not allow them to brown.

With a slotted spoon, remove the artichokes from the lemon-and-flour mixture and set aside. Drain the lemon-and-flour mixture into the casserole. Add the dill and salt. Stirring continuously with a wooden spoon, bring the liquid to the boil.

Place the artichokes side by side in the casserole and baste them thoroughly with the liquid. Reduce the heat to low. Cover the casserole and simmer gently for 20 minutes. Turn the artichokes over and simmer for another 25 minutes. The artichokes are cooked when their bases are tender when pierced with the point of a sharp knife.

Arrange the artichokes on a serving dish and pour the sauce over them.

Artichokes à la Grecque

Pickled baby artichokes make a piquant hors d'oeuvre or may be served as part of an antipasto. The artichokes must be very small, tender and completely edible.

4 SERVINGS

20 baby artichokes, outer leaves removed and the remaining leaves cut short
4 pints [5 pints] water
juice of 3½ lemons
5 fl. oz. [⅝ cup] olive oil
½ teaspoon coriander seeds
6 peppercorns
1 bay leaf
1 sprig of thyme
1 teaspoon salt

Put 3 pints of water and 1½ tablespoons of lemon juice into a large pan. Add the artichokes and bring to the boil over moderate heat. Boil for 10 minutes. Drain the artichokes in a colander and cool in running cold water. Drain again.

Put all the remaining ingredients in a large pan and bring to the boil over high heat. Add the artichokes. When the liquid comes to the boil again, lower the heat, cover and simmer for 20 minutes.

With a slotted spoon, remove the artichokes from the pan and place in a serving dish. Pour 6 tablespoons of the liquid from the pan over them. Chill thoroughly before serving.

Artichokes à la Provençale
ARTICHOKES WITH GARLIC AND TOMATOES

This is a classic French method of cooking artichokes. Served on its own it makes an attractive and unusual hors d'oeuvre. It is also an excellent vegetable accompaniment to grilled [broiled] chicken.

4 SERVINGS

4 artichokes
2 pints [5 cups] water
2½ teaspoons salt
2 tablespoons olive oil
4 slices bacon, rinds removed and cut into pieces
2 onions, finely chopped
2 garlic cloves, crushed
freshly ground black pepper
½ teaspoon dried basil
12 oz. canned tomatoes
1 tablespoon tomato purée
2 tablespoons brandy (optional)
4 fl. oz. [½ cup] white wine
8 fl. oz. [1 cup] chicken stock or water and 1 chicken stock cube
1 bouquet garni, consisting of 3 parsley sprigs, 1 spray of thyme and 1 bay leaf, tied together

Cut off the stems of the artichokes, remove the small leaves at the bases and cut off the tops of the leaves, leaving the artichokes about 3 inches high.

Slice the artichokes into quarters, and, with a spoon, scrape out the chokes. Put the water and 2 teaspoons of the salt into a large saucepan and bring to the boil. Add the artichokes and boil for 5 minutes. Drain the artichokes on kitchen paper towels and set aside.

Heat the oil in a large heavy saucepan or flameproof casserole over moderate heat. Add the bacon and fry until crisp. Stir in the onions and garlic and fry for 5 minutes or until the onions are soft.

Place the artichoke quarters into the casserole and spoon the bacon mixture over them. Stir in the remaining ½ teaspoon of salt and 6 grindings of black pepper. Add the basil, tomatoes, tomato purée and brandy, if used. Bring to the boil over high heat then reduce heat to low and simmer for 5 minutes.

Pour the wine and stock over the artichokes, add the bouquet garni. Cover and cook over low heat for ¾ hour.

If there is too much liquid raise the heat and boil quickly until the liquid has reduced slightly. Remove the bouquet garni before serving. Serve immediately.

Artichokes Stuffed with Pork and Almonds make a delicious, although expensive, main course.

Artichokes Stuffed with Pork and Almonds

This is an unusual and rather expensive way to serve artichokes. They may, however, be served as a main course for lunch or supper. Serve some melted butter mixed with a few drops of lemon juice into which the artichoke leaves and hearts can be dipped.

4 SERVINGS

4 large artichokes
1 lemon quartered
2 fl. oz. [¼ cup] lemon juice
enough boiling water to cover the artichokes
1 tablespoon salt
STUFFING
2 oz. [¼ cup] vegetable fat

½ lb. minced [ground] pork
1 medium-sized onion, chopped
2 oz. [1 cup] fresh breadcrumbs
2 tablespoons chopped parsley
½ teaspoon salt
    freshly ground black pepper
½ teaspoon celery salt
2 oz. [⅓ cup] blanched almonds,
    finely chopped
1 egg, lightly beaten
1 tablespoon vegetable oil

Wash and prepare the artichokes for boiling. Squeeze lemon juice over the cut areas to prevent them discolouring. Using a sharp knife, cut off the top third of each artichoke. Pull open the centre leaves carefully and pull out the yellow and purple leaves from the centres. Using a teaspoon, scrape and pull off all the fuzzy chokes to expose the heart. Squeeze a little lemon juice into the hollows. Push the leaves back together again.

Stand the artichokes in a large saucepan. If they do not fit snugly into the saucepan, tie a piece of string around each one so they will keep their shape while boiling.

Pour the boiling water and the remaining lemon juice over the artichokes so that they are completely covered. Add the salt. Cover the saucepan and simmer the artichokes, over medium heat, for 25 minutes, or until the bases are tender when pierced with a sharp knife. When the artichokes are cooked, remove them from the water with a slotted spoon and turn them upside down in a colander to drain.

While the artichokes are boiling, pre-heat the oven to moderate 350°F (Gas Mark 4, 180°C) and make the stuffing.

In a large, heavy frying-pan, melt the fat. Add the pork and the onions and sauté them until they are lightly browned. Remove the frying-pan from the heat and add the breadcrumbs, parsley, salt, 4 grindings of pepper, celery salt, almonds and beaten egg.

Stir the mixture well.

Place the artichokes in a baking dish and fill the centres with the stuffing.

Pour a little water around the artichokes. Brush the artichokes generously with oil. Cover the dish with aluminium foil and bake on the centre shelf of the oven for 30 to 40 minutes until the artichokes are tender.

Serve hot.

Artichokes Stuffed with Prawns and Spicy Mayonnaise

Cold artichokes filled with prawns and herbs and anchovy flavoured mayonnaise makes an attractive first course for a dinner party or a tasty and appetizing main dish for a summer lunch. This recipe uses a home-made mayonnaise but a bought one may be substituted if time is short.

6 SERVINGS

6 artichokes
    juice of 1 lemon
4 pints [5 pints] water
2 tablespoons salt
MAYONNAISE
6 egg yolks
$\frac{1}{2}$ teaspoon salt
    freshly ground pepper
$\frac{1}{4}$ teaspoon French mustard
1 teaspoon sugar
1 pint [2$\frac{1}{2}$ cups] olive oil
4 tablespoons wine vinegar
1 tablespoon lemon juice

2 tablespoons finely chopped chives
1 teaspoon chopped capers
1 garlic clove, crushed
1 tablespoon chopped fresh or 1$\frac{1}{2}$
    teaspoons dried tarragon
6 canned anchovies, drained and
    finely chopped
2 tablespoons chopped parsley
$\frac{1}{8}$ teaspoon cayenne pepper
2 lb. peeled prawns or shrimps (if
    frozen allow to thaw)
2 lemons, sliced

To make the mayonnaise, place the egg yolks in a medium-sized mixing bowl. Beat with a fork, rotary whisk or electric blender. Add the salt, 4 grindings of pepper, mustard and the sugar. Continue beating until the yolks are thick and creamy.

Still beating continuously, add 4

Artichokes Stuffed with Prawns is a very attractive cold dish.

tablespoons of oil very slowly by dripping it from a spoon. If you are using an electric blender, set the speed to slow when adding the oil. If the sauce becomes too thick to beat easily, dilute it with a few drops of vinegar. Beating constantly, add the remaining oil a little at a time, until it is incorporated into the egg yolks. Add the vinegar and lightly beat to mix.

Add the lemon juice, chives, capers, garlic, tarragon, anchovies, parsley and cayenne pepper to the mayonnaise and beat well with a wooden spoon.

Taste and add more salt and pepper if necessary.

Put 1$\frac{1}{2}$ lbs. prawns into a large bowl and stir in half of the dressing. Mix well and place in the refrigerator to chill.

Wash and prepare the artichokes for cooking. Dip the trimmed tops into the lemon juice. This prevents them from going brown.

Pour the water into a large saucepan, add the salt and bring to the boil. Place the artichokes in the water and boil for about 30 minutes or until they are cooked. Remove the artichokes with a slotted spoon and place upside down on kitchen paper towels and leave to drain and cool.

Gently pull the leaves of each artichoke apart and remove the yellow inner core. With a fork or spoon, scrape out the choke and discard it.

When the artichokes are really cold, fill the centre of each one with the prawn filling. Garnish each one with the remaining prawns or shrimps.

Serve on individual plates and place lemon slices around the edge. Serve the remaining filling separately.

Artichokes with Veal and Peppers

This is a decorative supper dish which is worth the time and effort required to prepare it. Serve a sauce with it of melted butter mixed with a few drops of lemon juice for the artichoke leaves and heart.

4 SERVINGS

4 artichokes
1 lemon, halved
2 fl. oz. [$\frac{1}{4}$ cup] lemon juice
    enough boiling water to cover the
    artichokes
1 tablespoon salt
STUFFING
3 tablespoons olive oil
1 onion, finely chopped
1 lb. minced [ground] veal
1 green pepper, halved, seeded and
    finely sliced
1 garlic clove, crushed

1 teaspoon salt
  freshly ground black pepper
½ teaspoon ground nutmeg
4 tomatoes, blanched, peeled and
  chopped
2 oz. [½ cup] grated Cheddar cheese

Wash and prepare the artichokes for boiling. Squeeze lemon juice over the cut areas to prevent them discolouring. Using a sharp knife, cut off the top one-third of the artichoke. Pull open the centre leaves carefully and pull out the yellow and purple leaves from the centre. Using a teaspoon, scrape and pull off all the fuzzy choke to expose the heart. Squeeze a little lemon juice into the hollow. Push the leaves back together again.

Stand the artichokes in a large saucepan. They must fit snugly into the saucepan so they keep their shape while boiling or tie a piece of string around each one.

Pour the boiling water and lemon juice over the artichokes so that they are completely covered. Add the salt. Cover and simmer the artichokes over medium heat for 25 minutes, or until the bases are tender when pierced with a sharp knife.

Meanwhile, heat the oil in a large saucepan. Add the onions to the oil and cook over medium heat, stirring, for 3 minutes. Add the veal and continue cooking until the meat is brown. Add the green pepper, garlic, salt, 4 grindings of pepper and the nutmeg and mix well.

Stir in the tomatoes and cheese. Reduce the heat to low and cover the saucepan. Simmer gently for 20 to 25 minutes, stirring occasionally.

While the veal mixture is cooking, remove the cooked artichokes from the water with a slotted spoon. Turn them upside down in a colander to drain. Keep the artichokes warm.

When the veal mixture is ready, fill the artichokes with it and serve hot.

Artichoke Hearts à l'Allemande

An elegant vegetable dish for lunch or dinner parties, Artichoke Hearts à l'Allemande may be served as an accompaniment to veal, cold meats or sautéed chicken.

4 SERVINGS

12 artichoke hearts
1½ pints [4 cups] cold water
 2 tablespoons lemon juice
 1 teaspoon salt
1½ oz. [3 tablespoons] butter
10 fl. oz. [1¼ cups] Allemande Sauce

Bring the water to a boil in a medium-sized saucepan. Add the lemon juice and salt. Drop the artichoke hearts into the water and simmer on a low heat for 10 minutes. Remove the saucepan from the heat and drain the artichoke hearts.

Artichoke Hearts in Butter are baked in the oven and flavoured with spring onions [scallions] or shallots.

Melt the butter in a medium-sized frying-pan. Add the artichoke hearts and sauté gently until they are tender. With a slotted spoon, transfer them to a heated serving dish. Pour the hot Allemande Sauce over them and serve immediately.

Artichoke Hearts in Butter

This is a simple, well-flavoured dish which can be served as a first course or as a vegetable accompaniment to chicken, veal or egg dishes.

4 SERVINGS

12 artichoke hearts, cooked and cut
   into quarters
 4 oz. [½ cup] butter
 4 tablespoons chopped shallots or
   spring onions [scallions]
½ teaspoon salt
   freshly ground pepper
 4 tablespoons chopped parsley

Preheat the oven to warm 325°F (Gas Mark 3, 170°C).

Melt the butter in a medium-sized, flameproof casserole. Put in the shallots, or spring onions, and the artichoke hearts

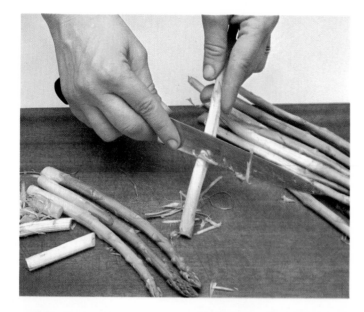

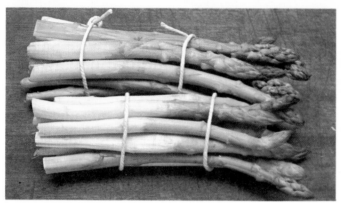

1. To prepare the asparagus, peel or scrape the stalks with a knife, thickly at the butt end and very thinly towards the tip.
2. Wash the stalks and tie them with string in neat bundles of not more than 10. Cut off the ends of the stalks evenly.
3. Stand the asparagus in a jar of boiling water and cover it with pierced aluminium foil. Place the jar in a pan of boiling water.
4. When the asparagus is cooked, take the bundles out of the jar, drain, remove the string and put the stalks on a serving plate.

and stir, making sure the hearts are well coated with the butter. Sprinkle on the salt and 4 grindings of pepper and mix well.

Cover the casserole and bake in the centre of the oven for 20 minutes. Sprinkle with parsley, and serve immediately.

Artichoke Hearts with Herbs

An unusual vegetable dish for a lunch or dinner party, this may accompany veal, roast or sautéed chicken and egg dishes.

4 SERVINGS

12 fresh artichoke hearts
1½ pints [4 cups] cold water
2 tablespoons lemon juice
1 teaspoon salt
1½ oz. [3 tablespoons] butter
½ teaspoon dried chervil
½ teaspoon chopped parsley

Bring the water to the boil in a medium-sized saucepan. Add the lemon juice and salt. Drop the artichoke hearts into the water and simmer for 10 minutes. Drain and slice the artichoke hearts.

Melt the butter in a heavy frying-pan

and very gently sauté the sliced artichoke hearts. Put them in a heated vegetable dish and sprinkle with the chervil and parsley.

Asafoetida

Asafoetida is a gum resin usually obtained from the plant ferula foetida which is native to Iran and Afghanistan. The resin is dried and in India and Iran it is used as a condiment. Asafoetida has an acrid taste and a strong garlic-like odour.

Asbestos Mat

Mats made of asbestos, a grey fibrous mineral, are noncombustible, reflect heat and are good insulators. For these reasons, the mats can be placed under a saucepan when an extremely low heat is required, or to prevent burning. They can also be used on the stove under a utensil which is not fireproof, to prevent it cracking.

Ashberry

This bright red berry is the fruit of the mountain ash. More commonly known as ROWAN BERRY, it is used to make jelly and to flavour preserves.

Ashe Reshte

NOODLE SOUP

Ashe Reshte (ah-sh RESH-teh), *a Persian recipe, is a tasty, unusual and filling soup. It is ideal to serve on cold winter evenings.*

4 SERVINGS

½ lb. minced [ground] beef
1 medium-sized onion, chopped finely
½ teaspoon ground cinnamon
grated rind of ½ lemon
freshly ground black pepper
1½ teaspoons salt
2 pints [5 cups] water
2 oz. [¼ cup] dried peas
2 oz. [¼ cup] lentils
4 oz. fine egg noodles
2 tablespoons chopped parsley
1 tablespoon dried mint

Put the minced beef, onion, ¼ teaspoon cinnamon, grated lemon rind, 4 grindings of black pepper and ½ teaspoon salt into a medium-sized mixing bowl. Using your hands, mix the ingredients well and shape into small balls the size of walnuts.

Put the water in a large pan with the dried peas and lentils and the remaining

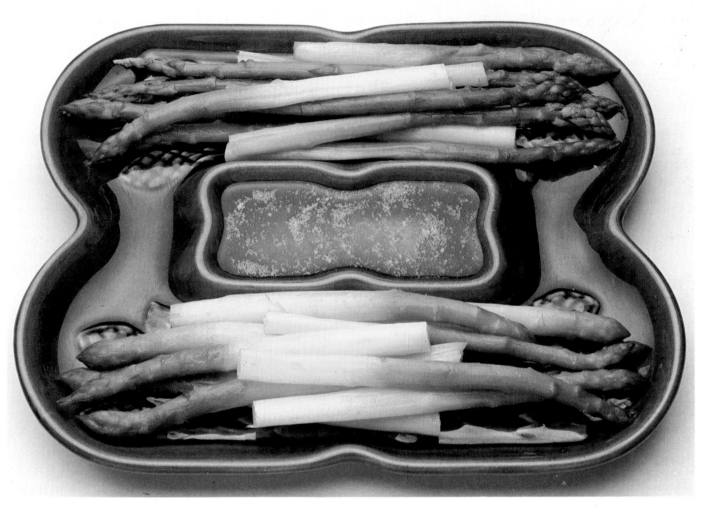

1 teaspoon of salt. Bring to the boil and simmer for 15 minutes. Add the meatballs, noodles, 3 grindings of pepper and the parsley. Simmer for 40 minutes. Add more boiling water if the soup is too thick.

Crush the dried mint with your fingers and add to the soup with the remaining cinnamon. Serve immediately.

Asparagus

Asparagus is a member of the lily family of which there are more than a hundred species. The best known species is garden asparagus, which is now grown in most temperate and subtropical regions of the world.

Wild asparagus was known to the early Greeks and to this day it grows on the Mediterranean coast. As a cultivated plant, asparagus was known in the second century B.C. and was highly prized as a vegetable by the Romans. But in the West extensive cultivation of the plant did not begin until the sixteenth century.

Although there are a number of varieties of asparagus, the best known for culinary purposes are French asparagus, especially the white Argenteuil asparagus and Lauris, grown in the Vaucluse

district in the South of France, English asparagus, which is a thin, green variety, Italian or Genoa asparagus, which is purplish in colour, and white Belgian asparagus.

To prepare asparagus, peel or scrape the stalks with a sharp knife. At the butt end, the asparagus may be peeled as much as $\frac{1}{16}$ of an inch. But the peeling should gradually become very thin towards the tip. Wash them carefully. Make bundles of no more than 10 stalks, tie the bundles in 2 places and cut the ends off the stalks evenly.

To cook asparagus, bring about 4 inches of salted water to the boil in a deep pan. Stand the bundle of asparagus in the pan so that the stalks are in the water and the tips are out of it. Cover partially, leaving space for the steam to escape, and cook for 15 to 20 minutes.

There are special asparagus pans on the market which are deep and narrow and have holes in the lid. If you do not have a special asparagus pan, you can use a glass jar. Fill the jar with boiling water and stand the asparagus in it. Place the jar in a pan with boiling water and cook for 30 minutes. When the asparagus is cooked, take out the bundle carefully, drain and cut the strings.

To serve asparagus, pile the hot, cooked stalks on a plate lined with a folded napkin. Estimate 6 stalks per person. Serve with melted butter or with a Hollandaise sauce. Cold asparagus is delicious served with a vinaigrette sauce.

Asparagus may be served alone as a first course. It also makes an excellent vegetable accompaniment to meat, fish and chicken dishes. It may also be served cold in place of a salad.

Asparagus au Beurre

As well as making a simple but elegant hors d'oeuvre, asparagus is a delicious vegetable accompaniment to meat and fish dishes. The season for fresh asparagus is a short one so frozen asparagus may be used in any other asparagus recipe.

4 SERVINGS

1 lb. frozen asparagus
2 pints [5 cups] water
1 tablespoon plus $\frac{1}{4}$ teaspoon salt
6 tablespoons hot, melted butter
   freshly ground pepper

Boil the water in a large saucepan and add 1 tablespoon of salt. Drop the asparagus into the water. When the water returns to the boil, boil rapidly for 4 minutes, or until the asparagus is almost tender.

If the asparagus is not to be served immediately, put in a colander and run cold water through it to prevent it from cooking further and to retain the colour and texture.

Just before serving, put the asparagus in a warmed serving dish and pour the butter over it. Taking care not to break the asparagus, gently toss it in the hot butter to finish the cooking and to coat it with butter. Sprinkle with ¼ teaspoon of salt and 4 grindings of pepper and serve.

Asparagus Cream Soup

This delicious soup is made with fresh asparagus, cream and eggs. The base is a home-made vegetable stock which should cook for at least 2 hours.

4 SERVINGS

2 lb. asparagus
1 small onion, finely sliced
10 fl. oz. [1¼ cups] water
1 teaspoon salt
4 grindings fresh black pepper
4 tablespoons flour
2 tablespoons butter
2 egg yolks
5 fl. oz. single [light] cream
STOCK
1 tablespoon butter
1 lb. carrots, sliced in large pieces
1 lb. onions, peeled and sliced
½ head celery, sliced
1 small turnip, sliced in large pieces
6 peppercorns
 a bouquet garni, consisting of 4 sprigs of parsley, a sprig of thyme and 1 bay leaf tied together
1 teaspoon salt
5 pints [6¼ pints] hot water

For the stock, melt the butter in a large pan. Add the slices of carrot, onions, celery and turnip to the pan. Cook over low heat, stirring occasionally, until the vegetables are brown. Add the peppercorns, bouquet garni, salt and hot water. Bring to the boil, half cover the pan and simmer for 2 hours, or until the stock has a good flavour and has reduced to 1½ pints [2 pints]. Strain before using.

For the soup, wash and trim the asparagus. Cut off 2 inches from the tips of the asparagus and put them aside. Peel stalks and cut into 1-inch lengths.

Put the sliced onion and asparagus stalks in a medium-sized saucepan. Add

the strained stock and simmer over low heat for 30 minutes.

Meanwhile, put the water and ½ teaspoon of salt into another medium-sized saucepan and bring to a boil. Drop in the asparagus tips and boil for 5 minutes, or until they are tender. Drain.

Pour the asparagus stock through a fine sieve into a medium-sized bowl. With the back of a wooden spoon, rub the asparagus stalks and the onion through the sieve. Rinse the saucepan and pour back the sieved stock. Reheat the stock, adding the remaining ½ teaspoon of salt and the pepper.

Put the flour and the butter in a small bowl and work them together into a soft paste. Roll it into small pellets.

Remove the stock from the heat and add the butter-and-flour pellets one at a time, stirring continuously with a wooden spoon. When the stock is thoroughly blended and smooth, replace it on moderate heat and continue to stir until it comes to a boil. Remove the stock from the heat.

In a medium-sized bowl, beat the egg yolks and stir in the cream. Stirring constantly, add ½ pint of hot stock, a spoonful at a time, to the egg-and-cream mixture. Still stirring continuously, pour this mixture into the stock. Over a very low heat, whisk the soup for 2 minutes. Do not allow it to boil or it will curdle. Add the asparagus tips and serve.

Asparagus au Gratin
ASPARAGUS WITH CHEESE SAUCE

Asparagus au Gratin (oh GRAH-tan) *may be served as a first course or as a vegetable dish with the main course for lunch or dinner. It goes well served with chicken breasts, veal escalopes, brains, sweetbreads and egg dishes.*

4 SERVINGS

3 lb. fresh asparagus
1 blade of mace or ¼ teaspoon ground mace
1 bay leaf
1 shallot, sliced
5 peppercorns
10 fl. oz. [1¼ cups] milk
1 tablespoon butter
2 tablespoons flour
1½ oz. [½ cup] Gruyère cheese, grated
2 tablespoons single [light] cream
½ teaspoon prepared mustard
¼ teaspoon salt
3 grindings fresh pepper
2 tablespoons grated Parmesan cheese

Put the mace, bay leaf, peppercorns,

shallot and the milk in a medium-sized saucepan. Place on low heat and allow to simmer very gently for 8 minutes.

Prepare the asparagus and cook until tender.

In a heavy, medium-sized saucepan, melt the butter over low heat. Remove from the heat and with a wooden spoon, stir in the flour. Return the saucepan to the heat and cook for 2 minutes, stirring continuously.

Pour the milk through a strainer, a little at a time, into the butter-and-flour mixture and continue stirring over moderate heat. When all the milk has been stirred in, bring the mixture to a boil. Reduce the heat and simmer gently for 3 minutes. Remove the saucepan from the heat and stir in the Gruyère cheese, cream, mustard, salt and pepper.

Arrange the cooked asparagus in a fireproof serving dish. Pour the hot sauce over the asparagus. Sprinkle the Parmesan over the top and brown under a moderate grill [broiler], or until the top is golden brown.

Serve immediately.

Asparagus aux Oeufs
ASPARAGUS WITH EGGS

A delicately-flavoured dish, Asparagus aux oeufs (oz-erf) is an elegant way to serve this vegetable. It makes a good first course or a light lunch or supper dish. This sauce is quick and easily prepared.

6 SERVINGS

3 lb. fresh asparagus
3 hard-boiled eggs, shells removed and chopped
2 tablespoons finely chopped parsley
½ teaspoon salt
4 grindings fresh black pepper
6 oz. [¾ cup] butter, melted and cooled
2 tablespoons lemon juice

Prepare the asparagus and boil until it is tender.

Meanwhile with a fork, blend the eggs, parsley, ½ teaspoon of salt and pepper in a medium-sized mixing bowl. Stirring constantly, add the melted butter. Continue stirring until the sauce is smooth, and add the lemon juice.

Drain and transfer the asparagus to a large, heated serving dish. Pour on the sauce and serve immediately.

Asparagus Cream Soup is made with fresh aparagus stalks, stock and cream and is thickened with eggs. It is garnished with the asparagus tips.

Asparagus Polonaise

Vegetables Polonaise are sprinkled with buttered breadcrumbs and sieved eggs. Asparagus is most delicious served with this classic garnish.

4 SERVINGS

3 oz. [⅜ cup] butter
1 oz. [⅓ cup] fine breadcrumbs, made from stale bread
2 lb. asparagus, cooked and drained
1 hard-boiled egg, sieved
2 tablespoons chopped parsley

Melt the butter in a small saucepan. Add the breadcrumbs and sauté until they are lightly browned.

Sprinkle the crumbs and butter over hot, freshly cooked asparagus and then sprinkle with the sieved egg and chopped parsley.

Serve immediately.

Asparagus with Sour Cream

Served with grilled meat, chicken or fish, this casserole, which is very easy to prepare, will make the most simple meal quite elegant.

1 tablespoon margarine
3 lb. asparagus, cooked and drained
½ teaspoon garlic salt
freshly ground black pepper
12 fl. oz. [1½ cups] sour cream
6 oz. [2 cups] dry breadcrumbs
3 tablespoons melted butter
1 tablespoon chopped parsley

Preheat oven to moderate 350°F (Gas Mark 4, 180°C).

Grease an ovenproof casserole with the margarine. Place the asparagus in the casserole. Sprinkle with garlic salt and 2 to 3 grindings of pepper and stir in the sour cream.

Mix the breadcrumbs with the melted butter and spread over the asparagus.

Bake for about 40 minutes or until the crumbs are golden brown. Sprinkle with the parsley before serving.

Asparagus Timbale

This savoury asparagus custard, accompanied by Hollandaise sauce, makes an excellent light lunch or supper dish, or may be served as an accompaniment to grilled chicken or fish. The sauce should be served while it is still warm.

Asparagus Polonaise is a simple dish of fresh, boiled asparagus with an egg and sautéed breadcrumb garnish.

4 SERVINGS

3 lb. fresh, boiled asparagus, or
1 lb. frozen asparagus
4 eggs
¾ teaspoon salt
1 teaspoon grated nutmeg
4 fl. oz. single [light] cream
8 fl. oz. [1 cup] chicken stock or milk
SAUCE
5 tablespoons wine vinegar
6 peppercorns
1 bay leaf
6 oz. [¾ cup] butter
3 egg yolks
pinch of salt

Preheat the oven to warm 325°F (Gas Mark 3, 170°C). Lightly butter a 2½-pint ring mould or soufflé dish.

If you are using fresh asparagus, cut off tough part of the stalks and discard.

Cut the asparagus into ½-inch pieces and set aside. In a medium-sized mixing bowl, using a whisk or rotary beater, whisk the eggs with the salt and grated nutmeg. Gradually add the cream and the stock, or milk, beating all the time. Fold in the asparagus pieces.

Pour the mixture into the greased mould or soufflé dish. Place the mould or soufflé dish in a baking pan of boiling water and bake for 35 minutes, or until the custard is set. Test by plunging a warm, dry knife into the centre of the custard. If it comes out clean, the custard is set. If you use a ring mould, test the custard after 20 minutes of cooking.

Remove the custard from the oven and let it stand for 5 minutes. Run a knife round the edge of the custard and un-mould it on to a heated serving dish.

While the custard is cooking, make the sauce. Put the vinegar, peppercorns and bay leaf in a small saucepan and cook, over moderate heat, until the vinegar is reduced to 1¼ tablespoons. Strain and set aside.

In a small bowl, beat the butter until it is soft. In another bowl, beat the egg yolks with a wire whisk or wooden spoon. Add a heaped teaspoon of softened butter and a pinch of salt to the egg yolks. Cream well. Stir in the strained vinegar.

Put the bowl in a saucepan containing warm water and place over low heat. The water should heat gradually, but never come to boiling point. Stir the mixture until it begins to thicken. Add the remaining butter, cut in small pieces, stirring continually. When all the butter has been added, taste the sauce. Add a little more salt if necessary. If the sauce is too sharp, add a little more butter. If the sauce is too thick, add a tablespoon or two of cream to dilute it. Serve the sauce separately.

Asparagus Pea

Also called Winged Pea and Goa Bean, the asparagus pea is the seed of a vine of which one variety is native to India and one to Southern Europe. The green-winged pods are eaten when they are between 1 and 3 inches in length. Although this vegetable is not related to the asparagus, it does have a similar flavour. Asparagus peas should be boiled in salted water for 10 to 15 minutes, drained and served with melted butter.

Aspic

Aspic is a jelly (the French term is *gelée*) made from strong chicken, veal, beef or fish stock. This stock is so strong in gelatinous matter that it is not necessary to add any gelatine. There are occasions, however, when to save time or money it is advisable to use gelatine. The quantity of gelatine used for the firmest aspic is usually ½ ounce to 1 pint

of liquid. For decorative aspics, the proportion is ½ ounce to 1½ pints of liquid and for jellied soups, ½ ounce to 2 pints of liquid.

Aspic jelly is transparent and light coloured and is used as an ingredient or an accompaniment to many cold dishes. Because it is used mainly for decorative purposes, the consistency and clarity of the aspic are important. The stock is made clear by simmering with egg whites and straining before it is allowed to set.

Before using, the jelly must be tested for consistency. Pour ½ inch of jelly into a small, chilled bowl or saucer and place it in the refrigerator for 10 to 15 minutes. Then cut it into pieces and leave it at room temperature for 10 minutes. The jelly should then be fairly stiff if it is going to be used to line a mould, less stiff, but able to hold its shape, if it is to be used as an aspic to coat various dishes, and softly holding its shape if it is required for a jellied soup. Time is required when working with jelly, for if the decoration is complicated, several coats of jelly may be required and this may take several hours.

Chopped aspic makes an attractive border or bed for many cold dishes. To make chopped aspic, put a ½-inch of jelly in a tin. When it is set, cut it into small cubes with a knife. In the same way, decorative cutouts in the shape of diamonds or triangles can be made.

Sprays of tarragon and fennel leaves are often used for decoration in aspic, as are pimentoes, carrots, the yolks and whites of hard-boiled eggs, olives and truffles. A layer of jelly is spooned over the chilled food, the decoration is then dipped into the almost set jelly, placed in position, chilled to setting point and then covered with a final layer or two of jelly.

Aspic–I

This is an elaborate recipe for making aspic. The setting depends upon the gelatinous matter in the ingredients. Both the preparation and the cooking take a long time.

ABOUT 3½-4 PINTS

1 calf's foot, skinned and cleaned
5 lb. veal or beef bones and meat, chopped into 3-inch pieces, poultry carcasses and giblets
4 oz. pork rind
2 carrots, scraped
2 onions, peeled
2 celery stalks
2 leeks

1 bouquet garni, consisting of ½ teaspoon thyme, ½ teaspoon tarragon, 1 bay leaf, 6 sprigs of parsley, 2 garlic cloves, and 2 cloves, tied in a piece of cheese cloth
2 teaspoons salt
2 egg whites and shells
2 oz. minced [ground] beef
1½ teaspoons dried tarragon
4 fl. oz. [½ cup] Madeira

Wash and scrub the calf's foot. Soak it in cold water for 8 hours, changing the water several times. Put it in a medium-sized pan, cover it with water and boil for 5 minutes. Rinse in cold water and set aside.

Put the bones and meat in a large pan with enough cold water to cover by 2 inches. Slowly bring to the boil. Remove the scum with a large spoon. When the scum stops forming, add the calf's foot, the pork rind, vegetables and seasonings. Add more water, if necessary, to cover all the ingredients by 1 inch. Bring to the simmer and remove the scum.

Cover with a lid, leaving space for the steam to escape. Cook for 5 hours, simmering very gently. Occasionally, remove the scum and fat and, by adding boiling water, keep the level of the liquid above that of the ingredients.

Strain the stock into a bowl and leave to cool. Remove the fat which has hardened on top when the stock is cool. The stock is now ready for clarification.

Scald a large enamel or glass saucepan and a wire whisk with boiling water. Pour 4½ pints [5½ pints] of the stock into the saucepan. Place the pan over moderate heat and bring the stock to the boil.

Meanwhile, in a small mixing bowl, lightly beat the egg whites with a fork.

When the stock is boiling, add the egg whites and shells. Using the whisk, whisk vigorously in an anti-clockwise movement. As soon as the stock begins to boil again, stop whisking and allow it to rise to the top of the pan.

Remove the pan from the heat and allow the stock to settle.

Repeat the boiling process twice more, being careful not to break the egg white crust that will form. After the third boiling, remove the pan from the heat and leave it for 5 minutes.

Line a large strainer or colander with a scalded clean flannel cloth and place it over a large mixing bowl. Slowly strain the stock through the strainer or colander without squeezing the cloth (this will make the aspic cloudy). Do not break the egg white crust.

If the stock is not perfectly clear, strain it again through the cloth and egg white

crust into another bowl.

Remove the strainer or colander and stir in the Madeira.

When the aspic cools, keep it in the refrigerator, covered, until you are ready to use it.

Aspic—II

This is a recipe for a very quick, easy and inexpensive aspic jelly. Although the result lacks the flavour of aspic made from bone stock, it is quite acceptable.

APPROXIMATELY $\frac{3}{4}$ PINT

1 chicken stock cube
$\frac{1}{2}$ pint [1$\frac{1}{4}$ cups] boiling water
$\frac{1}{2}$ oz. [2 tablespoons] gelatine
3 fl. oz. [$\frac{3}{8}$ cup] dry white wine

Put the stock cube in a mixing bowl. Add the boiling water and stir to dissolve the cube.

Put the gelatine in a cup and pour a little of the hot stock into it. Stir until all the gelatine has dissolved and add it to the rest of the stock. Taste the stock and add salt if necessary.

Mix in the wine and leave the aspic to cool. When it is cool, cover the bowl and refrigerate. The aspic is now ready for use.

Aspic de Pommes
APPLE ASPIC

A dessert with a pleasing texture, Aspic de Pommes (as-peek d'pohm) requires no gelatine to make it set. The pectin in the apples makes a firm jelly which can be unmoulded before serving.

6 SERVINGS

1 teaspoon vegetable oil
4 oz. [$\frac{2}{3}$ cup] mixed glacé fruit, cherries, angelica, pineapple or orange
4 fl. oz. [$\frac{1}{2}$ cup] water
1 lb. [2 cups] sugar
2 tablespoons lemon juice
3 lb. firm cooking apples
1 teaspoon grated lemon rind
2 fl. oz. [$\frac{1}{4}$ cup] sweet sherry
8 fl. oz. double cream [1 cup heavy cream] beaten

Grease a 1$\frac{1}{2}$-pint mould with 1 teaspoon oil.

Reserving a few cherries and some angelica for decoration, chop the rest together and set aside.

Put the water, sugar and lemon juice into a large pan and, over moderate heat, stir to dissolve the sugar. When the sugar is completely dissolved, remove the pan from the heat.

A mould of apple purée flavoured with sherry, Aspic de Pommes is decorated with glacé cherries and angelica.

Peel, core and quarter the apples and cut the quarters into thin slices. Drop the apple slices into the syrup as you cut them to prevent them from discolouring.

Put the pan back on the stove, raise the heat to high and, stirring continuously to prevent the apples from sticking and burning, boil rapidly for 20 minutes.

Press the apple pulp through a sieve. Stir in the sherry, and the chopped mixed fruit and the grated lemon rind.

Pour the mixture into the mould and chill in the refrigerator for at least 5 hours.

Before serving, run a knife round the edge of the mould. Place a serving plate on top of the mould and turn it upside-down to unmould the aspic. Decorate the aspic with the remaining cherries and angelica and serve with lightly whipped cream.

Assiette Anglaise

The French culinary term for an assortment of cold meats served on one plate, *Assiette Anglaise* (AH-see-YET on-glaze) always includes a slice of York ham, a slice of beef tongue, a slice of roast beef and, sometimes, slices of galantine and brawn. It is garnished with chopped aspic and cress and is usually served at lunch.

Asti Spumante

One of Italy's best known sparkling white wines, Asti Spumante (ah-stee spoo-MAHN-teh) is made from Muscat grapes, which are grown in the vineyards of Asti and other Piedmontese vineyards. Always sweet and sometimes very sweet, it is preferable to drink this wine well chilled with the dessert or fruit course at the end of a meal.

Asynpoeding

VINEGAR PUDDING

A South African pudding, Asynpoeding (ah-sane-poo-ding) is an unusual ginger flavoured dessert baked with a vinegar flavoured syrup. Serve hot with custard.

8 SERVINGS

6 oz. [¾ cup] butter
6 oz. [¾ cup] sugar
3 eggs
¼ teaspoon salt
14 oz. [3½ cups] sifted flour
2 teaspoons ground ginger
2 teaspoons bicarbonate of soda [baking soda]
    a little milk
6 oz. [½ cup] pineapple jam
SYRUP
1 pint [2½ cups] cold water
4 fl. oz. [½ cup] white vinegar
12 oz. [1½ cups] sugar

Preheat the oven to fairly hot 400°F (Gas Mark 6, 200°C).

In a medium-sized mixing bowl, using a wooden spoon, cream the butter well and gradually add the sugar. Beat in the eggs, one at a time, beating thoroughly. Sift in salt, flour, ginger and mix.

In a small bowl, blend the bicarbonate of soda with a little milk and add to the egg-and-flour mixture.

Blend the ingredients into a dough. On a floured surface, roll out the dough into a rectangular shape, about 5 inches wide and 12 inches long. Spread the dough evenly with the pineapple jam and roll up as for a jam roll. Cut into 2-inch slices and place on the bottom of an ovenproof casserole dish.

Mix the cold water, vinegar and sugar together. Pour over the pudding in the casserole. Cover and bake in the centre of the oven for 1½ hours. Serve immediately.

Athenian Walnut Cake

Crunchy with walnuts and steeped in brandy and syrup, this Greek cake may be served with coffee, or as a dessert.

6 TO 8 SERVINGS

2 oz. [¼ cup] butter
5 oz. [⅝ cup] sugar
4 eggs
1 teaspoon ground cinnamon
8 oz. [1½ cups] walnuts, chopped
8 oz. [2 cups] sifted flour
SYRUP
6 oz. [¾ cup] sugar
10 fl. oz. [1¼ cups] water
4 fl. oz. [½ cup] brandy

Preheat the oven to moderate 350°F (Gas Mark 4, 180°C). Grease a medium-sized loaf or cake tin with a little butter and dust with flour.

In a medium-sized mixing bowl, beat the butter and sugar together with a wooden spoon until they are well creamed. Separate the egg yolks from the whites and set the whites aside. Add the yolks, one at a time, to the creamed butter and sugar and mix thoroughly.

Using a whisk or rotary beater, beat the egg whites until they are stiff. Add half of the egg whites and the cinnamon to the creamed mixture and mix well.

Set aside 2 tablespoons of chopped walnuts. Mix the rest of the walnuts and flour together and add gradually to the creamed mixture, mixing thoroughly. Fold in the remaining egg whites.

Put the mixture in the cake tin and sprinkle the top with the remaining 2 tablespoons of chopped walnuts. Bake for 1¼ hours or until the cake is cooked. Test by inserting a thin warmed skewer into

An adaptation of a Greek recipe, Athenian Walnut Cake is steeped in sugar syrup and brandy.

the centre of the cake. If it is clean and dry when removed, the cake is ready.

To make the syrup, dissolve the sugar in the water in a small saucepan over a low heat. When the sugar is completely dissolved, raise the heat and boil rapidly until the syrup thickens. Remove from the heat and mix in the brandy.

When the cake is cooked, remove it from the tin and place it upside down in a deep dish.

With a skewer, pierce the bottom of the cake in many places. Pour the hot syrup slowly over the cake while it is still hot. Set the cake aside to cool and to absorb the syrup. Turn right side up and serve cold.

Athénienne, à l'

À l'Athénienne (ah LAH-tay-nee-YEN) is a French term which is used to describe dishes which are flavoured with onions, aubergine [eggplant], tomatoes and sweet peppers cooked in olive oil.

Atholl Brose

A Scottish drink of oatmeal steeped in boiling water, strained and added to whisky, cream and honey, Atholl Brose is traditionally considered a good cure for a cold.

Aubergine [Eggplant]

The fruit of a plant native to Southern Asia, the aubergine is now widely grown in tropical, subtropical and warm temperate regions of the world. A member of the potato family, it is also known as eggplant, brinjal, melanzana, garden egg and patlican. There are many varieties of aubergines, which range from dark purple to pale mauve, and from yellow to white. They vary in shape from long and thin to pear shaped and quite round. The long, purple variety of aubergine is the one most commonly eaten.

Aubergines may be cooked whole in the skins or sliced and fried, baked, grilled or stuffed. They may also be stewed with mutton or lamb. The aubergine is one of the most popular vegetables in the world. It is eaten in the Far East, South Asia, Eastern Europe and America.

In the West, aubergines are usually sliced or chopped, sprinkled with salt and left to drain. The slices are then dried before cooking. Salting and draining removes some of the bitterness as well as the excess moisture, therefore requiring less fat for frying.

Only firm, smooth, shiny aubergines of uniform colour should be selected for cooking.

Aubergines Farcies Duxelles

BAKED AUBERGINES STUFFED WITH MUSHROOMS

Aubergines Farcies Duxelles (oh-bair-jeen FAHR-see doo-sell) *may be served as a first course or as an accompaniment to roast lamb or grilled, sautéed or roast chicken. This dish may be prepared the day before it is baked.*

It is also an ideal dish for freezing. When the aubergines are stuffed, allow them to cool. Place in the freezer and leave until hard, then wrap in aluminium foil. Return to the freezer to store. To serve them, place in a casserole and sprinkle with the cheese and breadcrumbs. Cook in the oven until hot throughout.

6 SERVINGS

3 large aubergines [eggplants]
1¼ tablespoons salt
3½ tablespoons olive oil
1 onion, finely chopped
1 garlic clove, crushed
1½ oz. [3 tablespoons] butter
1 lb. mushrooms, chopped
   freshly ground black pepper
6 oz. [¾ cup] cottage cheese
3 tablespoons chopped parsley
¼ teaspoon dried thyme
2 tablespoons grated Parmesan cheese
4 tablespoons white breadcrumbs

Remove the green stems from the aubergines and cut them in half lengthwise. With a sharp knife, make cuts in the pulp to within ¼ inch of the skin. Sprinkle with 1 tablespoon of salt and lay the aubergines, cut-sides down, on kitchen paper towels for 30 minutes to drain.

Squeeze the aubergines to remove as much liquid as possible and dry on kitchen paper towels. Put the aubergines, skin side down, in a flameproof dish. Pour a little olive oil over each one. Pour a little water into the dish to just cover the bottom.

Place under the grill [broiler] and cook for about 10 minutes until they are soft. Remove from the dish.

Using a spoon, scoop the flesh out into a bowl, leaving the skins intact. Roughly chop the flesh.

Preheat the oven to fairly hot 400°F (Gas Mark 6, 200°C).

Put the remaining olive oil in a large frying-pan. Fry the onion and garlic slowly over low heat for about 5 minutes or until it is tender but not browned.

Add all of the butter to the frying-pan and add the mushrooms. Sauté the mixture gently for another 5 minutes. Season with the remaining salt and 3 grindings of

pepper. Remove from the heat and stir the aubergine flesh into the mushroom-and-onion mixture.

In a small bowl, mash the cottage cheese with a fork. Stir into the aubergine mixture. Add the parsley and thyme. Add more salt and pepper if necessary.

Fill the aubergine shells with the mushroom mixture. Sprinkle with the grated cheese and breadcrumbs. Grease a clean flameproof dish with a little butter. Put the filled aubergines into the dish and cover with aluminium foil. Cook in the oven for 20 minutes, remove the foil and cook for a further 10 minutes or until the crumbs are crisp, golden and brown.

Aubergines Farcies Provençale

A tasty vegetarian luncheon dish, Aubergines Farcies Provençale (oh-bair-jeen fahr-see proh-von-sahl) *is easy to make and inexpensive when aubergines are in season.*

4 SERVINGS

4 aubergines [eggplants]
   water
2 tablespoons olive oil
2 small onions, chopped
2 cloves garlic, crushed
4 large tomatoes, blanched, peeled and chopped
12 green olives, stoned
½ teaspoon salt
   freshly ground black pepper
2 oz. [½ cup] grated cheese
1 oz. [⅓ cup] dry breadcrumbs
1 oz. [2 tablespoons] butter

Preheat the oven to moderate 350°F (Gas Mark 4, 180°C).

Put the aubergines in a large saucepan. Cover them with water and bring to the boil. Cover and cook over low heat for 15 minutes. Drain the aubergines and cut them in halves lengthways. Scoop out the pulp carefully, leaving shells ¼-inch thick. Set aside.

Heat the oil in a large frying-pan over moderate heat. Add the onions and cook slowly until they are soft but not brown. Add the garlic, tomatoes, olives, aubergine pulp, salt and 4 grindings of pepper. Simmer for 10 minutes, stirring occasionally.

Fill the aubergine shells with the mixture, sprinkle with the cheese and breadcrumbs, dot with the butter and place in an ovenproof dish. Bake for 30 minutes or until brown. Serve hot.

Filled with mushrooms and onions, Aubergines Farcies Duxelles are sprinkled with cheese and baked.

Aubergine Fritters—I

These fritters are a crisp and tasty accompaniment to serve with chicken, fish and rice dishes.

6 SERVINGS

  3 aubergines [eggplants]
    salt
BATTER
  4 oz. [1 cup] flour
  ¼ teaspoon salt
    a pinch of turmeric
  2 egg yolks
  1 tablespoon oil
  5 fl. oz. [⅝ cup] milk
  1 egg white
  1 pint [2½ cups] cooking oil

Cut the aubergines into thin slices, sprinkle with salt and place in a colander to drain for 30 minutes.

Prepare the batter by sifting the flour, salt and turmeric into a medium-sized bowl. Make a well in the centre of the flour mixture and pour in the egg yolks and oil. With a wooden spoon, or wire whisk, beat the egg yolks and oil until they are mixed, slowly incorporating the flour. Add the milk a little at a time and continue beating until the batter is smooth. Cover and set aside in a cool place for 30 minutes.

Put the egg white in a small bowl and whisk until stiff. Fold into the batter.

Dry the aubergine slices with kitchen paper towels. Heat the oil in a deep frying-pan until it is very hot. Dip the aubergine slices in the batter and fry them in the oil until they are crisp and light golden in colour. When the fritters are cooked, drain them on kitchen paper towels, arrange on a warmed vegetable dish and serve hot.

Aubergine Fritters—II

This is another way to make aubergine fritters. They should be well seasoned and spicy and may accompany a rice and chicken dish.

4 SERVINGS

  1 large aubergine [eggplant]
  4 fl. oz. [½ cup] water
  1 onion, grated or chopped very
    finely
  ¼ teaspoon cayenne pepper
  ¼ teaspoon ground turmeric
  ½ teaspoon salt
  1 egg, lightly beaten
1½ oz. [⅓ cup] flour
  1 teaspoon baking powder
    milk
  5 tablespoons oil

Peel the aubergine and cut into cubes.

Put the cubes in a small saucepan with the water and cook, covered, for 15 minutes, or until tender. Drain and put the cubes in a mixing bowl. With a fork mash the aubergine well. Mix in the onion, cayenne pepper, turmeric, salt and egg. Add the flour and baking powder and stir in enough milk to make a thick batter.

Heat the oil in a large frying-pan. When the oil is very hot drop in the aubergine batter a tablespoonful at a time and fry the fritters on each side until they are brown. Remove the fritters with tongs or a slotted spoon and drain on kitchen paper towels. Serve immediately.

Aubergines Gratinées

An excellent vegetarian dish, Aubergines Gratinées (oh-bair-jeen GRAH-tee-nay) can be served either as a main course on its own or as an accompaniment to meat or chicken. The tomato sauce can be prepared well in advance and the dish put together an hour before it is required.

4 SERVINGS

4 aubergines [eggplant]
1 tablespoon salt
  flour
3 fl. oz. [⅜ cup] vegetable oil
5 oz. [1¼ cups] cheese, grated
1 oz. [⅓ cup] white breadcrumbs
1 oz. [2 tablespoons] butter
SAUCE
1½ oz. [3 tablespoons] butter
1 small onion, finely chopped

3 tablespoons flour
12 oz. canned tomatoes
2 teaspoons tomatoe purée
½ teaspoon dried basil
  freshly ground black pepper
½ teaspoon salt

Slice the aubergines into rounds ¼-inch thick. Sprinkle the slices with salt and leave on a plate to drain for 30 minutes.

For the sauce, melt the butter in a saucepan, add the onions and fry over moderate heat, stirring occasionally, until the onions are soft. Add the flour and cook for 1 minute.

Strain the liquid from the tomatoes and stir into the onion mixture. Add the tomatoes, tomatoe purée, basil, 4 gridings of pepper and the salt. Bring to the boil stirring all the time. Lower the heat, cover the pan and simmer the sauce for 15-20 minutes.

Preheat the oven to moderate 350°F (Gas Mark 4, 180°C).

Dry the aubergine slices with kitchen paper towels. Dip the slices into the flour to coat well. Heat the vegetable oil in a large frying-pan over high heat. When the oil is very hot put in the slices of aubergine, a few at a time. Turn them over with kitchen tongs after a few seconds. When well fried, remove, drain on kitchen paper towels and keep hot until all the slices are fried. Add more oil to the frying-pan if necessary.

Put a layer of sauce in the bottom of a medium-sized ovenproof casserole. Sprinkle with some of the cheese and then put in a layer of aubergine slices.

Aubergines Gratinées is a tasty casserole of aubergines with tomato sauce topped with cheese and breadcrumbs.

Continue with these layers until the ingredients are used. Finish with a layer of tomato sauce. Sprinkle with cheese and breadcrumbs. Dot with a little butter. Bake in the oven for 25 minutes or until golden brown.

Aubergines Grillées

GRILLED AUBERGINES [EGGPLANT]

Grilled aubergines may be served as a vegetable or can be used as a foundation for escalopes, noisettes, tournedos or other small pieces of meat.

4 SERVINGS

2 aubergines [eggplant]
salt
5 fl. oz. [⅝ cup] olive oil
1 tablespoon chopped parsley

Peel the aubergines. Cut them into thick slices. Sprinkle both sides of each slice with salt and leave to drain in a colander for 30 minutes. When drained, rinse the slices in cold, running water and pat dry in a clean cloth, or kitchen paper towels.

Coat the slices of aubergine with olive oil and place in a shallow flameproof dish. Place under a heated grill [broiler] and cook for 3 minutes. Turn the slices, add more oil if too dry, and cook until the slices are soft. Sprinkle with parsley.

Aubergine and Lamb Casserole

This is a tasty way of using leftover lamb and makes an interesting supper dish. You can substitute beef stock for the chicken stock. Serve with boiled potatoes and a green salad.

4 SERVINGS

2 aubergines [eggplant]
1 tablespoon plus ½ teaspoon salt
1 lb. mushrooms
2 oz. [¼ cup] butter
1 medium-sized onion, chopped
1 garlic clove, crushed
4 tablespoons flour
1 pint [2½ cups] chicken stock
1 green pepper, seeded and
  chopped
1 lb. cooked lamb, diced
1 teaspoon dried oregano
½ teaspoon dried rosemary
4 tablespoons fresh breadcrumbs
½ teaspoon freshly ground black
  pepper

Cut the aubergines into 1-inch cubes. Place the cubes in a colander, sprinkle with 1 tablespoon of salt and leave to drain for 30 minutes. Rinse under cold running water and dry on kitchen paper towels.

Preheat the oven to fairly hot 400°F (Gas Mark 6, 200°C).

Chop the mushrooms into thick slices. Melt 1 tablespoon of butter in a medium-sized frying-pan and fry the mushrooms for 10 minutes. Set aside.

Melt 2 tablespoons butter in a medium-sized saucepan and fry the onion and garlic until they are golden. Add the flour and stir with a wooden spoon until it is well blended. Stirring constantly, gradually add the chicken stock to the pan. Continue cooking until the sauce is thick and smooth.

Place the aubergine cubes, mushrooms, green pepper, lamb, oregano, rosemary, ½ teaspoon of salt and the pepper into an ovenproof casserole.

Pour the sauce into the casserole and stir gently to mix.

Cover the top with the breadcrumbs, dot with the remaining butter and bake in the oven for 30 minutes or until the top is golden.

Aubergine and Lamb Stew

Aubergines and lamb are an excellent combination. In this stew, the addition of coriander seed, mint and garlic enhances their flavour. A bowl of chilled yogurt, to which

half a diced cucumber has been added, makes an excellent accompanying salad.

4 SERVINGS

2 aubergines [eggplant]
1 tablespoon plus ½ teaspoon salt
5 tablespoons olive oil
2 lb. lean, boned leg or shoulder
  of lamb, cut into 1-inch cubes
2 teaspoons coriander
  seeds, coarsely crushed
1 large onion, sliced
1 garlic clove, crushed
2 tablespoons chopped fresh mint
1 lb. tomatoes, blanched, peeled
  and chopped or 14 oz. canned
  peeled tomatoes, drained
  freshly ground black pepper

Cut the aubergines into 1-inch cubes. Place the cubes in a colander, sprinkle with 1 tablespoon of salt, put a plate with a weight on it on top of the aubergines and leave to drain for 30 minutes. Pat the cubes dry with kitchen paper towels before cooking.

Heat the oil in a large frying-pan. Add the lamb cubes, a few at a time, and the crushed coriander seeds. When all the lamb has been browned, remove the cubes with a slotted spoon, put on a plate and set aside. Add the onion to the pan and fry until golden. Add the garlic and all the mint and cook for 1 minute. Add the aubergine cubes and fry, stirring frequently, for 10 minutes.

Return the lamb to the pan with the tomatoes, ½ teaspoon of salt and 6 grindings of black pepper. Cover, lower

Aubergines, garlic, parsley and olive oil combine to make this unusual and attractive Aubergine Salad.

the heat and cook for 1 hour. If the stew seems too liquid, simmer without a cover for the last 20 minutes.

Aubergine Salad

This Greek dish is usually served as a meze, or appetizer, as an accompaniment to an aperitif. Traditionally, flat Greek bread is dipped into the aubergine purée. It can also be served as a salad. If you find the natural greyish colour of the purée unattractive, add 2 or 3 drops of red food colouring.

4 TO 6 SERVINGS

2 large aubergines [eggplant]
1 large garlic clove, crushed
2 fl. oz. [¼ cup] olive oil
  juice of 1 lemon
1 teaspoon salt
4 parsley sprigs, chopped

Preheat the oven to moderate 350°F (Gas Mark 4, 180°C).

Place the whole, unpeeled aubergines on a baking sheet and bake for about 40 minutes, or until they are soft. When the aubergines are cool enough to handle, cut them in half lengthways and scoop out the pulp. Mash the pulp to a purée in a mortar or by pushing through a sieve.

Put the purée in a medium-sized mixing bowl. Mix in the crushed garlic. Beat in the oil a little at a time. Add half the lemon juice, the salt and parsley. Mix well and taste. Add the rest of the lemon juice if necessary.

Aubergines Sautéed

This is a quick and easy way to serve this vegetable. Sautéed aubergines go well with light meat or fish dishes.

4 SERVINGS

3 aubergines [eggplant]
2 tablespoons salt
4 tablespoons flour
6 tablespoons cooking oil
2 tablespoons chopped parsley

With a sharp knife, peel the aubergines. Cut them into ¾-inch cubes.

Put the cubes into a colander, sprinkle them with salt and leave them to drain for 30 minutes.

Dry the aubergines on kitchen paper towels and sprinkle them with the flour.

Heat the oil in a heavy, medium-sized frying-pan over moderate heat. Put in the aubergine cubes and fry them briskly for 10 minutes, or until they are tender.

Remove the aubergine cubes with a slotted spoon. Put them in a warmed vegetable dish and sprinkle on the parsley.

Aubergine Soufflés

An elegant and tasty first course, these individual Aubergine Soufflés can also be served as an accompaniment to a main dish of meat, chicken or fish. The aubergine shells are not for eating in this dish because they may not be completely cooked by the time the soufflés are ready.

4 SERVINGS

2 aubergines [eggplant]
1 pint [2½ cups] boiling water
½ tablespoon vinegar
1½ oz. [¾ cup] fresh breadcrumbs
2 egg yolks, beaten
1 tablespoon melted butter
2 oz. [½ cup] grated cheese
½ teaspoon salt
  freshly ground black pepper
½ teaspoon dried basil
2 egg whites
2 tablespoons dried breadcrumbs
1 tablespoon butter, cut into pieces

Low Cal

Preheat the oven to fairly hot 375°F (Gas Mark 5, 190°C).

Cut the aubergines in halves lengthways with a sharp knife. Scoop out the pulp, leaving a shell ¼-inch thick. Set the shells aside.

Put the pulp into a medium-sized saucepan and cover with 1 pint of boiling water. Add the vinegar and

simmer for 15 minutes or until the pulp is tender.

Drain the pulp and put it in a large bowl. With a fork mash it to a purée. Add the fresh breadcrumbs, egg yolks, melted butter, grated cheese, salt, 4 grindings of black pepper and the dried basil. Mix well. If the mixture is too stiff add a spoonful of the cooking liquid.

Beat the egg whites in a small bowl with a whisk until they are stiff. Fold them into the aubergine mixture.

Fill the aubergine shells with the mixture. Sprinkle the dried breadcrumbs over the top, dot with small pieces of butter and place in an ovenproof dish. Put the dish in a large baking pan which has a little water in it and bake for 30 minutes. Serve immediately.

Aubergines à la Tunisienne

This dish is equally delicious served either hot or cold. Aubergines à la Tunisienne (oh-bair-jeen ah lah too-NEEZ-yen) goes well with lamb dishes and is especially good with lamb kebabs.

4 SERVINGS

3 aubergines [eggplant]
1 tablespoon plus ½ teaspoon salt
4 tablespoons olive oil
2 onions, sliced
1 garlic clove, chopped
¼ teaspoon cayenne pepper
¼ teaspoon ground cloves
½ teaspoon ground cumin
1 lb. tomatoes, peeled and chopped
1 teaspoon ground coriander
1 tablespoon fresh chopped mint
2 tablespoons raisins
½ teaspoon black pepper
2 tablespoons chopped parsley

Cut the aubergines into cubes. Sprinkle with 1 tablespoon salt and put in a colander to drain for 30 minutes. Dry the cubes on kitchen paper towels.

Heat the oil in a large frying-pan over moderate heat. Add the onions and fry until soft. Add the garlic, the cayenne pepper, cloves and cumin and cook for 2 minutes. Add the aubergine cubes. Stir well and brown the cubes lightly on all sides. Add the tomatoes, coriander, mint, raisins, remaining salt and the pepper. Cook gently, stirring occasionally, until almost all the liquid has evaporated. Stir in the parsley.

Serve hot or cold.

Aubergines à la Tunisienne is an exotic and spicy accompaniment to any lamb dish.

Aubergines à la Turque

Stuffed with a spicy mixture of meat and rice and served with a thick tomato sauce, Aubergines à la Turque (oh-bair-jeen ah lah toork) is an easy-to-make supper dish.

4 SERVINGS

4 aubergines [eggplant]
2 teaspoons salt
5 tablespoons olive oil
1 onion, chopped
1 garlic clove, crushed
1 lb. minced [ground] lamb
1 tablespoon chopped parsley
¼ teaspoon cayenne pepper
grated rind of 1 lemon
1 teaspoon salt
½ teaspoon black pepper
4 oz. [2 cups] cooked rice
juice of 1 lemon
SAUCE
1 tablespoon olive oil
1 onion, minced
1 garlic clove, crushed
½ teaspoon dried basil
14 oz. canned peeled Italian tomatoes
½ teaspoon salt

First make the sauce. In a small saucepan, over moderate heat, fry the onion in the oil until golden brown. Add the garlic and basil and fry for 1 minute. Add the tomatoes and salt. Stir well and bring to the boil. Cover, lower the heat and simmer for 1 hour, or until the sauce has thickened. Stir occasionally with a wooden spoon, mashing the tomatoes with the back of the spoon.

Wash the aubergines and, with a sharp knife, cut them in half lengthways right through the stalk. Scoop out the pulp, but be careful not to damage the shells. Sprinkle the inside of the shells with a little salt. Place them upside down on a plate and set aside. Put the pulp in a bowl and set aside.

Heat 4 tablespoons of olive oil in a large frying-pan over high heat. Add the onion, lower the heat and fry until golden brown. Add the garlic and fry for 1 minute. Add the meat and brown it thoroughly. Add the aubergine pulp, parsley, cayenne pepper, grated lemon rind, salt and pepper. Stir to mix, lower the heat, cover and simmer for 25 minutes. Stir in the boiled rice and mix well.

Preheat the oven to fairly hot 375°F (Gas Mark 5, 190°C). Wipe the aubergine shells with kitchen paper towels. Brush them liberally all over with the remaining olive oil and place them in a large baking dish. Fill them with the meat-and-rice mixture. Sprinkle a little lemon juice over the top and bake for 40 minutes, or

until the shells are cooked and the top brown.

Serve with the tomato sauce.

Au Beurre

Au beurre (oh burr) is the French term for any dish cooked in butter or served with butter.

Au Beurre Noir

Au beurre noir (oh burr nwahr) is the French description of a dish served with black or nut-brown butter. Black butter is made by cooking butter in a pan until it becomes dark brown. Vinegar, salt and pepper are added and the sauce is then cooked until it is reduced by half. *Beurre noir* is used as a sauce for eggs, fish and some vegetables.

Au Blanc

Au blanc (oh blonk) is to keep white while cooking by using a *blanc*, the French name for a solution of salted water, lemon juice and flour, which is used for the preliminary cooking of any food which discolours. The term *au blanc* also applies to food cooked or served in a white sauce.

Au Brun

Au brun (oh broon) is the French term for a dish cooked in or served with a brown sauce. This sauce is sometimes called ESPAGNOLE and accompanies steak, cutlets, game, some vegetables and eggs.

Au Four

Au four (oh foor) is a French cookery term which means 'baked in the oven'.

Aufschnitt

Aufschnitt (owf-schnit) is a German term which refers to a variety of cold meats and sausages sold in German delicatessen shops.

Au Gras

A dish cooked in a rich meat gravy or meat stock is referred to by the French term *au gras* (oh grah).

Au Gratin

Au gratin (oh grah-tan) is the French cookery term for a dish which has been browned on top. Such a dish is usually covered with a sauce, sprinkled with bread-crumbs or grated cheese and baked in an oven or browned under a grill.

Au Jus

Au jus (oh joo) is the French term for meat served with its natural juices or gravy.

Au Lait

A dish or drink, such as coffee, which is served or cooked with milk is referred to by the French term *au lait* (oh lay).

Au Maigre

Au maigre (oh MAY-gr') is the French cookery term for a dish cooked without meat or meat stock and is, therefore, suitable for serving during Lent.

Au Naturel

Plainly cooked or simply cooked food is known by the French term, *au naturel* (oh nah-too-RELL).

Augolemono Soup

EGG AND LEMON SOUP

  ①

Augolemono (ahv-GOH-le-MOH-noh) *is a traditional Greek soup with an unusual*

lemon flavour. The alternative spelling is *Avgolemono.*

6 SERVINGS

3 oz. [⅜ cup] long-grain rice
3 pints [7½ cups] chicken stock
4 eggs
  juice of 2 lemons
¼ teaspoon black pepper
2 parsley sprigs, chopped

Wash the rice thoroughly. Soak it in cold water for 30 minutes and drain it.

Put the stock in a large saucepan and bring it to a boil. Add the rice and simmer over low heat for 15 minutes, or until the rice is tender. Remove the pan from the heat.

Break the eggs into a medium-sized mixing bowl and beat with a wire whisk until they are well beaten.

Gradually add the lemon juice, beating continuously. Add a few spoonfuls of stock, a little at a time, beating constantly until it is well mixed. Stir this mixture into the saucepan containing the rest of the stock.

Over moderate heat, cook the soup for two or three minutes. Do not let it boil or it will curdle. Add the pepper, sprinkle with chopped parsley and serve immediately.

A traditional first course in Greece, lemon-flavoured Augolemono Soup tastes as delicious as it looks.

Aurore Sauce

  ①

This sauce, which can be served with fish, meat, eggs or vegetables, is based on a velouté sauce.

1 PINT

1½ tablespoons butter
3 tablespoons flour
10 fl. oz. [1¼ cups] chicken or veal
  stock
½ teaspoon salt
5 fl. oz. [⅝ cup] tomato purée
5 fl. oz. single [⅝ cup light] cream
3 egg yolks

Melt the butter in a small saucepan over moderate heat. When the butter is melted, remove the pan from the heat and stir in the flour. Return to the heat and cook for 4 minutes, stirring continuously. Gradually add the stock and the salt, stirring all the time. When the mixture is blended, bring to the boil and simmer for 5 minutes. Add the tomato purée.

In a small bowl, mix the cream and

egg yolks thoroughly. Add half of the hot sauce, a spoonful at a time, stirring continuously. When it is well mixed, pour the egg mixture slowly into the pan with the remaining sauce. Stir to blend and cook over low heat until the sauce is smooth and thick. Do not allow the sauce to boil.

Au Rouge

A French culinary term, *au rouge* (oh rooj) is applied to a dish served with or finished in a red sauce.

Australian Wines

Australia is a comparative newcomer to the world of wine. The first vine was planted in 1788, but not until the early nineteenth century was there any success in wine production. Now Australia exports wines in bulk, chiefly to Britain. These consist mainly of light table wines and dessert-type wines which are fortified with spirits. The southeast of Australia falls within the temperate zone and so is naturally endowed with good vineyard conditions. Australian wines are generally robust and full in flavour. The Hunter River area, in New South Wales, has the vineyards which provide the best Australian table wines, while the Murray River area, extending through New South Wales, Victoria and South Australia, is where the grapes for the finer fortified wines are grown. The Barossa Valley, where the annual wine festival is held, is one of the most famous growing areas.

Austrian Boiled Beef

This is a good Sunday lunch dish. Serve it with a hot horseradish sauce, red cabbage cooked with onions and apples, and boiled potatoes. The potatoes can be added to the pot and boiled with the meat. The stock, makes an excellent soup.

6 SERVINGS

4 pints [5 pints] water
1 teaspoon salt
1 carrot, scraped and cut in half
3 parsley sprigs
1 celery stalk
1 leek, wash and trim
1 bay leaf
6 peppercorns
3 to 4 lb. boneless top beef rump
2 oz. ox liver

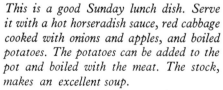

Put the water, salt, carrot, parsley, celery, leek, bay leaf and peppercorns in a large pot and bring to the boil. Add the

beef and the liver. The meat must be covered with water so add more if necessary. Bring to the boil again and skim off the scum.

Lower the heat, half cover the pot and simmer very gently for 2 to 2½ hours, or until the meat is tender. Add more boiling water whenever necessary during cooking to keep the beef covered at all times. For the last hour of cooking, cover the pot completely.

Remove the beef from the pan and serve on a heated dish.

Austrian Cabbage

This is an interesting and unusual way to cook dark green winter cabbage. Serve with roast pork or beefburgers.

4 SERVINGS

1 oz. [2 tablespoons] butter
1 onion, sliced
1 garlic clove, crushed
1 cabbage, shredded
10 fl. oz. [1¼ cups] sour cream
1 teaspoon paprika

Preheat the oven to moderate 350°F (Gas Mark 4, 180°C).

Melt the butter in a large saucepan over moderate heat. Add the onion and garlic and sauté until the onion is nearly soft. Add the cabbage. Stir to mix well and cook for 4 minutes.

Put the cabbage mixture into a baking dish. Mix the sour cream and paprika together and pour over the cabbage. Bake for 20 minutes. Serve hot.

Austrian Coffee Cake

This decorative and delicious dessert is very easy to make. Soaked in a mixture of coffee and brandy, the cake is decorated with whipped cream and walnuts.

4 SERVINGS

4 oz. [½ cup] butter
4 oz. [½ cup] plus 2 teaspoons sugar
2 eggs
4 oz. [1 cup] self-raising flour
2 oz. [¼ cup] crushed walnuts plus a few halves for decoration
6 fl. oz. [¾ cup] strong black coffee
2 fl. oz. [¼ cup] brandy
10 fl. oz. double cream [1¼ cups heavy cream]
½ teaspoon vanilla essence

Preheat the oven to moderate 350°F (Gas Mark 4, 180°C). Prepare a 7-inch cake tin by greasing the inside with a little butter and dusting with a little flour.

In a medium-sized bowl, beat the butter with a wooden spoon until it is soft. Add 4 ounces [½ cup] sugar and beat until the mixture is creamy. Add the eggs, 1 at a time, with 1 tablespoon of flour. Beat to mix and then fold in the remaining flour and the crushed walnuts. Turn the batter into the prepared cake tin. Bake for 50 minutes, or until a thin skewer inserted in the centre of the cake comes out clean.

Remove the cake from the tin and place on a rack to cool. Mix the brandy and coffee. Put the cake back in the cake tin and slowly pour the coffee and brandy over it. When all the liquid has been absorbed, turn out on to a dish.

Whip the cream with the remaining 2 teaspoons of the sugar and the vanilla essence. Using a spatula, spread the cream in whirls over the cake to cover it completely. Decorate with walnut halves.

Austrian Jam Doughnuts

Traditionally served during Fasching, a spring carnival in Austria and Germany, these jam doughnuts are light and delicious and may be served with morning coffee or afternoon tea.

ABOUT 24 DOUGHNTUS

½ oz. fresh yeast
3 tablespoons plus 1 teaspoon sugar
1 tablespoon warm water
1 lb. [4 cups] sifted flour, warmed
¼ teaspoon salt
6 egg yolks, well beaten
5 fl. oz. single [⅝ cup light] cream
1 tablespoon rum
1 teaspoon vanilla essence
1 teaspoon grated orange rind
1 teaspoon butter
12 oz. [1 cup] apricot jam
vegetable oil for deep frying
icing [confectioners'] sugar

Crumble the yeast into a small bowl and mash in 1 teaspoon of sugar with a kitchen fork. Add 1 tablespoon of water and cream the water and yeast together to form a smooth paste. Set the bowl aside in a warm, draught-free place for 15 to 20 minutes, or until the yeast has risen and is puffed up and frothy.

Sift the flour, the remaining sugar and the salt into a warmed, large mixing bowl. Make a well in the centre of the flour mixture and pour in the yeast and the egg yolks, cream, rum, vanilla essence and grated orange rind. Using your fingers or a spatula draw the flour into the liquid. Continue mixing until the mixture forms a firm dough.

For the Austrian Jam Doughnuts, cut 40 circles of dough and drop a teaspoon of apricot jam on to 20 of the circles.

Place a circle of dough on top of each one with jam on it and press the edges of the circles together.

Using a slightly smaller pastry cutter, trim the edges off the doughnuts to seal the circles together.

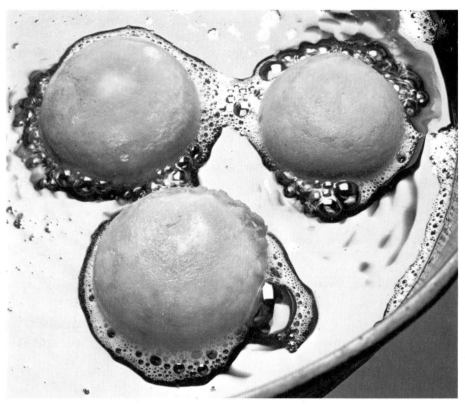

Fry the doughnuts until they are golden brown, crisp and puffy. Then turn them and fry on the other side.

Grease a large bowl with the butter. Shape the dough into a ball and put it into the bowl. Cover it with a clean, damp cloth. Set the bowl in a warm place and leave it for 1 to 1½ hours, or until the dough has nearly doubled in size.

Punch the dough down in the bowl to deflate it and turn it out on to a lightly floured board.

With a rolling pin, roll the dough into a circle, ¼-inch thick. Using a lightly floured 3-inch pastry cutter, cut circles of dough. Collect up the remaining dough and shape into a ball. Roll it out ¼-inch thick and cut out more circles of dough.

Put 1 heaped teaspoon of the jam on to the centres of half the circles of dough. Place another circle on top of each one

and press the outer edges of the two circles together.

With a slightly smaller pastry cutter, trim the edges off the doughnuts. Place waxed paper on baking sheets and dust them lightly with flour. Put the doughnuts on them about 1 inch apart. Place the doughnuts in a warm place for 30 minutes, or until they have risen and become slightly puffy.

Put the vegetable oil in a heavy frying-pan over moderate heat.

When the oil becomes hot ease the

doughnuts into the pan a few at a time. Do not crowd the pan.

The doughuts will puff up and after about 1 minute they should be golden brown on the underside. Turn the doughnuts over and fry them for a minute longer until they are golden all over.

Drain the doughnuts on several layers of kitchen paper towels on a plate, as they are cooked. Continue until all the doughnuts are fried, adding more fat to the frying-pan if necessary.

Arrange the doughnuts on a warmed plate, dust with the icing [confectioners'] sugar and serve hot.

Austrian Pudding

This is a delicious dessert and a good way to use leftover cake.

4 TO 6 SERVINGS

1 tablespoon plus 1 teaspoon butter, softened
1 lb. raspberries
6 oz. [¾ cup] sugar
4 egg yolks
4 oz. [1 cup] cake crumbs
2 oz. [½ cup] almonds, ground
1 tablespoon single [light] cream
4 egg whites
2 oz. [¼ cup] glacé cherries, halved

Preheat the oven to moderate 350°F (Gas Mark 4, 180°C). Grease a medium-sized soufflé dish with 1 teaspoon of butter.

Mix the raspberries with 3 ounces of sugar. Put them in the soufflé dish and set aside.

Place the egg yolks in a medium-sized mixing bowl with the remaining 3 ounces of sugar and beat with a wire whisk until the mixture is thick and creamy. Mix in the cake crumbs, ground almonds, cream and the remaining butter.

In another mixing bowl, whisk the egg whites until they are stiff. Fold the eggs whites into the pudding mixture and pour over the raspberries. Decorate the top with the glacé cherries and bake for 50 minutes, or until the pudding is firm and golden brown. Serve hot.

Austrian Wines

Austria produces mostly light white wines, many of which are exported to Germany. Austria's greatest wine, however, is considered to be Ruster Ausbruch, a golden dessert wine with a sweet and spicy aroma. The Heuriger, a fresh young wine, is the best-known product of Austrian vineyards.

Many of the Austrian wines are drunk when they are quite new. From the Wachau, one of the most beautiful wine areas in the world, come wines made from the Riesling grapes of the Rhine, which are similar in character to the German Rhine wines. The pleasant white wine of Gumpoldskirchen is one of the internationally better-known Austrian exports.

Au Vert

A French culinary term, *au vert* (oh vair) refers to any dish which is served with a green sauce.

Aviyal

VEGETABLE CURRY

An Indian dish of mixed vegetables cooked with coconut and spices, Aviyal (ah-VEE-yahl) should be served with boiled rice. You may use a combination of any vegetables, carrots, beans, aubergines [eggplant], turnips, cauliflower, green peppers, potatoes, spring onions [scallions] and okra.

4 SERVINGS

4 tablespoons cooking oil
1 teaspoon mustard seeds
1 onion, minced
1 green chilli, minced
2-inch piece of fresh ginger, peeled and minced
2 garlic cloves, peeled and cut into quarters lengthways
1½ teaspoons ground turmeric
1 tablespoon ground coriander
1½ lb. mixed vegetables, sliced

Low Cal

1 teaspoon salt
8 oz. [1 cup] fresh coconut puréed in an electric blender with
6 fl. oz. [¾ cup] water, or 1-inch slice creamed coconut
2 tablespoons coriander leaves, chopped (optional)

Heat the oil in a large saucepan over high heat. Add the mustard seeds, ginger and garlic and fry for 30 seconds. Add the onion and green chilli, reduce the heat and, stirring occasionally, fry gently for 10 minutes, or until the onion is golden.

Add the turmeric and ground coriander and cook for 1 minute. Add the vegetables and stir to mix well with the fried spices. Add the salt and the coconut purée and stir to mix. If the mixture is too dry, add 1 or 2 spoonfuls of water. Cover and simmer for 30 minutes or until the vegetables are tender. Sprinkle with the chopped coriander leaves and serve.

A spicy combination of flavours, Aviyal is a tasty and attractive Indian vegetable curry.

Avocado

The avocado is a delicately-flavoured, subtropical fruit that is best eaten when the flesh has ripened to the consistency of soft butter and is light yellow-green in colour. The large, brown-skinned stone and the thick green or black skin are never used. However, if you place the base of the stone in water until it sprouts roots and shoots, and then plant it in soil, it will grow into a small, decorative tree.

The fruit of a small to medium-sized tree native to Central America, avocados are now widely grown in tropical and subtropical areas such as the southern states of America, Mexico, Israel, South Africa and Australia.

Avocados are exceptionally rich in protein, Vitamin A and Vitamin B. Although high in calories, they have almost no carbohydrate content. They also contain a rare, highly digestible oil which is not found in other fruits.

The flesh of the avocado can be used in salads, sauces, soups and desserts. Diced or sliced, avocados are an attractive garnish for clear soups and hot dishes.

To halve an avocado, cut in half lengthways round the stone. Holding the two halves, gently twist them apart. Then remove the stone with the point of a knife. To prevent the flesh from darkening, rub it with a little lemon juice. Half an unpeeled avocado filled with a chicken or seafood salad, or with curried meat or chicken, tastes as good as it looks.

The most simple avocado recipe is the fruit eaten by itself with an oil and vinegar dressing.

Avocado Aspic

Serve this decorative aspic as part of a buffet supper or as a salad course at dinner.

6 TO 8 SERVINGS

    1 oz. gelatine
    4 fl. oz. [½ cup] cold water
    1¼ pints [3 cups] chicken stock
    2 avocados
      lemon juice
    2 teaspoons finely chopped onion
    2 celery stalks, diced
    2 tablespoons diced cucumber
    2 tablespoons canned diced
      pineapple

In a medium-sized saucepan, soften the gelatine in the cold water. Heat, stirring until the gelatine is dissolved. Add the chicken stock and cool the mixture.

Cut the avocados in half, peel and remove the stones. Slice the avocado halves into thin even slices. Sprinkle with lemon juice.

Cover the bottom of a ring mould with a layer of gelatine and chill until it is set. Keep the remaining gelatine in a warm place so it will not set.

Arrange the avocado slices on top and cover with a layer of the gelatine. Chill until it is set.

Arrange more slices around the sides and add a thin layer of gelatine to hold them in position.

Chop any remaining avocado and mix it with all remaining ingredients and the remaining gelatine. Turn into the decorated mould and chill until firm.

Before serving, dip the mould quickly into hot water. Unmould on a bed of lettuce leaves on a serving plate.

Avocado Chicken Soup

A delicious and delicately flavoured soup, this can be served as the start to an otherwise heavy meal. Do not place the soup over direct heat after the avocado mixture is added.

4 SERVINGS

    1½ pints [3 cups] chicken stock, fresh
      or made from a stock cube
    1 small onion, finely minced
    2 avocados, peeled and stoned
    1 tablespoon butter, softened
    1 teaspoon salt
    4 grindings of black pepper
    2 teaspoons lemon juice

Simmer the chicken stock and onion in a covered saucepan for 30 minutes.

Purée the avocados by pushing them through a sieve. Combine the purée with the butter, salt, pepper and lemon juice.

Remove the stock from the heat and fold in the avocado mixture.

Serve immediately in heated bowls.

Avocado Chicken Supreme

A good way to use leftover chicken or turkey, this dish could be served as a first course or as a light lunch or supper entrée.

4 SERVINGS

    2 oz. [¼ cup] butter
    2 tablespoons flour
    10 fl. oz. [1¼ cups] milk
    ½ teaspoon salt
    ¼ teaspoon white pepper
    ½ teaspoon dried tarragon
    12 oz. [1½ cups] chicken, cooked and
      diced
    3 tablespoons chopped mushrooms
    1 tablespoon chopped green pepper

    2 large avocados
      juice of ½ lemon
    2 tablespoons dry breadcrumbs

Preheat the oven to moderate 350°F (Gas Mark 4, 180°C).

In a medium-sized saucepan, melt 2 tablespoons of the butter over low heat. Stir in the flour to make a smooth paste. Gradually add the milk, stirring constantly until the sauce thickens. When the sauce boils add the salt, pepper, tarragon, chicken, mushrooms and green pepper. Simmer for 4 minutes.

Cut the unpeeled avocados in half lengthways. Remove the stones and rub the cut surfaces with the lemon juice.

Fill the cavities with the chicken mixture. Sprinkle the top with the breadcrumbs and dot with the remaining butter. Put the avocados in a baking dish with ½ inch boiling water. Bake in the oven for 10 minutes.

Avocado and Courgette [Zucchini] Salad

An unusual and decorative salad which could be served with any veal or beef dish, the courgettes can be cooked the day before you are going to use them.

4 SERVINGS

    1 lb. courgettes [zucchini]
    1 pint [2½ cups] water
    2 teaspoons salt
    1 garlic clove, crushed
    ¼ teaspoon dried tarragon
    ¼ teaspoon black pepper
    ½ teaspoon sugar
    2 tablespoons white wine vinegar
    6 tablespoons olive oil
    1 avocado
    12 stuffed green olives
      lettuce leaves
    4 sprigs watercress

Wash the courgettes. Cut off the ends. Cut into slices ½-inch thick. In a saucepan, bring the water to the boil. Add 1 teaspoon of salt and the courgettes. Cover and cook for about 6 minutes. Drain the courgettes, put them in a bowl and allow to cool.

In a cup, mix the remaining salt, garlic, tarragon, pepper, sugar, vinegar and oil. Pour over the courgettes and toss well. Leave the courgettes to marinate in the refrigerator for 6 hours or overnight.

Peel and stone the avocado and cut it

A striking combination of greens, this Avocado and Courgette Salad goes well with any main dish.

into slices. Drain the courgettes and reserve the marinade. Cut the olives in half. Put the lettuce leaves on individual plates and arrange the courgettes, avocado and olives on top.

Garnish with watercress. Serve with the marinade separately.

Avocado Dip—I

This inexpensive, quickly made dip or spread can be served at cocktail parties or with pre-dinner drinks, accompanied by potato crisps, biscuits, toast slices, celery or other vegetable sticks.

ABOUT 32 OUNCES

4 medium-sized avocados
2 tablespoons lemon juice
2 tablespoons grated onion
⅛ teaspoon Tabasco sauce
¼ teaspoon salt
⅛ teaspoon black pepper

Peel and stone the avocados. Using a wooden spoon, push the avocado flesh through a sieve into a bowl. Mix in the lemon juice, grated onion, Tabasco sauce, salt and pepper. Cover the bowl and refrigerate until well chilled.

Avocado Dip—II

Spicy and delicious, this dip is quickly made. It can be prepared early in the day and covered and refrigerated until it is to be served.

ABOUT 24 OUNCES

3 medium-sized avocados
3 tablespoons mayonnaise
¼ teaspoon salt
¼ teaspoon pepper
¼ teaspoon chilli sauce
1 garlic clove, crushed
1 teaspoon prepared mustard
2 teaspoons lemon juice

Peel and stone the avocados. Using a wooden spoon, push the avocado flesh through a sieve into a bowl. Mix in the mayonnaise, salt, pepper, chilli sauce, garlic, mustard and lemon juice. Cover the bowl and refrigerate.

Avocado Herb Salad Dressing

A good way to use a soft, slightly over-ripe avocado, this dressing can be used for a simple lettuce and tomato salad.

ABOUT 8 OUNCES

1 teaspoon salt
4 grindings black pepper
½ teaspoon dried basil
½ teaspoon dried oregano
2 fl. oz. vinegar
6 fl. oz. [¾ cup] olive oil
1 medium-sized avocado, peeled, stone and puréed

In a small bowl, mix the salt, pepper, basil, oregano, vinegar and oil.

Gradually add the mashed avocado to the dressing until well blended.

Avocado with Jellied Consommé

An unusual first course for a summer lunch or dinner, jellied tomato consommé piled into avocado halves and garnished with watercress is elegant but inexpensive.

6 SERVINGS

14 oz. canned, peeled tomatoes
1 onion, sliced
½ teaspoon dried basil
4 allspice berries
1 bay leaf
½ oz. gelatine
12 fl. oz. [1½ cups] condensed consommé
½ teaspoon salt
½ teaspoon black pepper
3 avocados
juice of ½ lemon

Put the tomatoes, onion, basil, allspice and bay leaf in a medium-sized pan and bring to the boil. Lower the heat and simmer uncovered for 40 minutes. Strain through a sieve into a bowl.

In a cup, mix the gelatine with 4 table-spoons of the hot tomato liquid. When it has dissolved add it to the bowl.

Warm the consommé and add it with the salt and pepper to the tomato liquid. Mix well and pour the mixture into a shallow dish. Chill in the refrigerator until it sets.

Cut the avocados in half lengthways and remove the stones. Sprinkle the cut surfaces with the lemon juice.

This inexpensive Avocado Dip takes only a few minutes to prepare and is ideal to serve with drinks.

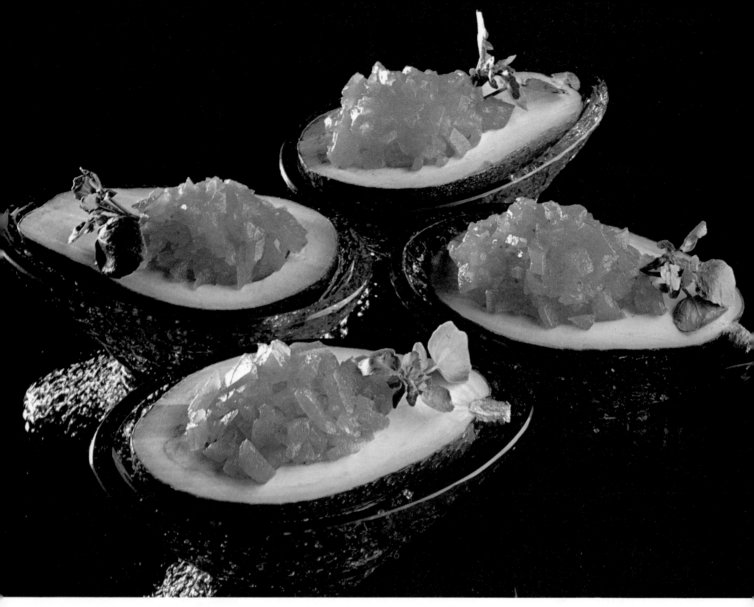

Chop the jellied consommé and pile it into the avocado halves. Garnish with watercress.

Avocado Soup

An easy-to-make, inexpensive, cold soup, this may be served at the start of a summer lunch or dinner. It may be garnished with chives, dill or parsley.

6 SERVINGS

1 large avocado
1½ pints [3¾ cups] chicken stock, fresh or made from a stock cube
1 teaspoon grated onion
⅛ teaspoon cayenne pepper
5 fl. oz. single [⅝ cup light] cream
1 tablespoon chopped dill

Peel and stone the avocado. Using a wooden spoon, push the avocado through a sieve into a bowl.

Add the stock, onion and cayenne pepper. Beat well with a whisk until the mixture is smooth. Alternatively, blend the ingredients in an electric blender. Mix in the cream.

Pour the soup into individual soup bowls. Put the bowls in the refrigerator and chill thoroughly. Garnish with the dill and serve.

Azerbaijan Pilaff

This pilaff from Azerbaijan is delicately flavoured with sesame seeds and a little ginger. It makes an excellent accompaniment to roast chicken, roast lamb or a curry.

4 SERVINGS

2 oz. [¼ cup] butter
10 oz. [1½ cups] long-grain rice, washed, soaked for 30 minutes in water and drained
½ teaspoon ground ginger
1½ teaspoons sesame seeds
1 pint [2½ cups] chicken stock
½ teaspoon salt
½ teaspoon black pepper
2 oz. [½ cup] slivered, toasted almonds

Preheat the oven to moderate 350°F (Gas Mark 4, 180°C).

Melt the butter in a flameproof

Avocado halves filled with jellied tomato consommé is an elegant, yet easy and inexpensive first course.

casserole dish over moderate heat. Add the rice and cook for 10 minutes, stirring all the time. Add the ginger and sesame seeds and cook for 3 minutes. Pour in the stock, salt and pepper and bring to the boil, stirring constantly.

Put the casserole in the oven uncovered for 35 minutes or until all the liquid is absorbed and the rice is cooked. Toss the rice with a fork after 10 minutes and again after 20 minutes. Taste and add more salt if necessary. Sprinkle with the almonds and serve immediately.

Azarole

A member of the hawthorn family, the azarole tree grows in France, Italy, Algeria and Spain, where its fruit is used to make preserves and flavour liqueurs. The fruit resembles that of the hawthorn, but it is slightly larger. Its haws are usually orange-yellow or reddish in colour and have an apple-like flavour.

B

Baba

A rich, light-textured cake, a baba is made with flour, yeast, butter and eggs, and baked in the oven. It is said that the baba was invented by Stanislaus Leszczynski, King of Poland in 1704, when he poured rum over a dry yeast cake, naming it Ali Baba after the hero of his favourite story from *The Thousand and One Nights*. Introduced to Paris at the beginning of the nineteenth century, it became very popular and was known as a baba.

Baked in small or large round moulds, babas are soaked with syrup which is flavoured with rum or kirsch. They can be glazed with apricot jam, decorated with glacé fruit and served with Crème Chantilly.

Baba au Rhum

The best-known baba, Baba au Rhum (bah-bah oh rum) makes a delicious dessert for a lunch or dinner party. Babas can be baked a day or two in advance of serving, but should be reheated in a cool oven for 5 minutes so that they are warm when they are soaked in syrup.

MAKES 12 SMALL BABAS

BABA DOUGH
2 oz. [¼ cup] butter
7 oz. [1¾ cups] flour
¼ teaspoon salt
1 sachet easy-blend dried yeast
2 eggs, beaten
1 tablespoon milk
  butter for greasing
SAUCE
11 fl. oz. [1⅜ cups] water
5 oz. [⅝ cup] sugar
5 fl. oz. [⅝ cup] dark rum (light rum can also be used)
APRICOT GLAZE
4 tablespoons apricot jam
5 tablespoons water
DECORATION
1 teaspoon lemon juice
  glacé cherries, to decorate
  toasted almond slivers, to decorate

To make the babas, melt the butter in a small heavy-based saucepan over a very low heat. Be careful not to brown the butter.

Set aside to cool.

Sift the flour, salt and dried yeast into a large mixing bowl. Make a well in the centre of the flour mixture and gradually pour in the beaten eggs, cooled melted butter and milk.

Blend all these ingredients thoroughly together with a wooden spoon, then beat and knead the dough with your hands, lifting it and slapping it. To begin with the dough will be quite sticky. If it is too sticky add a spoonful of flour. If it is too dry add a spoonful of milk.

When the dough begins to lose its stickiness, turn on to a lightly floured board and continue to knead. When it is completely elastic and can be stretched and twisted without breaking, roll it into a ball.

Butter a large mixing bowl and carefully place the ball of dough in it. With a sharp knife cut a cross on the surface of the dough and lightly sprinkle it with 1 teaspoon flour.

Cover the bowl with a clean cloth and leave in a warm draught-free place for 1½-2 hours, or until the dough has almost doubled in bulk. Press the dough with your fingers, if the impression remains the dough has risen sufficiently and is now ready for the second kneading. If the dough has not risen sufficiently, leave it for another 10 minutes and check again.

When the dough has risen enough, deflate it by kneading it gently for 2 more minutes.

Butter the insides of 12 individual baba moulds. Divide the dough into 12 portions and gently press each portion into a mould. The mould should only be two-thirds full.

Place the uncovered moulds in a warm, draught-free place and leave to rise for about 35-45 minutes, or until the dough

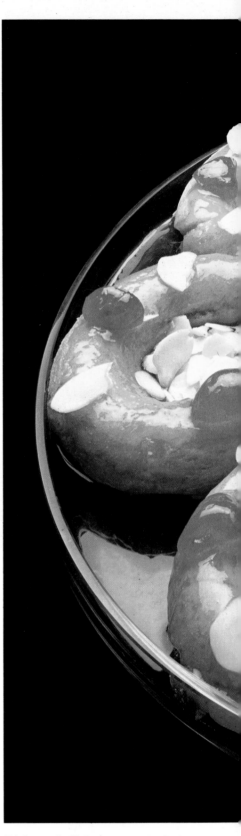

Rich and light-textured, Babas au Rhum are soaked in a rum-flavoured syrup and glazed with apricot jam.

has risen to just over the top of the baba moulds.

Preheat the oven to moderate 375°F (Gas Mark 5, 190°C).

Bake the risen dough in the middle of

the oven for 15 minutes, or until the babas are cooked, when the tops are brown and an inserted skewer comes out clean. Unmould them carefully on to a cake rack and set aside to allow them to cool slightly.

While the babas are cooling prepare the sauce; put the sugar and water in a heavy-based saucepan and gradually bring to the boil to completely dissolve the sugar.

Simmer for 5 minutes and remove from the heat.

Allow the syrup to cool completely and gradually stir in 4 fluid ounces [½ cup] of the rum.

Place the babas in a shallow dish large enough to hold them all comfortably and prick them all over with a fork. Pour the warm syrup over them and, basting with the syrup every few minutes, leave to soak

for 30-40 minutes or until the babas have absorbed enough syrup to be well moistened. Carefully transfer the babas to a rack and leave to drain.

To prepare the apricot glaze, put the jam and water in a small heavy-based saucepan and cook over medium heat for about 5 minutes, stirring constantly with a wooden spoon. Add the lemon juice and stir well, then strain through a fine nylon

sieve.

When the babas have drained, arrange them on a serving dish and sprinkle with the remaining rum. With a pastry brush, paint the babas with the apricot glaze. Decorate the outside of the babas with the glacé cherries and the toasted almond slivers, sprinkling the almonds in the centre and on top of the rings. Serve cold, with cream if liked.

If the babas are made in dariole moulds, decorate the tops with cherries and the sides with almonds.

Baba aux Fraises

Baba aux Fraises (bah-bah oh fraze) *is a delicious way to serve a rum baba when strawberries are in season, but other soft fruits, or a mixture of fruits, can be used. It is usually served with Crème Chantilly.*

12 SERVINGS

1 lb. fresh strawberries
   leftover baba syrup
1 large rum baba
CREME CHANTILLY
15 fl. oz. double cream [2 cups
   heavy cream]
1 teaspoon vanilla essence
   icing [confectioners'] sugar

Put the strawberries in a bowl and pour over the syrup. Leave for 20 minutes.

Put the rum baba on a serving dish. Fill the centre with the strawberries, putting a few around the baba.

To make the Crème Chantilly, place the cream and essence in a chilled bowl and, using a cold whisk, whip lightly, adding the icing sugar to taste. Serve the Crème Chantilly in a separate dish.

Baba aux Fraises, accompanied by Crème Chantilly, is an interesting way to serve a baba with strawberries.

Bacalhau

SALT COD CASSEROLE

A traditional Portuguese dish, Bacalhau (bah-kah-loah) *makes an unusual, tasty family lunch or dinner dish and may be served with a green salad. The salt cod should be bought the day before you wish to cook it, so that it can be soaked in cold water for 12 hours to remove some of the salt.*

4 SERVINGS

2 lb. salt cod
6 fl. oz. [¾ cup] olive oil
1½ lb. potatoes, peeled
1 lb. onions, cut in slices and
   separated into rings
1 lb. tomatoes, coarsley sliced
2 garlic cloves, finely chopped
½ teaspoon coarsley ground black
   pepper
10 black olives, stones removed
4 hard-boiled eggs, sliced
2 tablespoons finely chopped
   parsley

Put the cod in a medium-sized mixing bowl and cover with cold water. Leave covered for at least 12 hours to soak. Change the water every 3 or 4 hours, or whenever convenient.

Drain the cod and rinse it well to wash off the salt. Put the fish in a medium-sized saucepan, cover with water and bring to the boil over high heat. Lower the heat, cover the pan and simmer the cod for 15 minutes or until it is cooked.

Pour away the water and drain the cod

well. Skin and bone the fish. Flake it and set aside.

Preheat the oven to fairly hot 375°F (Gas Mark 5, 190°C).

Half fill a large saucepan with salted water and bring it to the boil. Add the potatoes and boil them for 15 to 20 minutes, or until they are just cooked. Drain and cut the potatoes into slices and set aside.

In a large frying-pan heat 4 tablespoons of the olive oil over moderate heat. When it is hot add the onions and fry for 5 minutes, stirring occasionally until they are soft but not brown. Add the tomatoes, garlic and pepper and cook stirring carefully for 4 minutes. Draw the pan off the heat.

Arrange the potato slices, the cod, onions and tomatoes in layers in the casserole until it is full. Pour the remaining oil over the top. Put the casserole in the centre of the oven and cook for 30 minutes or until all the ingredients are thoroughly heated and the top is brown.

Garnish the dish with the black olives, egg slices and chopped parsley. Serve hot.

Bacardi Rum

A light, white rum which was first produced in Cuba in 1862, Bacardi rum developed international popularity in the twentieth century. Bacardi is the main ingredient of the DAIQUIRI and many other cocktails. The chief producers of Bacardi today are the Bahamas and Puerto Rico.

Bacon

The word bacon usually refers to the cured meat from a specially bred pig. Most British bacon is cured in the Wiltshire style. The two sides of the pig are immersed for about five days in a tank of brine which is composed of salt, sodium nitrate, saltpetre and, sometimes, sugar. The bacon is then drained and matured for a further seven days. Many other cures, however, such as sweetcure and tendercure, have been developed in recent years. For the distinctive smoked flavour, cured bacon is hung over smouldering oak sawdust or chips for 12 hours.

Unsmoked bacon, commonly called green bacon, or white bacon, has a white rind and a milder flavour than smoked bacon, which has a brown rind. Country-smoked bacon is more heavily smoked than the commercial variety.

In Britain, a side of bacon is usually

A traditional Portuguese casserole made with salt cod, Bacalhau is a colourful main dish.

divided into the following cuts. From the fore end of the bacon, the cuts are called forehock and collar. Those from the middle of the bacon are called prime streaky, thin streaky, flank, top back, prime back, oyster back and long back. From the gammon, which is the hind quarter of a side of bacon, the cuts are called slipper, corner, prime middle and knuckle.

In America, there are only two types of bacon available. Smoked or hickory, smoked strips of bacon without rind, are very much like English rindless thin streaky bacon. Canadian bacon is cut from the eye of a pork loin and is more like ham.

The choicest bacon slices, or rashers, for frying or grilling are those from the back, which are called prime, long and top back. The fat and lean in these rashers are not intermixed, unlike streaky bacon which alternates streaks of lean and fat, but which can be fried or grilled.

Collar rashers are wider and leaner than streaky bacon. Often too coarse for grilling and frying, they are suitable for pies. Gammon rashers and steaks are cut thick and can be fried and grilled. Oyster or flank rashers are quite fatty and are used for larding poultry and meat.

The most suitable cuts of bacon for boiling or baking are the gammon cuts. A whole gammon usually weighs about 15 pounds and is divided into many cuts. The most popular are middle and corner gammon which are lean and boneless. The smaller, cheaper cuts, gammon slipper and gammon hock, include some bone.

Collar cuts of bacon, which can also be boiled or baked, are less expensive than gammon and include a good proportion of lean meat. The best collar cut, prime collar, is boneless and meaty. A cut called forehock has some bone and knuckle, is less tender than gammon, but is ideal for soups or stocks. It is also sold boned and rolled for boiling.

Bacon stored in a cool place should keep for 10 days in winter and up to four days in summer. Bacon fat can be kept in a covered jar in a cool place or in the refrigerator and used for frying eggs, liver, tomatoes or bread.

In many parts of the world, particularly

Bac

in England and America, bacon is traditionally served at breakfast with eggs, either fried or scrambled.

To fry bacon, cut off the rind with kitchen scissors, make little snips in the fat to prevent the rasher from excessive shrinking and arrange the rashers in a cold frying-pan in one layer, with the slices barely touching each other. No fat needs to be added unless you are cooking gammon or collar rashers. The bacon should be cooked over moderate heat until it is crisp. The rashers should be turned frequently to ensure even cooking. Bacon is not properly cooked until the fat has entirely lost its transparency. Drain the bacon on paper towels for 1 minute before serving.

To grill [broil] bacon, put it under a hot grill and cook, turning frequently, until the fat loses its transparency. Another method of cooking bacon, which is easy and ensures crispness, is to cook the bacon in a moderate oven on a rack set in a baking tin.

Fried or grilled bacon is delicious in a sandwich with lettuce and sliced tomatoes or served with calves' liver.

Cuts of bacon are frequently very salty and should be soaked in tepid water for at least two hours before boiling. The saltiness can also be removed by putting the cut of bacon in a saucepan of cold water and bringing it slowly to the boil. When it reaches boiling point, remove the saucepan from the heat and pour off the water. Refill the saucepan with cold water and boil the bacon for the required time. Cooking time for boiling bacon is 20 minutes to the pound, plus 20 minutes over.

British cuts of Bacon
1, 2, 9 boneless forehock joints
3 prime streaky   *4 thin streaky*
5 middle rashers   *6 middle gammon*
7 corner gammon   *8 forehock knuckle*
10 top back   *11 prime back*
12 gammon knuckle 13,14 collar joints
15 long back   *16 oyster back*
17 slipper gammon   *18 collar rashers*
19 flank   *20 bacon chops*
21 gammon steaks

Bac

Bacon, Baked

*Served hot or cold, baked bacon accom-
panied by creamed or sautéed potatoes and
broccoli or green beans, makes a delicious
and satisfying main course for lunch or
dinner. The bacon should be soaked in tepid
water for 2 hours before boiling to remove
excess salt.*

4 SERVINGS

3 lb. bacon gammon, collar or hock
5 fl. oz. [⅝ cup] vinegar
1 bay leaf
6 tablespoons brown sugar
  grated rind of 1 orange
  juice of 1 orange
⅛ teaspoon mace
20 cloves
5 fl. oz. [⅝ cup] cider

After soaking the bacon, place it in a
saucepan and cover with cold water. Add
the vinegar, bay leaf and 1 tablespoon
of sugar and bring to the boil. Remove
the scum from the surface of the water
and reduce heat to low.

Simmer very gently, partly covering
the saucepan, for 1 hour and 10 minutes,
removing the scum from the surface of
the water from time to time. Remove the
bacon from the water, peel off the thick
skin and put the bacon in a medium-
sized, ovenproof serving dish, the fat side
up.

Preheat the oven to moderate 350°F
(Gas Mark 4, 180°C).

In a small bowl, mix the remaining
brown sugar, grated orange rind, orange
juice and mace together. Push the
cloves into the fat of the bacon. Pour the
brown sugar-and-orange mixture over the
bacon and pour the cider round it.

Place in the centre of the oven and
bake for 40 minutes, basting from time
to time, or until the sugar is brown and
crisp. Serve the bacon hot in the dish in
which it has been cooked.

Bacon, Boiled

*Served hot, boiled bacon is delicious with
mustard, pickled onions, new potatoes and
young green beans or peas. It may also
accompany roast turkey or veal. Cold
boiled bacon is excellent accompanied by a
mixed salad and boiled new potatoes.*

4 SERVINGS

3 lb. bacon gammon, collar
  or hock
5 fl. oz. [⅝ cup] vinegar
6 cloves
1 bay leaf
1 tablespoon brown sugar

Soak the bacon in tepid water for 2 hours.
Place the soaked bacon in a saucepan
and cover with cold water. Add the
vinegar, cloves, bay leaf and sugar and
bring to a boil. Remove the scum from
the surface of the water and reduce heat
to low.

Simmer very gently, partly covering
the saucepan, for 1 hour and 30 minutes,
or until the bacon is very tender. Remove
the scum from the surface of the water
from time to time. Drain, peel off the
skin and place the bacon on a warmed
serving dish, if the bacon is to be served
hot. If it is to be served cold, allow the
bacon to cool in the water in which it has
been cooked. This ensures that the
meat remains moist. Drain well before
serving.

Bacon Dumplings

*These Austrian Bacon dumplings may be
served in chicken soup or cooked in boiling
salted water, and served with beef instead
of potatoes.*

16 DUMPLINGS

1 egg
4 tablespoons milk
6 slices white bread, trimmed
4 slices lean bacon, diced
2 small onions, finely chopped
2 oz. [½ cup] flour
½ teaspoon salt
2 tablespoons finely chopped
  parsley
½ teaspoon dried thyme
½ teaspoon finely grated lemon rind

In a small mixing bowl, lightly beat the
egg and milk together.

Put the bread in a medium-sized
mixing bowl and pour the egg-milk
mixture over it. Set aside.

In a small frying pan, over moderate
heat, fry the bacon dice for 4 or 5 minutes,
or until they are crisp and golden. Using
a slotted spoon, remove the bacon and set
aside to drain on kitchen paper towels.

Add the onions to the pan and fry them
gently for 5 minutes, or until they are
golden brown. Add the onion and the
bacon to the bread in the mixing bowl.

Add the flour, salt, parsley, thyme and
lemon rind. Mix well with a spoon. If the
mixture is too dry add a little more milk;
if it is too wet add a little more flour.

Using your hands mix all the ingredients well together. Taste the mixture
and add more salt if necessary. With
floured hands shape the mixture into
balls the size of walnuts.

Half fill a large saucepan with salted
water or soup and bring it to the boil over

high heat. Ease the dumplings in, lower
the heat and simmer uncovered for 8 to
10 minutes, or until they are cooked.

With a slotted spoon, remove the dumplings from the pan. Serve immediately.

Bacon and Egg Pie

*Delicious eaten hot or cold, this is an
easily-made pie. It is a good dish for light
lunches, suppers, or for a family picnic.*

4 SERVINGS

PASTRY
6 oz. [1½ cups] flour
¼ teaspoon salt
1½ oz. [¼ cup] butter,
  chilled
1½ oz. [¼ cup] vegetable fat
2 tablespoons iced water
FILLING
1 teaspoon butter
8 oz. streaky bacon
4 eggs
½ teaspoon black pepper
  a little beaten egg

Preheat the oven to fairly hot 400°F (Gas
Mark 6, 200°C).

To make the pastry, sift the flour and
salt into a medium-sized mixing bowl.
Add the butter and the vegetable fat and
cut into small pieces with a table knife.
With your fingers, rub the fat into the
flour until the mixture looks like fine
breadcrumbs. Add 1 tablespoon of the
iced water and mix it in with the knife.
Using your hands, mix and knead lightly
until the dough is smooth. If the dough
is too dry, add the remaining iced water.
Pat the dough into a ball, cover and put
in the refrigerator for 30 minutes.

Grease an 8 inch diameter tin with 1
teaspoon of butter.

Break off two thirds of the pastry and
set aside the smaller piece. On a floured
board, roll out the larger piece into a
round 2 inches larger than the sandwich
tin. Line the tin with the pastry and trim
the edges.

Trim the bacon rinds and chop the
bacon into small pieces. Arrange the
bacon pieces in the pastry shell, leaving
4 wells for the eggs. Break an egg into
each well. Sprinkle with pepper. Brush
the edge of the pastry with a little beaten
egg. Roll out the remaining pastry into a
circle and cover the pie. Trim the edges
and pinch them together to seal them and
make a decorative pattern. Brush the top
of the pie with the beaten egg and
decorate with pastry shapes. Make a slit,
with a knife, in the centre of the pie to
allow the steam to escape.

Place the pie in the centre of the oven

102

and bake for 40 minutes. When the top of the pie becomes sufficiently brown, cover with aluminium foil and continue baking. Serve hot or cold.

Bacon and Liver Rolls

Tasty and inexpensive appetizers or hors d'oeuvre, these may also be served as a accompaniment to an entrée of roast chicken.

20 ROLLS

10 fl. oz. [1¼ cups] water
½ teaspoon salt
8 oz. chicken livers
2 hard-boiled eggs
2 tablespoons chopped onion
2 teaspoons chopped parsley
¼ teaspoon salt
  freshly ground black pepper
2 tablespoons butter, softened
½ teaspoon lemon juice
1 teaspoon brandy
10 bacon slices, cut in halves

In a medium-sized saucepan, bring the water to the boil. Add the salt and the chicken livers. Boil them for 7 minutes

Rolls of bacon filled with a rich liver mixture, Bacon and Liver Rolls make a tasty hors d'oeuvre.

or until they are just cooked. Drain the livers.

Using the back of a spoon, rub the hard-boiled eggs and the chicken livers through a fine sieve into a bowl. Add the onions, parsley, salt, 4 grindings of pepper, butter, lemon juice and brandy. Stir the mixture well and chill it in the refrigerator for 30 minutes.

Spread the chicken liver mixture on the strips of bacon. Roll up the bacon strips and put a wooden cocktail stick through the centre of each one. Place the rolls under a fairly hot grill and, turning them occasionally, cook them for 10 minutes, or until the bacon is crisp. Serve hot.

Bacon Whole-Wheat Scones

These bacon-flavoured scones may be served hot with a hearty soup for a light family lunch or supper. The dough can

be prepared well in advance and baked just before serving.

16 SCONES

5 oz. [1¼ cups] wholewheat flour
5 oz. [1¼ cups] plain flour
1 tablespoon baking powder
¼ teaspoon salt
3 oz. [⅔ cup] white vegetable fat [shortening]
8 oz. [½ lb.] streaky bacon, crisply fried
5 fl. oz. [⅝ cup] milk

Preheat the oven to very hot 450°F (Gas Mark 8, 230°C).

Sift the flours, baking powder and salt into a bowl. Rub in the fat until the mixture resembles breadcrumbs. Crumble the bacon and add to the flour mixture.

Gradually stir in sufficient milk to give a soft dough. Turn on to a lightly floured surface and knead lightly. Carefully roll the dough to ½ inch thick and cut into individual scones.

Place on a baking sheet, bake for about 15 minutes and serve hot.

The dry mixture can be prepared in advance. Then add the liquid, knead, cut out and bake when needed – a good idea for a brunch snack.

For a richer tasting scone, substitute butter for the white vegetable fat [shortening].

Badami Gosht

LAMB COOKED WITH ALMONDS

An adaptation of an Indian recipe, Badami Gosht (ba-DAH-mee gohsht) is fragrant and spicy lamb cooked with almonds. It makes a good lunch or dinner dish and may be served with chapatis, or bread, and with vegetables, such as aubergines or spinach. The usual cooking medium for this dish is clarified butter, which is called ghee in India.

If ghee is not available, cooking oil may be substituted.

If creamed coconut is not available, soak 4 tablespoons desiccated [shredded] coconut in 12 tablespoons of water for 1 hour or until the coconut is moist and has absorbed all the water.

4 SERVINGS

5 tablespoons clarified butter or vegetable oil
2 cinnamon sticks
6 cloves
  seeds of 6 cardamoms
1 large onion, finely chopped
2 garlic cloves, crushed
1½ inch piece root ginger, peeled and finely minced
1½ lb. boned leg of lamb, cut into 1-inch cubes
10 fl. oz. [1¼ cups] yogurt
1 teaspoon saffron threads soaked in 2 tablespoons of boiling water
½ teaspoon chilli powder
3 oz. [½ cup] ground almonds
1 teaspoon salt
1-inch slice creamed coconut dissolved in 10 fl. oz. [1¼ cup] hot water
2 whole dried red chillis

In a medium-sized saucepan heat the oil over moderate heat. Add the cinnamon, cloves and cardamom seeds and cook for 1 minute.

Add the onion and, stirring continuously, fry for 7 minutes until the onion is soft. Add the garlic and ginger and continue frying and stirring until the onions are golden brown.

Add the lamb cubes, a few at a time, and fry well, stirring frequently, until they are well browned.

Put the yogurt into a small bowl. Pour in the saffron, the soaking water and the chilli powder and beat well.

In another small bowl mix the almonds with enough water to make a paste.

Pour the yogurt mixture over the lamb cubes in the pan and stir to mix. Cook for a minute and stir in the almond paste and salt. Simmer for 15 minutes.

Add the dissolved coconut cream and

Badami Gosht, a fragant Indian lamb dish, is coloured with saffron and flavoured with almonds and coconut.

the whole red chillis. Lower the heat and simmer, uncovered, for 30 to 40 minutes or until the lamb is tender.

Cover the pan for the last 10 minutes of cooking. Serve hot.

Badminton Cup

This is a refreshing, cold, summer drink.

1¾ PINTS

½ medium-sized cucumber, peeled and sliced
4 oz. icing [1 cup confectioners'] sugar
juice of 1 lemon
⅛ teaspoon grated nutmeg
2 fl. oz. [¼ cup] Curaçao
1 bottle claret
6 fl. oz. [¾ cup] soda-water
2 borage sprigs, if available

Put the cucumber, sugar, lemon juice, nutmeg, Curaçao and claret into a large bowl. Stir to dissolve the sugar. Pour in the soda-water and some ice. Add the borage, if it is available.

Baghali Polo

LAMB WITH RICE AND DILL

Dill is traditionally used in Iranian cooking and it gives this lamb and rice dish a delicious aroma. Baghali Polo may be served as a main dish for lunch or dinner and is usually accompanied by a large bowl of chilled yogurt. You may also serve a tomato, cucumber and onion salad, made with a sharp dressing.

6 SERVINGS

4 tablespoons vegetable oil
2 lb. lean, boned lamb, cut into
    1-inch cubes
2 onions, sliced
12 fl. oz. [1½ cups] water
1 teaspoon salt
¼ teaspoon ground cinnamon
½ teaspoon black pepper
1 lb. [2½ cups] long-grain rice,
    washed, soaked in water for 30
    minutes and drained
1 lb. fresh or frozen Lima or broad
    beans
3 tablespoons chopped fresh dill or
    2 teaspoons dried dill

In a large flameproof casserole, heat the oil over moderate heat. Add the lamb cubes, a few at a time, As they brown, transfer them with a slotted spoon to a plate.

Add the onions to the casserole and fry them for 10 minutes, stirring occasionally, until they are brown.

Return the lamb to the casserole and mix in ½ teaspoon salt, the cinnamon,

pepper and water. Reduce the heat to low, cover the pan and simmer for 35 minutes, or until the lamb is tender.

Put the lamb, onion and cooking liquid into a bowl and set aside.

Preheat the oven to moderate 350°F (Gas Mark 4, 180°C).

Half fill a large saucepan with water and bring to the boil over high heat. Add the rice and remaining salt, parboil for 1½ minutes and drain. In the same pan parboil the beans for 10 to 15 minutes or 1 minute if the beans are frozen.

Put half the rice into the casserole and spoon the beans and dill on top. With a slotted spoon, transfer the lamb and onions to the casserole. Spread the remaining beans, dill and rice on top of the meat and pour over the liquid in which the lamb was cooked.

Put the casserole over high heat and bring to the boil.

Remove the casserole, cover it and put it in the oven for 30 minutes, or until the rice is cooked and all the liquid absorbed. Serve immediately.

Bagna Cauda

ANCHOVY AND GARLIC DIP

An Italian dish, Bagna Cauda (BAHN yah KOW-dah) is served hot as a dip for cold raw vegetables. It is ideal for a summer party or as a first course for a dinner party. An assortment of such vegetables as cucumbers, carrots, peppers, celery, French beans, cauliflower and broccoli are suitable for dipping. Wash and peel where necessary and cut into strips the right size for dipping. Break the cauliflower and broccoli into flowerets. Wrap the vegetables in a clean, damp cloth and chill in the refrigerator. Arrange on a serving plate and serve with Italian breadsticks.

12 FLUID OUNCES

4 oz. [½ cup] butter
2 tablespoons olive oil
3 garlic cloves, finely chopped
6 anchovy fillets, finely chopped
5 fl. oz. single [⅝ cup light] cream
1 small truffle, finely chopped,
    optional

In a small saucepan, heat the butter and the oil. Add the anchovies and the garlic and cook over low heat, stirring and mashing with a wooden spoon.

When the anchovies have become very soft, or almost a paste, add the cream and the truffle. Heat thoroughly but do not let the sauce boil.

Serve in a bowl placed over a plate warmer or in a small, heat-proof dish over a spirit lamp.

Bain-Marie

A bain-marie (ban mah-ree) is a large, shallow pan half-filled with hot water in which smaller pans containing sauces, custards and other dishes which cannot be re-heated on direct heat are put to keep hot until required.

The bain-marie is placed on the top of the stove on a very low heat or in a warm oven.

The bain-marie resembles a double boiler, but is superior when all-round heat is required for cooking, as in the case of custards, some mousses and fish or meat loaves.

Bake Blind

The term bake blind applies to the method of baking pastry shells without their fillings.

After the pie dish or flan ring is lined with pastry, it should be chilled in the refrigerator for about 30 minutes so that the dough is well set.

The base of the shell is then pricked all over with a fork. It is then lined with crumpled aluminium foil, or greaseproof paper, and filled with dried beans or uncooked rice, kept specially for this purpose.

About 5 minutes before the shell has finished cooking, the foil, or paper, and beans are removed and the baking continued so that the pastry can colour.

Baked Alaska

An impressive dessert, Baked Alaska is sponge cake topped with ice-cream and covered with meringue. It is not difficult to prepare but it does need very speedy, last-minute preparation before serving. This famous dessert was probably invented by the 18th-century scientist Count Rumford, in Europe. It did not get its present name until 1867, when it was included in menus to celebrate the purchase of the new state. In France it is called Omelette Norvege, after Norway, another country with a very cold climate.

8 SERVINGS

4 oz. [1 cup] self-raising flour
¼ teaspoon salt
1 teaspoon baking powder
4 oz. [½ cup] butter, at room
    temperature
4 oz. castor [½ cup superfine] sugar
2 eggs
½ teaspoon vanilla essence [extract]
1 pint [2½ cups] vanilla ice cream,
    or your favourite flavour
4 tablespoons raspberry jam, or
    your favourite flavour

½ lb. fresh or thawed raspberries
(optional)

MERINGUE

4 egg whites

9 oz. castor [1⅛ cups superfine] sugar

Preheat the oven to warm 325°F (Gas Mark 3, 170°C). Grease and line the base of an 8-inch sandwich tin.

To prepare the sponge base, sift the flour, salt and baking powder into a large mixing bowl. Add the butter, castor sugar, eggs and vanilla and beat by hand or in a food processor until the ingredients are thoroughly blended.

Put the mixture into the prepared tin and smooth the top. Bake for 30-35 minutes, until the cake feels firm to the touch. Turn out on to a wire rack and leave until cold. Wash and dry the cake tin.

Meanwhile, soften the ice cream. Pack it firmly into the clean cake tin and return to the freezer while the sponge cake base

is cooling.

When the cake is cold, split in half horizontally and place on a baking sheet. Sandwich the two halves together with raspberry jam.

If you are using raspberries arrange them carefully in a single layer on top of the cake. Make sure thawed raspberries, if using, are well drained.

Remove the ice cream from the freezer and let stand for 5 minutes. Quickly unmould the ice cream on top of the cake. Return the ice cream and cake to the freezer and freeze for 30 minutes.

Preheat the oven to very hot 450°F (Gas Mark 8, 230°C). To make meringue, put the egg whites in a large clean bowl and whisk until stiff. Whisk in the sugar a little at a time until the meringue

---

An impressive-looking dessert, Baked Alaska is a sponge cake topped with ice-cream and meringue.

is stiff and glossy.

Remove the cake from the freezer and quickly cover the entire surface with meringue, making sure there is no cake or ice cream showing. Fluff up the surface decoratively. Place the blade of a flat-bladed knife against the meringue and pull it away with a sharp movement to produce a little peak. Repeat over the entire surface.

Bake for 3 minutes or until the meringue turns brown on the tips. Serve at once.

Vary the combinations of jam and fruit. Using either canned or fresh fruit. Sprinkle the meringue with toasted chopped almonds, chopped walnuts or finely chopped hazelnuts before baking.

Do not freeze the assembled cake for longer than 30 minutes because if you use fruit it will freeze and be unpleasant to eat. The fruit can be omitted if you wish, instead dribble 4 tablespoons liqueur over the cake.

Bakewell Tart

This is a traditional English dessert from the 'Rutland Arms' pub in a small Derbyshire market town.

6 TO 8 SERVINGS

6 oz. [1½ cups] flour
¼ teaspoon salt
3 oz. [6 tablespoons] butter, cut into small pieces
1 tablespoon cold water
2 tablespoons raspberry or strawberry jam

FILLING

2 oz. [¼ cup] butter
2 oz. [¼ cup] castor sugar
1 egg, beaten
¼ teaspoon almond essence
4 tablespoons breadcrumbs
2 oz. [½ cup] ground almonds
icing [confectioners'] sugar, to decorate

Preheat the oven to 375°F (Gas Mark 5, 190°C). Grease an 8-inch loose-bottomed flan tin with butter.

Sift the flour and salt into a bowl, add the butter and rub in until the mixture resembles fine breadcrumbs.

Sprinkle with cold water and mix in with a knife. Using your hands, mix and knead the pastry until smooth. If it is too dry, add more cold water. Roll into a ball, wrap in foil and chill for 15 minutes.

On a lightly floured board, roll out the pastry, lift it on the rolling pin and ease it into the tin. Trim the edges, spread the jam over the base and chill.

To make the filling, cream the butter and sugar together until light and fluffy. Gradually beat in the egg, a little at a time, beating well after each addition.

Add the almond essence, crumbs and ground almonds and mix to a soft consistency, adding a little water if necessary. Fill the lined flan tin and level the surface with the back of a spoon.

Bake for 30-40 minutes or until the filling is set. Cool slightly, then sprinkle with icing sugar to decorate. Serve with custard or whipped cream, if wished.

Baking

Baking is a method of cooking food in an oven by dry heat. Bread, biscuits, pies, cakes and tarts are all baked. Meat is also baked, although the term roasting is more generally used to describe the cooking of meat in an oven.

Baking Powder

Baking powder is the name given to a number of mixtures which are used as

leavening agents for bread, cakes and pastries. They all contain a proportion of bicarbonate of soda, commonly called baking soda, and an acid such as tartrate, phosphate or alum. When this mixture is moistened and heated, a chemical reaction takes place which produces carbon dioxide, causing the dough to rise.

Baking Powder Biscuits

An American recipe, Baking Powder Biscuits are like English scones. They may be served hot with butter for lunch or supper, or with jam for tea.

8 BISCUITS

7 oz. [1¾ cups] flour, plus extra for dusting
2 teaspoons baking powder
1 teaspoon salt
1 oz. [2 tablespoons] butter, chilled
1 oz. [2 tablespoons] hard margarine
5 fl. oz. [⅝ cup] milk

Preheat the oven to fairly hot 400°F (Gas Mark 6, 200°C); place a shelf above centre.

Sift the flour, baking powder and salt into a mixing bowl. Add the butter and margarine and cut them into the flour. Lightly rub the fat into the flour until the mixture resembles breadcrumbs.

Stir in enough milk to make a soft, light

An unusual type of scone, American Baking Powder Biscuits are delicious served hot with butter and jam.

dough. Add more milk if the dough is too dry, or more flour if it is too sticky.

Turn the dough on to a floured surface and knead it well until it is smooth.

Roll out the dough to ¾ inch thick. Using a floured cutter, stamp out 8 rounds, rerolling the dough as necessary.

Place the biscuits on an ungreased baking sheet, prick with a fork and bake for 10-12 minutes.

Baking Soda

Baking soda is the common name for BICARBONATE OF SODA.

Baklava

A rich cake made of thin layers of crisp pastry, filled with chopped almonds or walnuts and steeped in syrup or honey, baklava is made throughout the Middle East and Greece.

Baklava varies in detail from country to country, town to town and even from one household to the next. But in one respect it must always be the same. The pastry must be paper thin, for that is the secret of good baklava.

Balkan Champagne Cup

This is an icy party punch, easy to make but expensive.

20 SERVINGS

1 piece lemon rind
  juice of 2 lemons
2 tablespoons icing [confectioners']
  sugar
1 piece cucumber peel
12 fl. oz. [1½ cups] cold soda-water
2 bottles dry red wine
1 bottle champagne

Mix the lemon rind and lemon juice with the icing sugar and cucumber peel in a large punch bowl. Add the soda-water, wine and champagne.

Immediately before serving, add a block of ice.

Balkan Chicken Pilaff

This pilaff depends on a strong chicken stock for its flavour. For convenience, cook the chicken and make the stock the day before. Serve the pilaff with a ratatouille and a salad of yogurt with chopped cucumber and mint leaves.

6 SERVINGS

STOCK
1 small chicken
1 teaspoon salt
1 onion, cut in half
2 whole carrots
4 peppercorns
PILAFF
1 lb. [2½ cups] rice, washed,
  soaked in water for 30 minutes
  and drained
3 oz. [⅜ cup] butter
1 onion, finely chopped
2 tomatoes, peeled and chopped
1 teaspoon salt
  freshly ground black pepper
1 teaspoon dried basil
2 oz. [¼ cup] walnuts, chopped

First make the stock. Put the chicken in a pot large enough to hold it comfortably. Pour in enough water to half cover it. Add the salt, onion, carrots and peppercorns and bring to the boil. Lower the heat and simmer the chicken for 40 minutes or until it is tender. Let the chicken cool in the stock.

When the chicken is cool enough to handle, remove it from the stock. Put it on a board and cut off all the meat. Put the meat in a covered bowl and refrigerate.

Return the chicken bones to the pan, adding more water if necessary to cover, and simmer for 1½ hours. Strain the stock into a bowl, cool, cover and refrigerate. When the fat hardens on the top of the stock, skim it off with a spoon.

To make the pilaff, heat 1½ pints of the stock until it boils. Cut the meat of the chicken into strips.

Melt the butter in a large flameproof casserole over moderate heat. Add the chopped onion and fry until it is golden. Add the chicken strips, stir and cook for 2 minutes. Add the tomatoes, salt, 6 grindings of pepper, basil and walnuts and cook for 1 minute. Add the rice and cook for 2 minutes, stirring continuously. Pour in the hot stock, raise the heat and bring the rice to the boil. When it is bubbling briskly, cover with a tight-fitting lid, lower the heat to very low and simmer for 25 minutes, or until all the liquid is absorbed and the rice is cooked. Serve straight from the casserole.

Balloon Whisk

Also called a wire wisk, a balloon whisk is particularly useful for beating egg whites, cream, sauces, batters and soups, as it incorporates more air and increases the volume. Balloon whisks are widely available in several sizes and are curved to fit round bowls.

Ballotine

The term ballotine (bah-loh-teen) should, correctly, only be applied to meat which has been boned, stuffed and rolled. It is, however, often used to describe a certain kind of GALANTINE which is usually served hot, but can also be served cold.

Balm

Balm is the name given to several plants of the mint family. The one most commonly used for flavouring food is LEMON BALM.

Bamboo Shoots

A popular vegetable in the Far East, bamboo shoots are a common ingredient in Chinese cookery. The ivory-coloured, conical-shaped shoots of tropical bamboo are usually about three-inches wide and four-inches long.

In the Far East, bamboo shoots are usually eaten fresh, cooked like asparagus. They are canned and exported and are available in Oriental provisions stores. The best ones are the large wedges which have been packed in water. Canned bamboo shoots require very little cooking.

Once the can is opened, the shoots should be drained and kept in the refrigerator in fresh water in a covered jar. If the water is changed every day the bamboo shoots can be stored for about 10 days.

Bamboo Shoots with Mushrooms

This Chinese recipe for Bamboo Shoots with Mushrooms is easy to make. It may be

Served with rice or egg noodles, Bamboo Shoots with Pork is an interesting Chinese dish.

served as part of a Chinese meal and it also makes an unusual vegetable accompaniment to grilled or roasted meat.

4 SERVINGS

12 oz. canned bamboo shoots, drained
12 dried mushrooms
 4 tablespoons groundnut oil
 2 tablespoons sherry
 4 tablespoons soy sauce
 1 tablespoon sugar
 ¼ teaspoon monosodium glutamate (optional)
 3 fl. oz. [⅜ cup] water

Cut the bamboo shoots into thin slivers. Soak the mushrooms in hot water for 5 minutes. Drain them well. Remove the stalks, and, if the mushrooms are large, cut them in half.

Heat a heavy frying-pan over high heat for 30 seconds. Add the oil and swirl it around the pan. Add the bamboo shoots and mushrooms and fry, stirring frequently, for 5 minutes.

Add the sherry, soy sauce, sugar, monosodium glutamate and water. Cover the pan and simmer, over low heat, for 20 minutes.

Serve hot.

Bamboo Shoots with Pork

A Chinese dish, Bamboo Shoots with Pork is delicious served with other Chinese dishes and boiled rice or fine egg noodles. As is the case in many Chinese recipes, the pork, leek and bamboo shoots must be shredded. This means that they must be cut into fine, thread-like strips.

4 SERVINGS

1½ lb. lean pork, shredded
 6 tablespoons soy sauce
 1 tablespoon sherry
 2 teaspoons cornflour [cornstarch]
 1 leek, shredded
 1 lb. canned bamboo shoots, shredded
 5 fl. oz. [⅝ cup] groundnut oil
 2 teaspoons sugar

Combine 2 tablespoons of soy sauce, the sherry and cornflour. Add the shredded pork and mix well.

Heat a large, heavy frying-pan over high heat for 30 seconds. Add the oil and swirl it around the pan.

Add the pork and the leek and, stirring frequently, fry for 5 minutes, or until the pork is well browned. Stir in the bamboo shoots.

Stir in the remaining soy sauce and sugar. Lower the heat and simmer for 10 minutes, stirring frequently.

Serve immediately.

Baked Bananas, easy and inexpensive to make, go well with roast or fried chicken, roast pork or baked fish.

Banana

The edible fruit of the banana tree, the banana is one of the most popular fruits in tropical countries where it is prized for its flavour, nutrition and cheapness.

The banana tree was known in antiquity. It is said that the serpent which tempted Eve in the Garden of Eden hid in a bunch of bananas and, therefore, one of its botanical names is *Musa paradisiaca*. The banana tree is also called *Musa sapientum* because the sages of ancient India rested in its shade and ate its fruit. The banana was known to the Greeks and Romans and Pliny, the Roman historian, recorded that the Greeks who accompanied Alexander on his expedition to India saw it there.

Native to Southeast Asia, the banana spread to the West coast of Africa, the Canary Islands and to the Americas.

Today there are more than 300 varieties of banana, all growing in hot, damp, tropical regions. The chief sources of commercial banana production are in Central America, although the best tasting bananas still come from South Asia.

Bananas are exported while they are still green and the fruit is ripened in heated warehouses. Bananas which are green at the tip are slightly under-ripe.

They should be kept in a warm place and not eaten until the skins are completely yellow or even slightly dotted with brown.

Bananas contain Vitamin C as well as a small amount of other vitamins. They have a high proportion of starch, which turns to sugar as the fruit ripens.

Bananas may be used as a vegetable or a fruit. They are delicious sliced and served with cream. They are used in many ways in cold desserts and salads and can also be baked or fried.

Bananas, Baked

Bananas baked in their skins make an unusual and delicious accompaniment to roast or fried chicken, roast pork or baked fish.

6 SERVINGS

6 large bananas, unpeeled
1 tablespoon vegetable oil

Preheat the oven to warm 325°F (Gas Mark 3, 170°C).

Rub the banana skins lightly all over with a little oil. Brush the bottom of an ovenproof dish with the remaining oil. Lay the bananas in the dish and place it in the centre of the oven.

Bake the bananas for 30 to 40 minutes or until they are soft and their skins turn black.

Serve hot with one strip of peel rolled back.

Bananas Baked with Custard

Bananas baked with bread and custard is a simple dessert that children will love.

6 SERVINGS

- 1 teaspoon butter
- 4 bananas
- 6 thin slices buttered bread
- 2 oz. [$\frac{1}{3}$ cup] raisins
- 1 pint [$2\frac{1}{2}$ cups] milk
- 2 whole eggs plus 2 yolks
- 2 tablespoons soft brown sugar
- $\frac{1}{2}$ teaspoon grated nutmeg

Grease a medium-sized baking dish with the butter. Peel the bananas and slice into rounds. Halve the bread slices. Put the layers of the bread, bananas and raisins in the baking dish, ending with a layer of bread.

In a small pan heat the milk over moderate heat. In a medium-sized mixing bowl, beat the eggs, egg yolks and sugar together. Slowly pour in the milk, stirring continuously. Pour the milk-egg mixture into the baking dish and leave to stand for 30 minutes.

Preheat the oven to fairly hot 375°F (Gas Mark 5, 190°C).

Dust the top of the pudding with the nutmeg and bake in the oven for 30 minutes. Serve hot or cold.

Bananas Baked in Orange Juice

This dessert of bananas baked in orange juice is delicious served with vanilla ice-cream. Ripe but firm bananas and, if possible, freshly shredded coconut should be used for this dish.

4 SERVINGS

- 1 tablespoon plus 1 teaspoon butter
- 6 bananas
- 2 teaspoons cornflour [cornstarch]
- 3 tablespoons Curaçao
- 4 fl. oz. [$\frac{1}{2}$ cup] fresh orange juice
- grated rind of 1 orange
- 2 oz. [$\frac{1}{2}$ cup] shredded fresh or desiccated coconut
- 2 tablespoons soft brown sugar

Preheat the oven to fairly hot 375°F (Gas Mark 5, 190°C).

Grease a medium-sized baking dish with 1 teaspoon butter. Peel the bananas, cut them in half lengthways and then cut them across into quarters. Place them in the baking dish.

Dissolve the cornflour in the orange juice. Mix in the Curaçao and pour over the bananas. Sprinkle with the orange rind, coconut and brown sugar. Dot with the butter and bake in the oven for 30 minutes or until the bananas are tender and the sauce thick.

Serve hot.

Bananas Beauharnais

BANANAS BAKED IN RUM AND CREAM

A rich dessert, Bananas Beauharnais (bow-ahr-nay) *is excellent for a lunch or dinner party. It is usually served hot, but it is equally good cold.*

4 SERVINGS

- 6 bananas
- 1 tablespoon castor sugar
- 6 tablespoons white rum
- 4 oz. [$\frac{1}{2}$ cup] crushed macaroons
- 1 tablespoon melted butter
- 10 fl. oz. double cream [$1\frac{1}{4}$ cups heavy cream]

Preheat the oven to moderate 350°F (Gas Mark 4, 180°C). Grease a medium-sized baking dish with a little butter.

Peel the bananas and put them in the baking dish. Sprinkle them with the sugar and the rum. Bake for 15 minutes.

Remove the dish from the oven and allow to cool for 10 minutes.

Reset the oven to warm 325°F (Gas Mark 3, 170°C).

Mix the crushed macaroons with the melted butter. Pour the cream over the bananas. Sprinkle the macaroon mixture on top of the cream. Return the dish to the oven and bake for another 20 minutes. Serve hot in the baking dish.

Bananas Caribbean

This spicy banana dessert is unusual and easy to make. Serve it with a creamy custard sauce or thick cream.

4 SERVINGS

- 2 tablespoons plus 1 teaspoon butter
- 6 bananas
- 2 oz. [$\frac{1}{4}$ cup] soft brown sugar
- 4 fl. oz. fresh orange juice
- grated rind of 1 orange
- $\frac{1}{2}$ teaspoon powdered cinnamon
- 4 tablespoons Curaçao
- 6 tablespoons rum

Preheat the oven to very hot 450°F (Gas Mark 8, 230°C). Grease a medium-sized baking dish with 1 teaspoon of butter.

Peel the bananas. Cut them in half lengthways. Place the bananas in the baking dish cut side up.

In a small bowl, mix together the sugar, orange juice and rind, cinnamon and Curaçao. Pour the mixture over the bananas. Dot with the remaining butter and bake, basting once, for 15 minutes or until the bananas are tender. Sprinkle the bananas with the rum and serve immediately.

Banana Cream Pie

This American banana pie is made with short crust pastry and topped with meringue. It is inexpensive and easy to make and it looks and tastes good.

6 SERVINGS

PASTRY

- 6 oz. [$1\frac{1}{2}$ cups] flour
- $\frac{1}{4}$ teaspoon salt
- $3\frac{1}{4}$ oz. [$\frac{1}{2}$ cup] vegetable fat or lard
- 2 tablespoons iced water

FILLING

- 2 ripe bananas, peeled and cut into slices
- 3 egg yolks
- 3 oz. [$\frac{3}{8}$ cup] castor sugar
- $\frac{1}{4}$ teaspoon salt
- 2 tablespoons cornflour [cornstarch]
- 1 tablespoon butter
- 16 fl. oz. [2 cups] milk
- 1 teaspoon vanilla essence or $\frac{1}{4}$ teaspoon grated nutmeg

TOPPING

- 3 egg whites
- 6 oz. [$\frac{3}{4}$ cup] castor sugar
- 2 tablespoons shredded almonds

Sift the flour and salt into a medium-sized mixing bowl. Add the vegetable fat and with your fingertips rub it into the flour until it resembles coarse breadcrumbs. Add a tablespoon of iced water and mix and knead the dough until it is smooth. Add more water if the dough is too dry. Roll the dough into a ball, cover it and chill it in the refrigerator for 30 minutes.

Preheat the oven to fairly hot 400°F (Gas Mark 6, 200°C).

On a floured board, roll the pastry out and line a 9-inch pie tin. Put the lined pie tin in the refrigerator for 10 minutes.

When you remove the pie-tin from the refrigerator, prick the bottom and sides of the pastry with a fork, line it with greaseproof paper and weigh it down with dried beans or peas. Bake the shell for 10 minutes.

Remove the greaseproof paper and bake for 5 minutes more, or until the shell is golden.

Reset the oven to cool 300°F (Gas

Bananas, coconut and orange combine to make Bananas Baked in Orange Juice a delicious dessert.

Banana Cream Pie, made with short-crust pastry and topped with meringue, is a tempting dessert.

Mark 2, 150°C).

To prepare the filling, beat the egg yolks in a medium-sized mixing bowl with a whisk or wooden spoon. Gradually beat in all of the sugar, salt, cornflour and butter.

Put the milk in a small saucepan and, over moderate heat, bring it almost to the boiling point. Pour the hot milk slowly into the egg mixture, stirring continuously. Place the bowl in a pan of boiling water and cook and stir the custard until it thickens. Cool the custard and then add the vanilla essence or nutmeg. Arrange the banana slices in the baked pie shell. Pour the custard over them.

Beat the egg whites in a small bowl with a rotary beater until they are stiff. Beat in one tablespoon of sugar and then fold in the remaining sugar. Pile the meringue on top of the custard and spread to cover the top completely. Sprinkle with the shredded almonds and bake for 15 to 20 minutes. or until the meringue is lightly browned.

Serve cold.

Bananas Creole

This cold dessert is a mould lined with slices of fresh pineapple and filled with a mousse flavoured with rum. It takes some time to prepare, but can be made well in advance and is an unusual and delicious dessert for a lunch or dinner party.

4 TO 6 SERVINGS

1 medium-sized pineapple
1 pint [2½ cups] water
8 oz. [1 cup] sugar
2 tablespoons light rum
4 bananas
MOUSSE
2 whole eggs plus 2 yolks
2 oz. [¼ cup] sugar
½ oz. gelatine
2 tablespoons hot orange juice
2 tablespoons light rum
5 fl. oz. double [heavy] cream, whipped

Peel the pineapple and cut into thin slices. Put the water and sugar in a medium-sized pan and, stirring continuously, dissolve the sugar over low heat. When the sugar is completely dissolved, raise the heat and bring the syrup to the boil. Boil for 5 minutes. Place the pineapple

slices gently in the syrup, add the rum, lower the heat and simmer for 15 minutes, or until the pineapple is tender. Remove the pineapple slices carefully, drain and set aside to cool.

Peel the bananas, cut them in half lengthways and lay them in a heatproof dish.

Bring the syrup to the boil and pour it over the bananas. Leave for 15 minutes, then drain the bananas and set them aside. Discard the syrup.

Line a plain mould with the pineapple slices and set aside.

Whisk the whole eggs, yolks and sugar in a medium-sized bowl. Place the bowl in a pan of simmering water, over low heat, and whisk until the egg-and-sugar mixture is thick.

Remove from the heat, place the bowl over crushed ice or cold water, and continue whisking until the mixture is cold.

Dissolve the gelatine in the orange juice and stir into the egg mixture with the rum. Fold in the whipped cream. Place the bowl on ice and stir. When the mousse is on the point of setting, pour it into the mould. Chill in the refrigerator until completely set. Unmould on to a serving dish, surround with the bananas and serve.

Bananas, Fried

A delicious garnish for chicken or meat, the bananas and the batter may be prepared in advance, but the bananas must be fried at the last minute.

4 SERVINGS

4 bananas
3 tablespoons olive oil
1½ tablespoons lemon juice
½ teaspoon salt
⅛ teaspoon paprika
BATTER
2 oz. [½ cup] flour
⅛ teaspoon salt
¼ teaspoon white pepper
4½ tablespoons vegetable oil
3 fl. oz. [⅜ cup] warm water

Peel the bananas and cut them in half lengthways. Place them in a dish. In a small bowl mix the olive oil, lemon juice, salt and paprika and pour it over the bananas. Leave the bananas to marinate for 20 minutes.

Meanwhile, prepare the batter. Sift the flour, salt and pepper into a small mixing bowl. With a wooden spoon, mix in ½ tablespoon of the oil and the water slowly. When the mixture is smooth, beat well. Leave the batter to stand for 30 minutes.

In a medium-sized frying-pan heat the remaining oil over moderate heat.

Drain the bananas and dip them in the batter. Fry them until they are golden on both sides. Drain on kitchen paper towels and serve immediately.

Banana Fritters

Banana Fritters flavoured with brandy make an unusual dessert. Use only firm bananas, otherwise the bananas will disintegrate if they are too soft.

4 SERVINGS

6 bananas
4 fl. oz. [½ cup] brandy
1 tablespoon brown sugar
BATTER
4 oz. [1 cup] flour
1 teaspoon salt
2 egg yolks plus 1 egg white
1 tablespoon olive oil
5 fl. oz. [⅝ cup] milk
4 tablespoons vegetable oil
2 tablespoons sugar

Peel the bananas, cut them in half lengthways and place in a dish. In a small bowl mix brandy with brown sugar. Pour over the bananas and leave to marinate for 20 minutes.

Sift the flour and salt into a medium-sized mixing bowl. Make a well in the centre of the flour and drop in the egg yolks and olive oil. Add the milk a little at a time and, beating continuously, gradually incorporate the liquid into the flour. Mix to a smooth batter. Cover the bowl and leave the batter to stand for 30 minutes.

Just before frying, beat the egg white with a wire whisk until it is stiff and fold it into the batter.

In a medium-sized frying-pan, heat the oil over moderate heat. Remove the banana halves from the marinade and dip them into the batter. Fry them in the hot fat until they are golden on both sides. Drain on kitchen paper towels, sprinkle with sugar and serve immediately.

Bananas with Orange

Easy to make, Bananas with Orange is a delicious dessert which should be served very hot with chilled orange butter and sponge fingers, shortbread or other plain, sweet biscuits [cookies].

4 SERVINGS

4 oz. [½ cup] butter
4 oz. [½ cup] plus 4 tablespoons
   soft, brown sugar
   grated rind of 1 orange
3 fl. oz. [⅜ cup] Cointreau
8 bananas
5 oranges

Preheat the oven to moderate 350°F (Gas Mark 4, 180°C).

Make the orange butter first. In a medium-sized mixing bowl, cream the

butter thoroughly with a wooden spoon. Slowly add 4 ounces [½ cup] sugar and the grated orange rind and beat well. Add 2 fluid ounces of Cointreau, beating until the mixture is smooth and all the liqueur is absorbed. Cover and refrigerate.

Peel the bananas and cut them into slices. Peel the oranges, remove all the pith and cut them into thin slices.

In an ovenproof dish, arrange the banana and orange slices in layers, sprinkling each layer with the remaining sugar. Add the remaining Cointreau. Bake in the oven for 25 minutes. Serve immediately with the orange butter.

Banana Pudding

This light and fluffy Banana Pudding is very quick to make and it requires no cooking. It should be served very cold.

6 SERVINGS

2 lb. ricotta cheese
6 bananas, mashed
2 teaspoons lemon juice
4 oz. icing [1 cup confectioners']
   sugar
2 tablespoons sweet white wine
½ teaspoon almond essence
1 oz. [¼ cup] flaked almonds
6 sponge fingers, crushed

Press the ricotta cheese through a fine strainer into a medium-sized bowl. Add the bananas, lemon juice, sugar, wine and

---

Bananas deep-fried in batter are a tempting and unusual garnish for almost any meat dish.

almond essence. Beat until the mixture is fluffy. Mix in the almonds.

Pour the mixture into a serving dish and sprinkle the sponge finger crumbs over the top. Cover and place in the refrigerator for 2-3 hours before serving.

Banana and Raspberry Cream

A simple, uncooked dessert with a fine balance of flavours, this may be served at a lunch or dinner party.

4 SERVINGS

6 bananas
1 lb. raspberries
10 fl. oz. double cream [1¼ cups heavy cream]
4 tablespoons castor sugar

Peel the bananas and cut them into rounds. Arrange the slices in a dish.

Mix the raspberries with the cream and push the mixture through a sieve. Mix in half the sugar. Taste to check the sweetness and add the rest of the sugar if necessary. Pour the cream mixture over the bananas. Chill well before serving.

Bananas in Sherry

A simple banana dessert, flavoured with honey and sherry, this is very easy to prepare.

4 SERVINGS

4 tablespoons melted butter
6 bananas
juice of 1 lemon
3 tablespoons clear honey
3 fl. oz. [⅜ cup] sherry

Preheat the oven to fairly hot 400°F (Gas Mark 6, 200°C). Grease a baking dish with 1 tablespoon butter.

Peel the bananas and cut them in half lengthways. Place them in the baking dish and pour the lemon juice over the top.

Mix the honey and sherry and remaining butter together and pour over the bananas. Bake for 20 minutes, or until the bananas are heated through. Baste twice during cooking. Serve hot.

More a cake than a bread, this Banana Walnut Bread is quick, easy and inexpensive to make.

Banana Walnut Loaf

A moist bread, Banana Walnut Loaf is very easy to make and good to serve at tea-time or with coffee.

ONE 9-INCH LOAF

5 oz. [⅝ cup] sugar
2 oz. [¼ cup] plus 1 teaspoon vegetable fat
3 eggs
4 bananas, mashed
8 oz. [2 cups] flour
1 teaspoon baking powder
½ teaspoon salt
¼ teaspoon bicarbonate of soda [baking soda]
6 oz. [1 cup] walnuts, chopped

Preheat the oven to moderate 350°F (Gas Mark 4, 180°C). Grease a 9-inch loaf tin with 1 teaspoon fat.

In a medium-sized mixing bowl, beat the sugar, vegetable fat and eggs together with a wooden spoon. Beat until it is light. Beat in the bananas.

Sift the flour, baking powder, salt and soda into the banana mixture and beat well. Stir in the walnuts.

Pour the mixture into the loaf tin and

bake for 1 hour, or until the loaf is done. Test by inserting a warm, dry skewer in the centre of the loaf. If it comes out clean, the loaf is ready. Turn the loaf out of the tin and allow to cool before slicing.

Banbury Cakes

These traditional English cakes are made of puff pastry and filled with dried fruit. They are light and crispy and may be served with tea or coffee.

MAKES 16 CAKES

PASTRY
8 oz. [2 cups] flour
¼ teaspoon salt
8 oz. [1 cup] unsalted butter
5 fl. oz. [⅝ cup] iced water

FILLING
2 oz. [¼ cup] butter
2 oz. [¼ cup] sugar
1 small egg yolk
2 oz. [⅓ cup] sultanas or raisins
2 oz. [⅓ cup] currants
1 oz. [⅓ cup] cake crumbs
1 oz. [¼ cup] candied peel, chopped
½ teaspoon ground ginger
¼ teaspoon ground nutmeg
  grated rind and juice of ½ lemon
1 egg white, lightly beaten

Sift the flour and salt into a medium-sized mixing bowl. With a table knife, cut 2 oz. [¼ cup] butter into the flour. Crumble the butter and flour with your fingers and, with the water, mix to a firm dough. Knead the dough to make it pliable. Cover with greaseproof or waxed paper and refrigerate for 15 minutes.

Put the remaining amount of butter between two pieces of greaseproof paper and beat it with the back of a spoon or a wooden mallet into a flat oblong slab about ¾-inch thick.

On a floured board, roll out the dough into a rectangular shape ¼-inch thick. Place the slab of butter in the centre of the dough and fold the dough over it to make a parcel. Refrigerate for 10 minutes.

Place the dough, with the folds downwards, on the board and roll out away from you into a rectangle. Fold the rectangle in 3, the open end facing you and roll out again. Refrigerate for 15 minutes. Repeat this twice more.

Preheat the oven to hot 425°F (Gas Mark 7, 220°C).

To prepare the filling, cream the butter and sugar in a small mixing bowl with a wooden spoon. When the mixture is well creamed, beat in the egg yolk. Mix in the sultanas, currants, cake crumbs, candied peel, ginger, nutmeg, lemon rind and lemon juice.

Puff pastry filled with a spicy, dried fruit mixture, Banbury Cakes are traditional English tea cakes.

On a floured board, roll out the dough thinly and cut it into 4-inch rounds. Dampen the edges with water and put a spoonful of mixture on to each round of pastry. Fold the pastry over the filling and turn upside down. Pat each cake into an oval shape and make 3 cuts in the tops. Place on a baking tin. Brush with beaten egg white, dust with a little sugar and bake for 20 to 25 minutes, or until the cakes are crisp and golden.

Remove the cakes and cool on a rack.

Bangra Masala
SPICED HERRINGS

This recipe for Bangra Masala (bahn-grah ma-sah-lah) is an adaptation of a recipe which comes from the west coast of India where in the winter and spring a herring-like fish called bangra *is abundant and cheap. It can be served as a main course accompanied by rice and spiced vegetables.*

4 SERVINGS

4 herrings, cleaned and gutted
2½ teaspoons salt
  juice of ½ lemon
3 tablespoons flour
1 teaspoon ground turmeric
4 to 6 tablespoons cooking oil

FILLING
3 tablespoons cooking oil
2 small onions, finely minced
1 large garlic clove, crushed
1½-inch piece fresh ginger, peeled and finely chopped
1 teaspoon ground turmeric
1 teaspoon ground coriander seeds
1 teaspoon chilli powder (optional)
1 teaspoon garam masala
6 tablespoons tomato purée
  juice of ½ lemon

Wash the herrings and wipe dry with kitchen paper towels. Sprinkle the inside of each fish with ½ teaspoon of salt and set aside.

To make the filling, heat the oil in a medium-sized frying-pan over moderate heat. Fry the onions until they are golden. Add the garlic and ginger and, stirring constantly, cook for 2 minutes. Add the turmeric, coriander, chilli powder (if you are using it) and garam masala and fry well for 8 minutes, stirring constantly. If the mixture gets too dry sprinkle with a little water and continue frying.

Add the tomato purée and lemon juice and, stirring, cook for 3 minutes. Remove from the heat and divide the filling into 4 equal portions. Spoon a portion inside each fish.

Gash the sides of the herrings with a sharp knife and rub in a little lemon juice. Mix the flour, turmeric and remaining salt on a plate. Dip the fish into the flour

Ban

mixture, rubbing it well into the gashes.

In a large frying-pan, heat the oil until it is hot enough to spit when the fish is put in. Fry the fish until it is cooked and crisp, approximately 10 minutes, or place under a hot grill.

Bannocks

A variety of large, round cake, or girdle-scone, from Scotland, bannocks can be made from oatmeal, wheat, barley or pease. Of the many varieties the best known are the Selkirk bannock, which is similar to a fruit bun, and the Pitcaithly bannock, which is like shortbread.

Banyuls

Banyuls is a popular French fortified dessert wine. The vineyards of Banyuls are on the lower slopes of the French Pyrénées. They provide three sweet wines—a red, a rosé and a white.

Hot Scottish Baps, split and buttered, are traditionally eaten at breakfast.

Baps

Soft, white, Scottish breakfast rolls, baps are delicious served hot with butter. They are simple to prepare, but they cannot be made in a hurry. Though baps are best served hot from the oven, they can be kept a short while and reheated.

8 ROLLS

1 lb. [4 cups] flour
½ teaspoon salt
5 fl. oz. [⅝ cup] plus 2 tablespoons milk
5 fl. oz. [⅝ cup] water
1 teaspoon sugar
1 tablespoon dried yeast
2 oz. [¼ cup] butter

Sift the flour and salt into a large mixing bowl. Put in a warm place.

Warm the milk and water, place in a bowl and add the sugar. Sprinkle the yeast on top. Leave in a warm place for 15 minutes or until it is frothy.

Rub the butter into the warm flour-and-salt mixture. Make a well in the middle of the flour and pour in the frothy yeast mixture. With your hands, mix into a

soft dough, adding 1 or 2 teaspoons more warm water if necessary.

Place the dough in a greased bowl, cover with a clean cloth and leave it to stand in a warm place for 1 hour or more until it doubles in size.

Preheat the oven to hot 425°F (Gas Mark 7, 220°C).

Grease a baking tin with a little butter and dust with flour. Remove the risen dough from the bowl and knead it on a floured surface. Divide it into 8 equal pieces. Knead each piece separately and pat it into an oval shape. Flatten each piece, place on the baking tin and leave in a warm place for 15 minutes.

Brush each bap with the remaining milk and bake in the oven for 15 to 20 minutes. Serve hot with butter.

Bara Brith

A traditional Welsh fruit cake, Bara Brith means 'speckled bread'. There are two varieties of Bara Brith. One is a rich fruit cake which is eaten at Christmas. The other is a popular bread or bun which is made with yeast.

Barbecue

Called *barbe à queue* by the French, this method of cooking was originally described as a way of roasting whole animals or fowls in the open. Spitted from beard, *barbe*, to tail, *queue*, the animal was roasted in a closed or open pit over heated stones, coals or a wood fire.

It is said that this cooking method was introduced into America by French buccaneers in the seventeenth century. It is more likely, however, that it was already being used by the American Indians.

Barbecueing is popular in the United States where, in good weather, food is cooked out-of-doors on braziers or grills over charcoal fires. Some equipment is necessary and appliances ranging from simple braziers to complicated electrically operated spits are widely available. Simple equipment, however, can be improvised.

Grilling, spit and skewer cooking, pit roasting and smoke cooking are the four main methods of barbecueing.

Grilling and spit and skewer cooking are the two methods most commonly used. Pit roasting has died out, except in New England where the clambake still remains popular and in Polynesia where the *luau* (loo-ow) is enjoyed.

Smoke cooking is a process which cooks the meat and flavours it at the same time. This is not practical for most people because a special oven, made of brick or metal, is required.

Barbecue is also a term now used to describe dishes in which meat, fish or fowl is marinated, then grilled or baked in the oven and basted or served with spicy, piquant sauces.

Barbecue Sauce

This is a good piquant sauce to serve hot with grilled meat or chicken. It can also be used for basting during grilling.

8 FLUID OUNCES

1 oz [2 tablespoons] butter
1 onion, chopped
1 garlic clove, crushed
½-inch piece fresh ginger, peeled and finely chopped
5 fl. oz. [⅝ cup] water
14 oz. canned tomatoes
1 large celery stalk, chopped
2 tablespoons lemon juice
2 tablespoons vinegar
2 tablespoons tomato purée
1½ tablespoons Worcestershire sauce
2 teaspoons brown sugar
½ teaspoon dried oregano
1 large bay leaf
1 teaspoon salt
¼ teaspoon nutmeg

Melt the butter in a small saucepan over moderate heat. Add the onion, garlic and ginger and fry until the onion is soft and translucent.

Add all the remaining ingredients, cover and cook over low heat for 40 minutes. Strain the sauce, taste, and add more salt and sugar if necessary.

Barbecued Beef, Chinese Style

Chinese Barbecued Beef is served on a bed of fried spinach. It is a dish which is delicious and pleasing to the eye.

4 SERVINGS

3 tablespoons soy sauce
3 tablespoons red wine
1-inch piece of fresh ginger, peeled and grated
2 teaspoons brown sugar
¼ teaspoon cayenne pepper
¼ teaspoon black pepper
1 lb. fillet of beef, cut into ½-inch slices
8 tablespoons vegetable oil
2 lb. spinach, washed and stalks removed
1 teaspoon salt

In a large bowl, combine the soy sauce, wine, ginger, sugar, cayenne and black pepper. Add the beef slices and leave to marinate for 2 hours, basting and turning them occasionally.

In a large, heavy frying-pan, heat 6 tablespoons of oil. Add the beef and, stirring frequently, fry over moderate heat for 5 to 10 minutes, depending upon how rare or well-done you want the meat.

In another heavy frying-pan heat the remaining oil and, stirring frequently with a wooden spoon, fry the spinach until it is tender. Roughly chop the spinach. Add the salt and mix well.

Arrange the spinach on a serving plate and spread the fried beef over it. Pour the beef juices over the spinach and beef. Serve hot.

Barbecued Chicken

Served with a green salad with vinaigrette dressing and sautéed or baked potatoes, Barbecued Chicken is an easy main course to prepare for a lunch or dinner party.

4 SERVINGS

2 small chickens
4 tablespoons vegetable oil
SAUCE
2 tablespoons olive oil
2 tablespoons Worcestershire sauce

2 tablespoons tomato purée
1 small onion, grated
3 tablespoons red wine
1 garlic clove, crushed
2 teaspoons paprika
½ teaspoon cayenne pepper
1 teaspoon salt
½ teaspoon black pepper
1 teaspoon brown sugar

Split the chickens in half. Wash them under cold, running water and dry them thoroughly.

Put the ingredients for the sauce in a large bowl and mix them together.

Preheat the grill to moderate. Put the chicken pieces in the grill pan, skin side down. Using a pastry brush, brush them with 2 tablespoons of the oil. Place under the grill and cook for 10 minutes.

Turn the chicken pieces. Brush the skin with the remaining oil and grill for 20 minutes. When they are golden brown, baste them with the sauce. Continue basting every few minutes until the chicken is completely cooked. Arrange the chicken on a warmed serving dish.

Strain the remaining sauce, with the pan juices, into a small saucepan. Heat gently, pour over the chicken and serve immediately.

Barbecued Duck

An excellent lunch or dinner dish, barbecued duck is roasted in the oven and basted with a piquant sauce. It may be served with broccoli and baked sweet potatoes.

4 SERVINGS

1 x 5 lb. duck
1 teaspoon dry mustard
¼ teaspoon cayenne pepper
½ teaspoon freshly ground black pepper
SAUCE
1 garlic clove, crushed
¼ teaspoon Tabasco sauce
2 tablespoons Worcestershire sauce
2 tablespoons tomato purée
4 tablespoons red wine
2 teaspoons paprika
grated rind and juice of 1 orange
2 tablespoons lemon juice
1 teaspoon brown sugar
¼ teaspoon black pepper
½ teaspoon salt
2 teaspoons arrowroot mixed with 1 tablespoon water

Preheat the oven to hot 425°F (Gas Mark 7, 220°C).

Rub the duck all over with the mustard, cayenne and black pepper. Prick the skin

all over with a fork, place the duck on a rack in a roasting pan and roast for 20 minutes.

Take the duck out of the oven, remove the rack and pour away the fat from the roasting pan. Put the duck back in the pan without the rack.

Mix all the ingredients for the sauce, except the arrowroot mixed with water, together in a small bowl and pour them over the duck.

Reduce the oven heat to moderate 350°F (Gas Mark 4, 180°C).

Return the duck to the oven and, basting every 15 minutes, roast it for 1 hour, or until the bird is tender.

Remove the duck from the oven, place it on a heated serving dish and keep hot.

Place the roasting pan on moderate heat. Stir in the arrowroot mixed with water and bring to the boil. Cook, stirring continuously, for 2 minutes. Pour the sauce over the duck and serve immediately.

Barbecued Fish

Grilled fish steaks served with a piquant sauce are an inexpensive lunch or dinner dish which is very quick to make. Serve the fish with peas, French beans or hot buttered broccoli and creamed potatoes.

4 SERVINGS

4 large cod or haddock steaks, about 8 oz. each
1 teaspoon salt
2 oz. [¼ cup] butter
SAUCE
8 fl. oz. [1 cup] red wine
⅛ teaspoon cayenne pepper
1 teaspoon prepared mustard
2 teaspoons chilli sauce
2 tablespoons lemon juice
1 teaspoon brown sugar
1 tablespoon capers
½ tablespoon salt

Preheat the grill to moderate. Sprinkle the fish steaks with salt and dot them with half of the butter, cut into small pieces.

Place the fish steaks on the rack of the grill pan. Place under the heat and grill the fish for about 4 minutes on each side. The fish is cooked when the flakes separate easily when tested with a fork. When the fish is cooked, remove it from the grill. Place the steaks on a serving dish and keep hot.

Left: A main dish for a dinner party, Barbecued Duck is roasted and basted with a piquant sauce.

Barbecued Fish is a tempting dish of grilled fish steaks, served with a piquant caper sauce.

Pour any juice from the grilling pan into a small saucepan. Add the remaining butter and melt it over moderate heat. Add all the ingredients for the sauce. Stir to mix and bring to the boil. Reduce the heat and simmer for 10 minutes. Pour the sauce over the fish steaks and serve immediately.

Barbecued Lamb

A spicy way of cooking lamb, this recipe includes commercially prepared sauces. The lamb, delicious hot or cold, may be served with new potatoes and whole new carrots.

6 SERVINGS

1 large garlic clove
1 x 3 to 4 lb. leg of lamb
2 teaspoons prepared mustard
½ teaspoon ground ginger
1 teaspoon salt
½ teaspoon freshly ground black pepper
2 tablespoons flour
SAUCE
4 tablespoons chutney
3 tablespoons Worcestershire sauce
2 tablespoons soy sauce
2 tablespoons tomato purée
2 tablespoons red wine
3 tablespoons melted butter
¼ teaspoon cayenne pepper
1 onion, finely chopped
1 teaspoon brown sugar

Preheat the oven to hot 425°F (Gas Mark 7, 220°C).

Cut the garlic clove into slices. With a sharp, pointed knife make slits in the meat and insert the slices of garlic. In a small bowl mix together the prepared mustard, the ginger, salt and pepper. Rub the mixture over the surface of the meat. Coat the meat with flour.

In another small bowl mix together all the ingredients for the sauce. Put the lamb in a roasting pan and place in the centre of the oven.

After 20 minutes lower the heat to fairly hot 375°F (Gas Mark 5, 190°C). Pour the sauce over the lamb and roast for 1 hour, or until the lamb is cooked, basting with the sauce every 15 minutes. If the basting liquid starts to dry up, add a little stock, water or wine. The sauce should be fairly thick.

To serve hot, place the meat on a warmed dish and pour the sauce over it. To serve cold, put the lamb on a cold plate, pour the sauce over it and allow it to cool before slicing.

Barbecued Pork

This is a simple dish to make for an informal dinner party. Barbecued Pork may be served with sautéed potatoes and broad, or French, beans.

6 SERVINGS

½ teaspoon ground ginger
¼ teaspoon cayenne pepper
½ teaspoon black pepper
2 teaspoons salt
1 tablespoon brown sugar
4 lb. loin of pork, boned and rolled
2 tablespoons vegetable oil
SAUCE
2 tablespoons chilli sauce
2 tablespoons soy sauce
2 tablespoons Worcestershire sauce
2 tablespoons tomato purée
2 teaspoons prepared mustard
1 tablespoon vinegar
1 teaspoon brown sugar
1 garlic clove, crushed
1 large bay leaf

Preheat the oven to moderate 350°F (Gas Mark 4, 180°C).

Mix together the ginger, cayenne, black pepper, salt and sugar in a small bowl. Rub the mixture all over the pork.

Heat the oil in a large flameproof casserole over moderate heat. Add the pork and brown it well on all sides. Drain all the oil from the casserole.

Mix all the ingredients for the sauce together. Pour the sauce over the pork. Cover the casserole and place it in the

middle of the oven. Cook for 1½ to 1¾ hours, basting occasionally.

To serve, carve the pork and place the slices on a heated serving dish. Bring the sauce in the casserole to the boil, skim off the fat and strain over the meat.

Barbecued Pork Chops

A tasty main dish, Barbecued Pork Chops are simple to make. Serve them with new potatoes and a green salad.

4 SERVINGS

2 tablespoons vegetable oil
½ oz. [1 tablespoon] butter
4 pork loin chops
5 fl. oz. [⅝ cup] tomato purée
1 onion, finely chopped
3 celery stalks, chopped
5 fl. oz. [⅝ cup] red wine
  juice of 1 lemon
1 tablespoon brown sugar
1 teaspoon prepared mustard
1 teaspoon salt
¼ teaspoon black pepper

Preheat the oven to moderate 350°F (Gas Mark 4, 180°C).

Heat the oil and butter in a large, heavy frying-pan. Add the pork chops and brown them on both sides. Remove them with kitchen tongs and place them in a shallow, ovenproof dish.

In a small bowl combine the rest of the ingredients and pour over the chops. Cover the dish and place in the centre of the oven. Bake for 1 hour and 20 minutes, basting occasionally. After 40 minutes remove the cover and cook uncovered for the rest of the cooking time.

Barbecued Prawns or Shrimps

Ideal to serve for a buffet or as an hors d'oeuvre, Barbecued Prawns are easy to prepare. The prawns are eaten by holding them by their tails and dipping them in the sauce.

4 SERVINGS

2 lb. large frozen prawns or shrimps, shelled
4 tablespoons white wine
4 tablespoons olive oil
2 tablespoons tomato purée
2 teaspoons marjoram
1 garlic clove, crushed
1 tablespoon finely chopped chives
1 teaspoon salt
¼ teaspoon black pepper

Place the prawns in a large shallow dish and leave to thaw for 1 to 2 hours at room

temperature. Drain the prawns and dry them with kitchen paper towels.

Mix the remaining ingredients for the sauce in a large bowl. Add the prawns to the sauce and stir them gently to coat them with the liquid. Leave the prawns to marinate for 4 hours.

Preheat the grill [broiler] to very hot.

Pour the prawns and the sauce into a shallow baking tin which will fit under the grill. Spread the prawns out evenly in the baking tin.

Put the baking tin under the grill.

Baked in a sweet and sour sauce, Barbecued Spareribs is an unusual, tasty and inexpensive dish which is easy to make.

Cook the prawns for about 3 minutes and baste frequently with the sauce. With a spoon, turn the prawns over, baste again and cook for a further 5 minutes or until they are lightly brown.

Using a slotted spoon, remove the prawns and arrange them on a heated serving dish. Spoon a little of the sauce over the top. Strain the remaining sauce into a sauceboat.

Barbecued Spareribs

Spareribs baked in a sweet and sour sauce make an easy and inexpensive main dish for lunch or dinner. Serve them on their own followed by a fresh mixed salad.

4 SERVINGS
2 tablespoons vegetable oil
1 garlic clove, crushed
1 large onion, finely chopped
5 fl. oz. [⅝ cup] tomato purée
3 tablespoons lemon juice
½ teaspoon salt
¼ teaspoon black pepper
½ teaspoon dried sage
4 tablespoons light brown sugar
4 fl. oz. [½ cup] beef stock
4 tablespoons Worcestershire sauce
2 teaspoons dry mustard
3 lb. spareribs of pork, cut into serving pieces

Preheat the oven to fairly hot 400°F (Gas Mark 6, 200°C).

Heat the oil in a large frying-pan over moderate heat. When the oil is hot, add the garlic and onion and cook for 3 minutes, stirring frequently until the onion is translucent and soft but not brown.

Add the tomato purée, lemon juice, salt, pepper, sage, sugar, beef stock, Worcestershire sauce and mustard to the mixture in the frying-pan and stir well. Simmer over low heat for 10 minutes, stirring frequently. Remove the frying-pan from the heat.

Put the spareribs on a rack in a large roasting tin. Pour the sauce evenly over the spareribs. Bake in the middle of the oven for 1 hour, or until the spareribs are brown and crisp, basting the ribs with the barbecue sauce every 15 minutes.

Serve hot.

Barbecued Veal Chops

This is an extremely easy and, at the same time, a very tasty way of preparing veal chops. For average size chops 20 minutes grilling is just right, but adjust the timing for very thick chops. Serve with a green vegetable.

4 SERVINGS

4 veal chops
1 onion, chopped
1 garlic clove, crushed
½ teaspoon ground coriander
½ teaspoon dried mixed herbs
¼ teaspoon chilli powder
1 tablespoon chopped parsley
1 teaspoon salt
¼ teaspoon black pepper
3 tablespoons olive oil
2 tablespoons vinegar
1 tablespoon tomato purée

Put the veal chops in a shallow dish. Mix all the remaining ingredients in a small mixing bowl and pour over the chops. Leave the meat to marinate for 3 hours at room temperature.

Heat the grill to hot. Remove the chops from the marinade and place them under the grill for 2 minutes. Lower the heat to moderate and cook for 8 minutes, marinating whenever the meat looks dry.

Turn the chops over and spread with the remaining marinade. Raise the heat to high again and grill them for 2 minutes. Lower the heat and continue grilling for 8 minutes more. Serve immediately.

Barbel

A river fish belonging to the carp family, barbel is so named because of the fleshy filaments, or barbels, hanging from its mouth or from the corners of its jaw.

The species of barbel found in European rivers rarely exceeds 16 pounds. The barbel of the Nile, however, weighs as much as 70 pounds. Gastronomically, barbel is a poor fish. Its insipid-tasting flesh is coarse and woolly and it has too many bones to make pleasant eating.

The most edible barbel is found in the Loire in France. The larger ones are most suited to poaching, braising or baking. The smaller-sized fish, known in France as *barbillons*, are usually grilled or fried.

Barberry

The berry of a plant called berberis, barberry grows in the temperate regions of the world. There are over 200 species of barberry, many of them prickly, ornamental evergreens.

The common barberry was introduced into the United States and Great Britain from temperate Europe and Asia, but, because the plant acts as host to a destructive wheat rust, its cultivation is forbidden in many places and a rust-resistant variety is grown instead.

Barberries are used in sauces, tarts and pies, and are also preserved in sugar. In Scandinavia the berries are a popular flavouring for drinks, sorbets and syrups.

In India, the Nepal and Asiatic barberries are dried in the sun and eaten like raisins. The Darwin barberry, from Chile, is widely grown in England as an ornamental shrub and bears quantities of edible little berries.

Bard

A culinary term, to bard is to cover the breast of a fowl or a piece of meat with slices of fatty bacon or pork to keep the meat moist and to protect it during cooking. The barding fat is removed before serving, except in the case of roast game.

Barley

A cultivated cereal as old as the earliest beginning of agriculture, barley is grown over a wider range of climate than any other grain. One of the five staple grains used for human consumption and malting, barley is most important as a livestock feed.

Barley is believed to have been used by prehistoric man for making beer. Today, more than 10 per cent of the world crop is used for this purpose.

When the husk is removed barley is called pot barley, scotch barley or hulled barley and is used in the preparation of stews, soups and haggis. Husked barley, steamed, rounded and polished in a mill, is known as pearl barley and is used to thicken soups and stews. Pearl barley ground into a fine flour, is called patent barley.

When barley is ground coarsely to make a wholemeal flour it is called barley meal and is used to make porridge and gruel. It is also used in the preparation of some kinds of bread. Pressed and flattened barley grains are called barley flakes and are used in making milk puddings and gruel.

Barley Bread

Barley Bread, which has a subtle, delicate flavour, is close-textured and retains its freshness for a number of days. Dried yeast is used in this recipe, but fresh yeast may be used instead if it is easily available (use double the quantity for fresh yeast).

ONE 3lb. LOAF
OR TWO 1½lb. LOAVES

1 large potato, quartered
1½ lb. [6 cups] strong white flour
½ teaspoon ground ginger
1 tablespoon salt
1 sachet easy-blend dried yeast
3 oz. [1 cup] barley flakes
12 fl. oz. [1½ cups] milk
4 teaspoons light soft brown sugar
¾ oz. [1½ tablespoons] butter, plus
    extra for greasing

Cook the potato in a little water until very soft. Drain, reserving the cooking liquor, and mash the potato with 5 fl. oz. [⅝ cup] of the liquid.

Sift the flour, ginger and salt into a bowl. Stir in the yeast and barley flakes.

Warm the milk, sugar and butter to blood heat, then stir into the potato to make a smooth paste. Pour the paste on to the flour and mix well to a smooth and elastic dough.

Turn on to a well floured surface and knead for about 10 minutes, adding up to 6 tablespoons more flour to the mixture as the dough becomes sticky.

Form into 1 large or 2 small loaf shapes. Put into 4½ pint greased loaf tin or 2 × 2¼ pint greased loaf tins. Cover with oiled cling film and leave in a warm place for 3-4 hours until it has doubled.

Preheat the oven to hot 425°F (Gas Mark 7, 220°C).

Uncover the loaf and bake for 10 minutes, then reduce the heat to fairly hot 400°F (Gas Mark 6, 200°C) and bake for 35 minutes or until the bread sounds hollow when tapped underneath. Turn out on to a wire rack and leave to cool completely.

If you want to freeze one of the loaves, wrap it in heavy-duty film. It will keep for 4 weeks. To thaw, loosen the wrapping. Leave at room temperature for 4 hours, or overnight in the refrigerator.

Barley Country Soup

This delicious soup with vegetables and barley is nourishing and filling so it makes a meal on its own. Serve it with crisp bread or toast. Other vegetables may be used if preferred and, if chicken livers are not available the soup is equally good if minced [ground] beef is added instead. The yoghurt stirred into the soup before serving gives it an extra special flavour.

6 TO 8 SERVINGS

2 oz. mushrooms, chopped
4 oz. chicken livers, chopped
2 large carrots, scraped and thinly sliced
2 parsnips, peeled and diced
1 small cauliflower, separated into flowerets and washed
1 large celery stalk, chopped
1 teaspoon oregano
¼ teaspoon nutmeg
1 bay leaf
1 teaspoon salt
¼ teaspoon black pepper
2½ pints [6¼ cups] cold water
1 pint [2½ cups] chicken stock
1½ oz. [3 tablespoons] butter
2 oz. [¼ cup] pearl barley
2 large potatoes, peeled, sliced and diced into ½-inch cubes
5 fl. oz. [⅝ cup] yoghurt
1 tablespoon chopped parsley

Put the mushrooms, chicken livers, carrots, parsnips, cauliflower, celery, oregano, nutmeg, bay leaf, salt and pepper

Low Cal

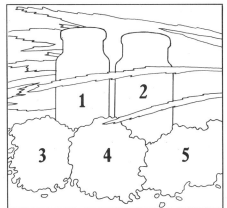

BARLEY
2 Barley meal
4 Flaked barley

1 Patent barley
3 Pearl barley
5 Pot barley

in a large heavy saucepan. Pour in the water and chicken stock. Place the pan over high heat and bring to the boil. Reduce the heat to low. Cover the pan and simmer for 30 minutes, or until the vegetables are cooked.

Remove the pan from the heat and strain the vegetables and livers into a medium-sized bowl. Return the liquid to the saucepan. Set the livers and vegetables aside.

In a small saucepan, melt the butter over moderate heat. Remove the pan from the heat and stir in the barley to coat it with the butter.

Add the barley to the stock in the saucepan and stir well. Place the pan over high heat and bring to the boil.

Reduce the heat to low. Cover the pan and simmer for 15 minutes, stirring occasionally.

Add the potatoes to the pan and simmer, covered, for a further 15 minutes, or until the potatoes are tender when pierced with a knife.

Return the reserved livers and vegetables to the pan and stir well to combine with the barley. Simmer for 10 minutes.

Remove the pan from the heat and pour the soup into a warmed soup tureen. With a metal spoon, lightly mix the yoghurt into the soup. Sprinkle with the parsley and serve immediately.

Barley and Mushroom Casserole

Cooked in this way, barley makes a delicious alternative to potatoes. It may be served with lamb, beef or poultry. Chopped fresh parsley or thyme may be added. For the best results, use fine or medium-sized pearl barley.

4 SERVINGS
2 oz. [¼ cup] butter
2 medium-sized onions, chopped
10 oz. mushrooms, wiped and sliced
7 oz. [1 cup] pearl barley
¾ teaspoon salt
¾ teaspoon black pepper
10 fl. oz. [1¼ cups] chicken stock

Preheat the oven to warm 325°F (Gas Mark 3, 170°C).

Melt the butter in a frying-pan over low heat. Add the onions and cook, stirring occasionally, for about 5 minutes, or until they are golden. Add the mushrooms and cook for 3 minutes.

Barley is an interesting change from potatoes or pasta. Try this savoury Barley and Mushroom Casserole.

Transfer the onions and mushrooms to an ovenproof casserole. Add the barley, salt, pepper. Pour in the stock and stir to mix the ingredients.

Cover the casserole and place in the oven. Cook for 40 minutes or until the barley is tender and all the liquid is absorbed.

Barley Sugar

A brittle toffee, barley sugar is made from sugar which is boiled with water and flavoured with lemon. Originally, barley sugar was made with barley water and sugar and was more acid in flavour than the modern sweet.

Barley Water

A drink made from blanched pearl barley simmered with water and flavoured with lemon and, sometimes, a little sugar, barley water is an easily digestible and nutritious beverage which is often given to invalids.

Barley Wine

This is the name given by some brewers to their best brew of beer. In Britain, barley wine is the name of a strong, sweet, bottled beer. In the United States, barley wine is known as malt liquor.

Barm Brack
IRISH FRUIT LOAF

A traditional Irish fruit loaf, Barm Brack is made with yeast. It is eaten all the year round in Ireland, but especially at Hallow-e'en when, traditionally, a gold ring is baked in it. Whoever finds the ring is supposed to be married within the year.

2 SMALL LOAVES
4 tablespoons plus 1 teaspoon sugar
10 fl. oz. [1¼ cups] tepid milk
½ oz. fresh yeast
1 lb. [4 cups] flour
½ teaspoon ground cinnamon
¼ teaspoon mixed spice
¼ teaspoon salt
1 oz. [2 tablespoons] butter
2 eggs, lightly beaten
6 oz. [1 cup] raisins
2 oz. [⅓ cup] currants
3 oz. [½ cup] candied peel
1 tablespoon caraway seeds
GLAZE
2 tablespoons sugar
3 tablespoons boiling water

In a small mixing bowl dissolve 1 teaspoon of sugar in the warm milk.

Crumble the yeast on top and mix with a spoon. Leave in a warm place for 20 minutes or until frothy.

Sift the flour with the remaining sugar, cinnamon, spice and salt into a large, warm mixing bowl. With your fingertips, rub in the butter. Make a well in the centre of the flour mixture. Pour in the frothing yeast and milk, and the beaten eggs. Mix well with a wooden spoon. Then, using your fingers, mix the dough into a ball.

Place the dough on a floured surface and knead well until it is smooth and elastic. Sprinkle the raisins, currants, candied peel and caraway seeds on to the dough and knead them in. Place the dough in a greased bowl, cover with a clean cloth or a polythene bag and leave in a warm place for 1 hour, or until the dough doubles in size.

Preheat the oven to fairly hot 400°F (Gas Mark 6, 200°C). Lightly grease two 1-pound bread tins.

Turn the risen dough on to a floured surface. Divide it into two portions. Lightly knead each portion, shape into rounds and put into the bread tins. Cover and leave in a warm place for 30 minutes.

Place the bread tins in the oven and bake for 1 hour.

To make the glaze, dissolve the sugar in the boiling water. Remove the loaves from the oven and brush the tops with the sugar-and-water syrup. Return the loaves to the oven for 3 minutes.

Turn the loaves on to a wire rack and leave to cool.

Baron of Beef

The cut of beef which consists of both sides of the back or two sirloins which is left uncut at the bone and roasted, a baron of beef can weigh from 50 to 100 pounds, depending on the size of the animal.

Today, a baron of beef is rarely served, except at banquets or at large restaurants. The term 'baron' is also applied to a large cut of mutton or lamb comprising the saddle and the two legs.

Barquettes

A French culinary term, *barquettes* are small oval or boat-shaped pastry shells. The shells may be filled with either sweet or savoury fillings and then baked in the oven. They may also be BAKED BLIND and then filled with crushed and sweetened fresh fruit such as strawberries, raspberries or gooseberries. Filled with prawns, shrimps, crayfish or mussels and topped with mayonnaise they make delicious hors d'oeuvre.

Barquettes aux Abricots
APRICOT TARTS

Attractive with a slightly tart, fresh taste, Barquettes aux Abricots (bahr-ket oh-zah-bree-koh), may be served with afternoon tea, or with coffee after dinner. Canned apricot halves may be substituted for fresh apricots, but they must be thoroughly drained and dried on kitchen paper towels before using. To make these tarts you will need a fluted, oval-shaped pastry cutter and 10 to 12 boat-shaped barquette moulds. The moulds are either deep with fluted edges or plain-edged and slightly shallower. The ones recommended for use in this recipe are about 2-inches long. It is possible, however, to get larger ones that are 3½-inches long. It is also possible to buy a cutter to match the size of the mould, which helps save time when lining the mould.

10 TO 12 SERVINGS

PASTRY
4 oz. [1 cup] flour
1 oz. icing [¼ cup confectioners'] sugar
2½ oz. [5 tablespoons] butter, cut into small pieces
2 egg yolks

FILLING
3 tablespoons finely ground almonds
5-6 fresh apricots, stoned and quartered
small bunch of ripe seedless grapes
6 tablespoons apricot jam
1 tablespoon brandy

Apricots in light, boat-shaped pastry, Barquettes aux Abricots are delicious with tea or coffee.

To make the pastry for the barquettes, sift the flour and sugar into a mixing bowl and make a well in the centre.

Add the butter and egg yolks. Using your fingertips, gradually blend into the flour, then knead until smooth. Wrap in cling film and chill for 30 minutes.

Roll out the pastry to ⅛ inch and use to line the barquette moulds. Prick the pastry and chill in the refrigerator for 10 minutes.

Preheat the oven to hot 400°F (Gas Mark 6, 200°C). Place the oven shelf above the centre.

Divide the ground almonds between the barquettes and arrange 2 apricot quarters, cut side down and a few grapes in each one.

Bake for 20 minutes. Leave the barquettes to cool in the moulds for 10 minutes, then remove the pastry from the moulds and cool on a wire rack.

Put the apricot jam and brandy in a small pan over a low heat until dissolved. Rub through a sieve, then spoon a little glaze over each barquette. Allow to set, completely.

Try various fruit to fill the barquettes such as plums, redcurrants, raspberries and grapes.

Barracouta
A large, rough-scaled, salt-water fish common in Australia and New Zealand waters, the barracouta is also caught off the South African coast where it is known as *snoek*. The flesh of the barracouta resembles that of tuna fish. It is eaten fresh, and is also smoked and canned.

Barracuda
Predatory, pike-like fish, barracuda inhabit tropical and semi-tropical seas. They range in size from 3 to 10 feet and have long, pointed jaws filled with razor-sharp teeth. The giant pike and the great barracuda, found in the South Pacific, are reputed to be the most vicious and their attacks on swimmers are often mistakenly attributed to sharks.

The barracuda is an excellent big-game fish because of its stamina and fighting spirit. It is also fished commercially and its meat sold both fresh and canned.

Barsac
Barsac is a sub-area within the SAUTERNES wine district in BORDEAUX which gives its name to a sweet, white wine. Barsac goes by the generic name of SAUTERNES.

Basil
There are over 50 varieties of basil, each differing in some way from the others, either in the shape or colour of the leaves or in the size of the plant. A native of tropical Asia, and known in India as *tulsi*, basil is regarded as a sacred plant and is used in religious ceremonies as well as medicinally.

Sweet basil is the variety of this herb which is most used in cooking. The leaves

have a spicy, clove-like flavour when they are fresh, but the taste alters when they are dried. Basil is traditionally used to flavour turtle soup and is also one of the main ingredients, with garlic, for flavouring Pistou, a popular soup in Provence. Basil has a particular affinity with tomatoes and makes an excellent ingredient in most tomato dishes.

Basil Baked Tomatoes

Tomatoes and onions baked with basil make a fragrant and tasty accompaniment to roast pork, lamb or chicken.

4 SERVINGS

3 oz. [⅜ cup] butter
2 large onions, thinly sliced and
   separated into rings
10 large tomatoes, thinly sliced
2 tablespoons chopped fresh basil,
   or 2 teaspoons dried basil
6 grindings black pepper
1 teaspoon salt
1 teaspoon sugar
3 oz. [1 cup] fresh breadcrumbs

Preheat the oven to fairly hot 400°F (Gas Mark 6, 200°C). Lightly grease an ovenproof dish with 1 tablespoon butter.

Melt 2 tablespoons butter in a large

Basil Baked Tomatoes is an unusual and fragrant accompaniment to pork, lamb or chicken.

frying-pan over low heat. Put in the onion rings and fry them for 10 minutes, or until they are tender but not brown. Remove the frying-pan from the heat.

Put a layer of onion rings on the bottom of the ovenproof dish, sprinkle with a little basil and cover with a layer of tomato slices. Add a little pepper, salt and a sprinkling of sugar. Dot with 1 tablespoon butter, cut into small pieces. Repeat the layers until all the ingredients have been used.

Cover the top with breadcrumbs and dot with the remaining butter. Place the dish in the oven and bake for 30 minutes. Serve hot.

Basil and Tomato Aspic

This smooth, fresh-tasting tomato aspic may be served with various cold meats together with other salads. An attractive dish to serve at a cold buffet lunch or dinner, it can be made two or three days in advance and kept in the refrigerator.

4 SERVINGS

1 pint [2½ cups] canned or bottled
   tomato juice
¾ oz. [3 tablespoons] gelatine
5 spring onions [scallions], chopped
1 tablespoon chopped fresh basil
   or 1 teaspoon dried basil
1 tablespoon brown sugar
   juice of ½ lemon
½ teaspoon salt
4 grindings black pepper
5 fl. oz. [⅝ cup] mayonnaise
6 radishes, sliced
½ cucumber, diced
1 apple, peeled, cored and diced
5 black olives, stoned and chopped

Warm 5 fluid ounces of the tomato juice in a small pan and pour it into a small bowl. Add the gelatine and stir to dissolve. Put the bowl over hot water and set aside.

Pour the remaining tomato juice into a small saucepan and bring it to the boil over moderate heat. Add the spring onions, basil, sugar, lemon juice, salt and black pepper, and simmer for 5 minutes.

Remove the pan from the heat and mix in the dissolved gelatine. Set aside to cool.

When the tomato mixture is cool, mix in the mayonnaise, radishes, cucumber, apple and olives.

127

Pour the mixture into a wet 1½-pint mould. Chill in the refrigerator for at least 2 hours before serving. To un-mould, run a knife around the edge of the mould and then dip the mould quickly into hot water. Place the serving plate on top of the mould and turn upside-down.

Basquaise, à la

A garnish for large cuts of meat, *à la Basquaise* (ah lah bahs-kayz) is composed of fried button mushrooms, moulded Anna potatoes and chopped ham.

Bass

The name of several voracious, spiny-finned sea and river fish, the bass best known in Europe is the sea bass. Also known as the sea wolf and sea perch and, in France, as the *bar*, it is caught in the Mediterranean and along the Atlantic coast of Europe. Because it has a super-ficial likeness to the salmon in shape and colouring, in England bass is some-times called sea salmon or white salmon.

Many varieties of bass live in the coastal waters, rivers and lakes of America. The striped bass, the large and small-mouthed black bass, and the calico bass make good eating and are considered excellent game by anglers. Gastrono-mically, the sea bass is the best of the species, with firm, lean, fine-textured flesh and a delicate flavour.

Large bass are poached and served hot with melted butter or a HOLLANDAISE SAUCE or cold with a SAUCE VERTE. Smaller bass can be grilled, baked or braised. Heavily spiced sauces should not be used because they will spoil the fish's delicate flavour. Nearly all ways of cook-ing salmon can be used for preparing bass.

Bass Baked in Lemon and Mushroom Sauce

Covered with a lemon and mushroom sauce and baked in the oven, sea bass is easy to prepare. Served with sautéed potatoes and petits pois *it makes a delicious main course for lunch or a dinner party. It may be accompanied by a full-bodied dry white wine.*

4 SERVINGS
8 bass fillets
2 oz. [¼ cup] butter
1 oz. [4 tablespoons] flour
1 teaspoon salt
¼ teaspoon white pepper
1½ pints [3¾ cups] tepid milk
1 bouquet garni consisting of 4

parsley sprigs, 1 thyme spray and 1 bay leaf tied together
4 tablespoons lemon juice
8 oz. mushrooms, wiped and sliced
1 lemon, quartered

Preheat the oven to moderate 350°F (Gas Mark 4, 180°C).

Wipe the fish with kitchen paper towels and place in a large, shallow oven-proof dish.

Melt the butter in a small saucepan over low heat. With a wooden spoon, stir in the flour, salt and pepper and cook for 1 minute. Gradually pour in the milk, stirring constantly. Bring to the boil. Add the bouquet garni, lemon juice and mush-rooms, and stir well. Simmer for 5 minutes.

Remove and discard the bouquet garni. Cover the fish with the sauce. Cover the dish and bake for 30 minutes. Garnish with lemon quarters.

Baste

A culinary term, to baste is to moisten food by spooning hot fat or liquid over it while it is cooking, usually in the oven. This improves its flavour and appearance. Long-handled spoons or basting syringes are available for this purpose.

Batatas à Portuguêsa

PORTUGUESE FRIED POTATOES

Fried in a mixture of butter and olive oil, Batatas à Portuguêsa (bah-tah-tah ah por-too-GAY-zah) make a pleasant accom-paniment to most meat dishes. In Portugal, these potatoes are traditionally arranged in a ring around the meat on the serving plate.

4 SERVINGS
3 oz. [⅜ cup] butter
4 tablespoons olive oil
2 lb. potatoes, peeled and sliced
1 small onion, thinly sliced
1 teaspoon salt
¼ teaspoon black pepper
1 tablespoon finely chopped chives

Put the butter and olive oil in a large, heavy frying-pan over moderate heat. When the butter melts add the sliced potatoes and onion.

Fry the potatoes and onion turning them frequently with a spatula for about 25 minutes, or until they are cooked and are crisp and a golden brown colour.

Remove the potatoes from the frying-pan. Pour off any excess fat. Place the potatoes and onion in a warmed serving dish. Sprinkle with the salt, pepper and chives, and serve immediately.

Bath Buns

These traditional buns, first made in the English spa of Bath at the beginning of the 18th century, have a craggy uneven shape and sugar lump topping.

12 BUNS
14 oz. [3½ cups] strong white flour
1 sachet easy-blend dried yeast
1 teaspoon castor sugar
6 fl. oz. [¾ cup] warm milk
½ teaspoon salt
2 oz. [4 tablespoons] butter, diced
3 oz. [⅜ cup] sugar
4 oz. [⅔ cup] currants
2 tablespoons chopped mixed peel
3 eggs
coarsely crushed sugar lumps
oil for greasing

Sift 4 oz. [1 cup] flour into a large bowl, then stir in the yeast and castor sugar. Pour in the milk and mix to a smooth bat-ter. Cover with greased plastic and leave to rise for about 20 minutes until frothy.

Sift the remaining flour with the salt, then rub in the butter. Stir in the sugar, currants and peel.

Lightly beat 2 eggs and add to the yeast batter with the flour and fruit mixture. Mix well with a wooden spoon to make a soft sticky dough. Beat for 10 minutes with the spoon or with the dough hook of a table-top mixer for 2 minutes.

Cover with greased cling film and leave to rise in a warm place for 1-1½ hours. Grease a large baking sheet with the vegetable oil.

Beat the risen dough with a wooden spoon for 2 minutes, then spoon on to the prepared baking sheet. Make 12 equal heaps and space them well apart to allow for expansion. Cover with greased cling film and leave to rise in a warm place for about 20 minutes, or until well risen.

Meanwhile, preheat the oven to fairly hot 375°F (Gas Mark 5, 190°C). Position the shelf above the centre.

Uncover the buns. Beat the remaining egg with a few drops of water and brush over the tops of the buns. Sprinkle with crushed sugar lumps. Bake the buns for about 20-25 minutes, until risen, golden brown and the undersides sound hollow when tapped with your knuckles. Return to the oven for 3-5 minutes if not done.

Transfer the buns to a wire rack and leave to cool. Serve buttered, if wished.

Bath Chap

The lower half of a pig's cheek, a bath chap is cured in the same way as bacon and is usually eaten cold. When it is not too fatty, a boiled bath chap, served cold,

Bath Buns, rich with currants and candied peel, are traditional English tea-time favourites.

---

is delicious and superior to pickled pork.

Although it is usually sold ready-cooked, cooking a bath chap at home is not complicated. A bath chap fresh from the pickle should be washed under cold, running water for 5 minutes. If it has been long-cured, however, it should be soaked in tepid water for at least 6 hours before boiling.

To cook a bath chap, place it in a large saucepan of cold water and bring the water to a boil. When the water is boiling, reduce the heat and simmer gently for 2½ hours.

Take the chap out of the saucepan and remove the skin. Sprinkle the fat side with browned breadcrumbs and bake in a

fairly hot oven 400°F (Gas Mark 6, 200°C) for about 30 minutes. Cooked in this way, a bath chap may be served hot or cold.

Bath Oliver

Large, thin, pale-coloured water biscuits, Bath Olivers are usually eaten with strong cheese. They were invented by a Dr. William Oliver of Bath in the eighteenth century for the benefit of his dyspeptic patients. The biscuits, now made commercially, are still stamped with an outline of Dr. Oliver's head.

Bâtonnets Aux Amandes

ALMOND CAKES

A type of petits fours, Bâtonnets aux

Amandes (bah-toh-nay oh-zah-mond) *are little fancy cakes in the shape of sticks. They may be served with after-dinner coffee or with an ice-cream dessert.*

MAKES ABOUT 80 STICKS

8 oz. [1¼ cups] blanched almonds
8 oz. [1 cup] castor sugar
1 egg white
2 fl. oz. [¼ cup] rum
ICING
1 egg white
4 tablespoons granulated sugar

Preheat the oven to moderate 350°F (Gas Mark 4, 180°C).

Lightly grease a large baking sheet and dust it with flour.

With a pestle and mortar, pound the almonds and sugar together. Add the egg white, and mix in with enough rum to make a stiff paste. Alternatively, if you have an electric blender, put in the almonds, sugar, egg white and rum and blend into a smooth paste.

Lightly dust a marble slab or working surface with flour. Place the almond paste on it and roll out with a rolling pin into a rectangle ⅛-inch thick. Cut the paste into strips ½-inch wide and 3-inches long.

Lightly beat the egg white in a saucer. Put the granulated sugar on a plate, dip the almond sticks into the beaten egg white and then into the granulated sugar. Place the almond sticks on the baking sheet and bake in the oven for 8 minutes.

Battenberg Cake

An attractive sponge cake in a two-coloured, chequer-board design, Battenberg Cake is usually iced with almond paste. Make the cake two days before you need it because it has to stand for at least 48 hours before it is cut.

6 SERVINGS

8 oz. [1 cup] butter
8 oz. [1 cup] castor sugar
4 eggs
8 oz. [2 cups] self-raising flour
½ teaspoon vanilla essence
2 to 4 tablespoons milk
2 tablespoons cocoa
2 tablespoons apricot jam
ALMOND PASTE
4 oz. icing [1 cup confectioners'] sugar
4 oz. [½ cup] castor sugar
8 oz. [1⅓ cups] ground almonds
1 teaspoon lemon juice
a few drops almond essence
1 egg, lightly beaten

Preheat the oven to fairly hot 375°F (Gas Mark 5, 190°C).

Bat

Prepare a 9-inch by 6-inch cake tin by cutting a piece of aluminium foil the exact length of the base, but 6 inches wider than the width. Fold a pleat in the middle so that the foil lies quite flat on the bottom of the tin and the pleat stands up, forming a wall which divides the tin into two oblongs of equal size.

With a wooden spoon, beat the butter and sugar in a medium-sized mixing bowl, until the mixture is light and creamy. Add the eggs, one at a time, along with 1 tablespoon of flour. Stir well to mix.

Fold in the remaining flour and the vanilla essence. Mix in a little milk, if it is necessary, to make the batter of a consistency that will drop easily off the spoon. Pour half the cake batter into one half of the prepared cake tin.

Mix the cocoa into the rest of the batter, add a spoonful of milk, if necessary, and pour it into the other half of the tin. Bake in the oven for 45 minutes. When the cake is cooked set it aside to cool.

While the cake is baking make the almond paste. Sift the icing sugar and the castor sugar together into a medium-sized mixing bowl. Mix in the ground almonds. Add the lemon juice, almond

For a Battenberg cake, divide the cake tin in half by pleating the foil lining down the middle.

Pour the white cake batter into one-half of the tin, and the cocoa-flavoured batter into the other.

Combine the almond paste ingredients and knead the mixture on a work surface dusted with icing sugar.

Remove the cake from the tin and carefully cut both pieces in half lengthways.

Join the brown and white halves of the cake together with the apricot jam and glaze the top of both halves.

Place the other two halves of the cake on top of the first two to make a chequer-board pattern.

Coat the cake with apricot jam and wrap the rolled-out almond paste around it.

The finished Battenberg cake should be kept in an air tight tin for two days before serving.

essence and enough beaten egg to bind all the ingredients into a paste.

Sprinkle your working surface with a little icing sugar and put the paste on it. Knead the almond paste until it is smooth. Be careful not to over-knead as the paste will become oily.

Remove the cake from the tin. Trim the two halves to equal size and cut each in half lengthways. Spread the side of one piece of white cake with the apricot jam and place a brown piece next to it. Spread jam on top of the two halves. Repeat with the other two halves of the cake, alternating the white and brown, and place on top of the jam covered layer to form a chequer-board pattern. Press gently together. Spread the remaining jam over the top and the sides of the cake.

On a lightly sugared board roll the almond paste into an oblong large enough to encase the cake. Wrap it round the cake, trimming the edges to leave the ends of the cake uncovered. Crimp the top edges to make a border and, with a knife, score a criss-cross pattern on the top. Keep the cake in a tin with a tight-fitting lid for two days before serving.

Batter

Consisting essentially of flour, milk and eggs, batter is a thick liquid mixture of a consistency that can be stirred, beaten or 'battered'. Batter forms a basis for pancakes, waffles, cakes and Yorkshire puddings. It is also used for coating fish or meat for frying or for making fritters.

When making batter, the proportion of liquid and oil or butter varies from recipe to recipe depending on how thick or thin the batter is required to be. The method, however, remains the same.

The flour, salt and sugar (if a sweet batter is being made) are sifted into a bowl. A well is made in the flour, exposing the bottom of the bowl. The eggs are then broken into the well and half the milk is poured in.

A wooden spoon or wire whisk are considered best for stirring. Only the eggs and milk are stirred at first and the flour is slowly incorporated, a little at a time. More milk is gradually added and the stirring is continued until the batter has a thick and creamy consistency.

When the batter has reached this stage, the mixture should be thoroughly beaten with a whisk. Oil, or cooled melted butter, and any remaining ingredients required by the recipe may then be added. The batter should be beaten for a few more minutes and then left to rest.

Batter should always be allowed to rest,

To prepare batter, sift the flour and salt into a bowl. Make a well in the flour and break the eggs into it.

Pour half the quantity of milk on to the eggs in the well of flour in the mixing bowl.

With a wooden spoon, or wire whisk, stir the eggs and milk and slowly incorporate the flour.

Gradually add more milk and continue stirring the batter until it is smooth and creamy.

preferably in a refrigerator, for at least one hour before use. If the recipe calls for a stiffly beaten egg white, this is folded into the batter just before it is used.

Batter for puddings and thick pancakes requires less liquid than batter for crêpes or light pancakes. Thicker batters are usually required for coating fish or meat for frying.

Pancake batters are best when cooled, melted butter is used, although oil may be substituted for savoury pancakes. For a lighter batter, water may sometimes replace a proportion of the milk. Stiffly beaten egg whites, added at the last moment, give pancakes a light and fluffy texture.

If a dry pancake is required the butter or oil may be omitted from the batter, but in this case the pan should be well greased. If the batter does contain oil or butter, the pan will require a little greasing.

Batter Pudding

This is a filling, hot dessert for a winter lunch or supper. Serve it with a hot jam or marmalade sauce, or sprinkled with brown sugar and dotted with butter.

4 SERVINGS

5 oz. [1¼ cups] flour
⅛ teaspoon salt
2 tablespoons sugar
½ teaspoon grated orange rind
2 egg yolks
5 fl. oz. [⅝ cup] milk
2 egg whites
1 tablespoon butter, softened

Sift the flour and salt into a medium-sized mixing bowl. Mix in the sugar and orange rind and make a deep well in the flour down to the bottom of the bowl.

Put the egg yolks into the well and add half the milk. Stir the mixture with a wooden spoon for 5 minutes, or until it has a creamy consistency. Add the rest of the milk and beat with a rotary beater for 5 more minutes.

Leave the batter to stand for 1 hour in a cool place.

In another medium-sized mixing bowl, using a wire whisk, beat the egg whites until they are stiff. With a spatula fold the whites into the batter.

Grease a medium-sized pudding basin with the butter and pour the batter into it. Cover the top with greaseproof or waxed paper and tie with string.

Place the pudding in a steamer or in a large pan filled with enough water to come half-way up the sides of the basin. Over moderate heat, bring the water to the boil.

Lower the heat, cover the pan and steam the pudding for 1½ hours, replenishing the water as it evaporates.

Remove the pudding basin from the steamer. Take off the greaseproof paper. Leave the pudding to stand for 1 minute before turning it out on to a warmed serving dish. Serve immediately.

Batuto

Finely chopped vegetables and herbs which are fried and mixed with diced pork or ham are the base of many Italian stews and soups, particularly in Roman cooking. This base when uncooked is called *batuto* (baht-too-toh). When it is cooked it is called *soffritto* (sohf-FREET-toh).

Bauernsuppe

GERMAN PEASANT SOUP

A country-style German soup, Bauernsuppe (bowrn-zoo-per) may be served either as a first or as a main course. The quantity given in this recipe will be sufficient for 4 people as a main course. Serve this hearty soup with crusty French bread.

6 SERVINGS

2 oz. [¼ cup] butter
2 lb. stewing steak, cut into small
   cubes
2 onions, chopped
1 bouquet garni, consisting of 4
   parsley sprigs, 1 thyme spray and
   1 bay leaf tied together
1 garlic clove, crushed
1 teaspoon paprika
1 teaspoon salt
1 oz. [4 tablespoons] flour
4½ pints [5½ pints] beef stock
2 large potatoes, peeled and diced
½ tablespoon finely chopped
   fresh dill
2 oz. [½ cup] grated Parmesan cheese

Melt the butter in a large, heavy pan over moderate heat. Add the meat cubes and fry them, turning occasionally with a spoon, until they are browned.

Add the onions, and fry for 8 minutes, or until they are soft and transparent. Add the bouquet garni, garlic, paprika and salt and stir well.

Mix in the flour, lower the heat and cook, stirring, for 5 minutes. Gradually stir in the stock. Bring to the boil. Cover the pan and simmer for 1 hour, stirring occasionally. Add the potatoes, cover and

A filling, meaty German soup, Bauernsuppe is served either as a soup or as a main course.

simmer for a further 45 minutes.

Ladle the soup into individual soup bowls. Sprinkle the top with the dill and grated cheese. Serve very hot.

Bavarian Strudel

PASTRY FILLED WITH APPLES

An inexpensive, apple-pastry dessert, Bavarian Strudel is quick and easy to make. Serve it hot with thick, cold cream or cold by itself.

4 SERVINGS

8 oz. [2 cups] sifted flour
2 tablespoons sugar
⅓ teaspoon salt
3 oz. [⅜ cup] butter, chilled
2 tablespoons vegetable fat
4 tablespoons milk
FILLING
2 lb. cooking apples, cored,
   peeled, and thinly sliced
2 oz. [⅓ cup] sultanas or raisins
   grated rind of 1 lemon
½ teaspoon mixed spice
4 oz. [½ cup] sugar
2 tablespoons fresh breadcrumbs
2 tablespoons milk for glazing
   icing [confectioners'] sugar

Preheat the oven to fairly hot 400°F (Gas Mark 6, 200°C).

Sift the flour, sugar and salt into a medium-sized mixing bowl. Rub the butter and vegetable fat into the flour with your fingertips until the mixture resembles fine breadcrumbs.

Pour in the milk and mix it in to make a dough. Knead and pat lightly until smooth. Wrap it in greaseproof or waxed paper and refrigerate for 20 minutes.

Mix the sliced apples, sultanas, lemon rind, mixed spice, sugar and breadcrumbs in a bowl.

On a floured surface, roll out the pastry into a long oblong shape about 5-inches wide. Place the pastry on a baking sheet. Spread the apple filling down the centre, lengthways. Fold the pastry over the filling, leaving the ends open so the filling can be seen.

Brush with milk and bake for 20 to 30 minutes, or until the pastry is golden.

Sprinkle the top of the strudel with icing sugar and cut into thick slices.

Bavarois

Bavarois (bah-vahr-wah) is a classic dessert. It is a rich egg custard blended with thick cream and lightly set gelatine and usually moulded. Bavarois can be flavoured with vanilla, coffee, orange, lemon, almond, pistachio, chocolate,

rum, liqueurs or fresh fruit purées. Chopped glacé fruits, chestnuts or fresh fruits can also be added. For a spectacular dinner party dessert, it is possible to make a combination of flavours and colours in a single mould and serve it with a fruit sauce.

This luscious dessert can be made in any metal mould with a sharply defined attractive shape. Oil the mould with a flavourless oil that will not affect the delicate taste of the bavarois. Almond oil (available from the chemist) is ideal. To unmould the bavarois, gently loosen the top edge with the tip of a sharp knife. Dip the mould, up to the rim, in very hot water for a second, then quickly turn out on to a *chilled* flat serving dish.

The decoration can be simple or elaborate, depending on the occasion, using whipped cream, fruits, nuts or chocolate. Flowers, such as marigolds and nasturtiums, add a touch of elegance.

Bavarois

BAVARIAN CREAM

A classic, moulded dessert, Bavarois (bah-vahr-wah), or Bavarian Cream, is a soft egg custard mixed with gelatine, whipped cream and flavouring. Properly prepared it has a smooth velvety quality and is regarded as one of the best moulded desserts.

4 TO 6 SERVINGS

1 teaspoon vegetable oil
1¼ pints [3 cups] milk
1 vanilla pod
5 tablespoons sugar
5 egg yolks
½ oz. [2 tablespoons] gelatine
3 tablespoons water
5 fl. oz. double [⅝ cup heavy] cream

Using a pastry brush, grease the inside of a 2-pint mould with the vegetable oil. Place the mould upside-down on kitchen paper towels to drain off the excess oil.

Put the milk and the vanilla pod into a medium-sized saucepan over moderate heat. When the milk is hot, but not boiling, remove it from the heat.

Put the sugar in a medium-sized mixing bowl. Make a well in the centre of the sugar. Drop the egg yolks, one at a time, into the well and, with a wooden spoon or spatula, beat the yolks, slowly incorporating the sugar. Continue this process until all the egg yolks and sugar are well mixed and beaten.

Remove the vanilla pod and, beating all the time, pour the milk in a thin stream on to the egg-and-sugar mixture.

Place a large pan, one-third full of water, on high heat. When the water is just about to boil, turn the heat to very low. The water must be hot but not simmering. Place the bowl with the egg-and-milk mixture in the water and, stirring slowly, cook until the custard is thick enough to coat the spoon. Be careful not to overheat the custard as it will curdle.

In a small saucepan over low heat dissolve the gelatine in the water. When the gelatine is completely dissolved, stir it into the custard.

Strain the custard through a sieve into a bowl. Place the bowl over ice in a bowl. Stir continuously until the custard thickens.

Whip the cream in a small bowl with a wire whisk until it is thick but not stiff. Lightly fold the cream into the thickening custard and pour the mixture into the mould.

Cover the mould with aluminium foil or waxed paper and refrigerate for 6 hours or until the Bavarian Cream is completely set.

To serve, dip the bottom of the mould into hot water for 1 second. Run a knife around the edge of the cream and turn it out on to a chilled serving dish.

Bavarois au Chocolat

CHOCOLATE BAVARIAN CREAM

Flavoured with dark chocolate and rum, Bavarois au Chocolat (bah-vahr-wah oh SHOH-koh-lah) *is a rich, cold dessert. Serve it in a serving dish and decorate with whipped cream and dark chocolate curls.*

An impressive dessert, Bavarois au Chocolat is richly flavoured with chocolate, coffee and rum.

4 TO 6 SERVINGS

vegetable oil
1¼ pints [3 cups] milk
4 oz. plain [semi-sweet] chocolate, grated
3 oz. [⅜ cup] castor sugar
4 egg yolks
½ oz. [2 tablespoons] gelatine
4 fl. oz. strong black coffee
1 teaspoon vanilla essence
5 fl. oz. double [⅝ cup heavy] cream
2 tablespoons rum

Using a pastry brush, grease the inside of a 2-pint mould with a little vegetable oil. Place the mould upside-down on

134

kitchen paper towels to drain off the excess oil.

In a medium-sized pan heat the milk and chocolate over moderate heat. Stir to dissolve the chocolate. Take the pan off the heat and set aside.

Put the sugar in a medium-sized mixing bowl. Make a well in the centre of the sugar. Drop the egg yolks, one at a time, into the well and, with a wooden spoon or spatula, beat the yolks, slowly incorporating the sugar. Continue this process until all the egg yolks and sugar are well mixed and beaten.

Pour the warm milk and chocolate mixture in a thin stream on to the egg-and-sugar mixture, beating all the time.

Place a large pan, one-third full of water, on high heat. When the water is just about to boil, turn the heat to very low. The water must be hot but not simmering. Place the bowl with the egg-and-milk mixture in the water and, stirring slowly, cook until the custard is thick enough to coat the spoon. Be careful not to overheat the custard as it will curdle.

Remove the custard from the heat and set aside.

In a small saucepan over low heat dissolve the gelatine in the coffee. Add the vanilla and stir to mix. When the gelatine is completely dissolved, stir it into the custard.

Strain the custard through a sieve into a bowl. Place the bowl over ice in a bowl. Stir continuously until the custard thickens.

Whip the cream in a small bowl with a wire whisk until it is thick but not stiff. Lightly fold the cream and the rum into the thickening custard and pour the mixture into the mould.

Cover the mould with aluminium foil or waxed paper and refrigerate for 6 hours or until the Bavarian Cream is completely set.

To serve, dip the bottom of the mould into hot water for 1 second, run a knife around the edge of the cream and turn it out on to a chilled serving dish.

Bavarois Clermont

BAVARIAN CREAM WITH MARRONS GLACÉS

Bavarois Clermont (bah-vahr-wah CLAIR-mohn), *which is flavoured with* marrons glacés, *preserved chestnuts, is a very elegant dessert for a dinner party.*

8 SERVINGS

1 teaspoon vegetable oil
1¼ pints [3 cups] milk
1 vanilla pod
4 oz. [½ cup] sugar

4 egg yolks
½ oz. [2 tablespoons] gelatine
4 tablespoons water
10 fl. oz. double cream [1¼ cups heavy cream], chilled
8 oz. marrons glacés, finely chopped

Using a pastry brush, grease the inside of a 3-pint mould with the vegetable oil. Place the mould upside down on a double layer of kitchen paper towels to drain off the oil.

Put the milk and the vanilla pod into a medium-sized saucepan over moderate heat. When the milk is hot, but not boiling, take the saucepan off the heat and set aside to cool.

Put the sugar in a medium-sized mixing bowl. Make a well in the centre of the sugar. Drop the egg yolks, one at a time, into the well and, with a wooden spoon or spatula, beat the yolks and sugar until the mixture is light and fluffy.

Remove the vanilla pod and slowly pour the milk on to the egg and sugar mixture, beating all the time.

In a small saucepan set over low heat, dissolve the gelatine in the water, stirring constantly. Remove the pan from the heat and set aside.

Place a large saucepan, one third full of water, on high heat. When the water is just about to boil, turn the heat to very low. The water must be hot but not simmering. Place the bowl with the egg and milk mixture in the water and, stirring slowly, cook until the custard is thick enough to coat the spoon. Be careful not to overheat the mixture or it will curdle.

Stir in the gelatine. Cook, stirring, for a further 2 to 3 minutes or until the mixture is smooth.

Strain the custard through a sieve into a medium-sized bowl. Place the bowl over ice in a bowl. With a wooden spoon, stir continuously until the custard begins to thicken.

With a wire whisk whip the cream in a medium-sized bowl until it is thick but not stiff. With a rubber spatula lightly fold the cream and the chopped marrons glacés into the thickened custard and pour the mixture into the mould.

Cover the mould with aluminium foil or waxed paper and refrigerate for 8 hours or overnight, until the Bavarian Cream is completely set.

To serve, dip the bottom of the mould into hot water for 1 second, run a knife around the edge of the cream and turn it out on to a chilled serving dish. Decorate the Bavarian Cream with additional stiffly whipped cream.

For a really spectacular decoration place whole marrons glacés around the bottom.

Bavarois à L'Orange

ORANGE BAVARIAN CREAM

This recipe for Bavarois à L'Orange (bah-vahr-wah ah lor-ronj) differs from other Bavarian Cream recipes because it incorporates the stiffly beaten egg whites into the custard. This gives a lighter texture to the finished cream. Fresh orange segments, soaked in syrup and orange liqueur, may be used as a garnish.

4 SERVINGS

1 large fresh orange
½ tablespoon gelatine
10 fl. oz. [1¼ cups] creamy milk
3 oz. [⅜ cup] castor sugar
4 egg yolks
5 fl. oz. [⅝ cup] thick cream
3 tablespoons Cointreau or Grand Marnier
oil for greasing

Very lightly oil a 1-pint mould. Prepare a double boiler with 1-inch boiling water.

Wash and dry the orange, then grate the rind from it with a fine grater. Squeeze the juice from the orange into a small bowl and sprinkle over the gelatine; leave to soften. Gently warm the milk.

Put the sugar and orange rind in a mixing bowl and make a well in the centre. Drop in the egg yolks, one at a time, and beat with a wooden spoon, slowly incorporating the sugar.

Pour warm milk in a thin stream on to the egg yolks, beating constantly. Place the bowl on top of the hot but not boiling water. Stirring slowly, cook the custard until it is thick enough to coat the back of the spoon. Do not overheat or the custard will curdle.

Immediately remove the thickened custard from the heat and stir in the softened gelatine, stirring until dissolved. Put some ice in a large bowl and stand the mixture in it to cool for about 15 minutes.

Meanwhile, whip the cream until it thickens slightly. Lightly fold the cream and orange liqueur into the thickening custard. Pour the mixture into the mould.

Cover with cling film and chill until set. Allow 5-6 hours or overnight.

Decorate the Orange Bavarois with mandarin orange segments well soaked in orange liqueur. Pipe a shell or star border in whipped cream round the base.

Bavarois Praline

BAVARIAN CREAM WITH CARAMELIZED ALMONDS

Served with whipped cream, Bavarois Praline (bah-vahr-wah prah-leen) is a

delicious dessert for a lunch or dinner party. Hazel nuts, or a mixture of hazel nuts and almonds, toasted and coated in caramel may be substituted for almonds. Praline may be stored for several weeks in a tightly covered jar.

A Strawberry Bavarian Cream may be made with this recipe by substituting strawberries for the praline and omitting the almond essence. Use 5 egg yolks instead of 7, because the strawberry purée will bind the Bavarian Cream. Dissolve the gelatine in 4 fluid ounces of orange juice. Force ½ pound of fresh strawberries through a fine sieve and fold 8 fluid ounces of the strawberry purée into the custard with the whipped cream.

6 TO 8 SERVINGS

PRALINE

2 teaspoons vegetable oil
3 oz. [⅜ cup] sugar
2 tablespoons water
3 oz. [½ cup] roasted almonds, shredded or ground

BAVARIAN CREAM

1 teaspoon vegetable oil
4 fl. oz. [½ cup] strong black coffee
½ oz. [2 tablespoons] gelatine
6 oz. [¾ cup] plus 1 tablespoon sugar
6 egg yolks
2 teaspoons cornflour [cornstarch]
12 fl. oz. [1½ cups] hot milk
5 egg whites
⅛ teaspoon salt
5 fl. oz. double [⅝ cup heavy] cream, chilled
1 tablespoon vanilla essence
¼ teaspoon almond essence

First make the praline. Grease a large baking sheet with the vegetable oil. Place the sugar and water in a small saucepan and, over moderate heat, cook for 4 minutes, or until the syrup turns light brown. Shake the pan occasionally. As soon as the syrup reaches the desired colour, remove the pan from the heat. Do not let the syrup darken too much or it will have a bitter taste.

Stir in the almonds and replace the pan on the heat. Bring the mixture to the boil and pour the syrup on to the baking sheet. Leave it to cool for 15 minutes. When it has cooled and hardened, break into pieces. Crush it to a fine powder with a pestle and mortar and set aside.

Using a pastry brush, grease the inside of a 2-pint mould with a little vegetable oil. Place the mould upside-down on kitchen paper towels to drain off the oil.

Pour the coffee into a bowl and sprinkle in the gelatine. Stir it well and place to one side to allow the gelatine to dissolve.

Put 6 ounces [¾ cup] of the sugar in a large mixing bowl. Make a well in the centre. Drop in the egg yolks, one at a

time, into the well and, with a wooden spoon or spatula, beat the yolks, slowly incorporating the sugar. Continue this process until all the egg yolks and sugar are well mixed and beaten and add the cornflour [cornstarch]. Pour the hot milk in a thin stream on to the egg-and-sugar mixture, beating all the time.

Place a large pan, one-third full of water, on high heat. When the water is just about to boil, turn the heat to very low. The water must be hot but not simmering. Place the bowl with the egg-and-milk mixture in the water and, stirring slowly, cook until the custard is thick enough to coat the spoon. Be careful not to overheat the custard as it will curdle.

Remove the custard from the heat and stir in the gelatine. Reserve 2 tablespoons of the crushed praline and stir the rest into the hot custard. Place the bowl in a larger bowl of ice cubes. Continue stirring until the custard is thick and almost set.

Put the egg whites in a medium-sized bowl with the salt. Beat them with a wire whisk, or rotary beater, until the whites stand up in soft peaks. Sprinkle the remaining tablespoon of sugar on to the egg whites and continue beating until the mixture is stiff. Fold the egg whites into the custard.

Whip the cream in a small bowl with a wire whisk until it is thick but not stiff. Lightly fold the thickened cream and the vanilla and the almond essence into the thickening custard and pour the mixture into the mould.

Cover the mould with aluminium foil or waxed paper and place in the refrigerator for 6 hours or until the Bavarian Cream is completely set.

To serve, dip the bottom of the mould in hot water for 1 second, run a knife around the edge of the cream and turn it out on to a chilled serving dish. Sprinkle the top with the reserved 2 tablespoons of crushed praline.

Bay Leaves

The dark green, fragrant leaves of the bay tree or sweet laurel (*Lauris Nobilis*), bay leaves are one of the most commonly

used culinary herbs. The tree is native to Italy, Greece and North Africa. It was introduced into Britain over 400 years ago and was taken to North America by the early settlers.

The sweet laurel was believed by the ancient Greeks to be the nymph Daphne and the tree was sacred to the god Apollo. The victors of the Pythian games were crowned with laurel leaves and laurel became the symbol of triumph in Greece and later in Rome.

The bay leaf is used as a flavouring for puddings, pies, stews, soups and court bouillons, and a leaf is always included in a bouquet garni.

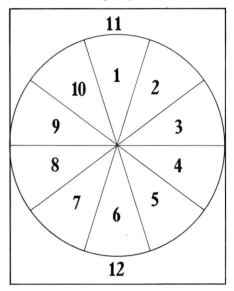

Beans
1 Oea Beans   *2 Flageolet*
3 Black Beans   *4 Broad Beans*
5 Haricot   *6 Pinto Beans*
7 Lima Beans   *8 Butter Beans*
9 Soya Beans   *10 Red Kidney Beans*
11 French Beans   *12 Runner Beans*

Bean

The seeds and pods of a wide variety of leguminous plants, beans are usually served as a vegetable. The seeds are a very good source of protein and of vitamin B and, when fresh, beans also contain vitamins A and C. In Europe until the sixteenth century, the only vegetable known as a bean was the broad bean. Today, however, the name applies to a large variety of this type of vegetable.

Among the various types of available beans are broad beans or Windsor beans, which are known as fava beans in the United States. Butter beans, large, flat and white, were originally found in South America. Flageolet, which are the pale green seeds of a choice variety of haricot or French beans, are usually sold dried in Britain. French beans are a smaller, more delicate bean than runner beans, but

they are of the same family and the pods as well as the seeds are eaten.

Haricot is the name given to a wide variety of bean plants, the best known being the French and kidney bean. In Britain this name is applied more particularly to the dried white seeds of dwarf or climbing haricot plants. In the United States these are known as navy beans.

Haricots vary considerably in size and can be green, brown, purple or red. Kidney beans are large, dark red, kidney-shaped beans which are often used for baked beans. Lima beans, originally from South America, are a delicate green or white colour and are of the haricot variety. The seeds may be eaten fresh or dried.

Oea beans, also known as black-eye peas or cow beans, are small, white peas with a black spot. They are used in cooking in the United States, particularly in the south. Pinto beans, which are

dappled pink in colour, and black beans are primarily eaten in Mexico where they are called *frijoles*. Runner beans, also called scarlet runners and string beans, are larger and longer than French beans. Soya beans, which are Chinese in origin, are rich in vegetable protein with a fairly high fat but low starch content.

Bean and Bacon Soup

This filling and tasty soup may be served at an informal lunch or dinner. It also makes a good main course, served with French bread, for a family lunch.

6 SERVINGS

12 oz. [1½ cups] dried butter [lima] beans
2 lb. bacon hock with bone
1 large onion, cut in quarters

1 large garlic clove, crushed
3½ pints [8¾ cups] water
1 bouquet garni, consisting of 4 parsley sprigs, 1 thyme spray, and 1 bay leaf tied together
½ teaspoon white pepper
20 large black olives, cut in half
3 tablespoons chopped parsley

Put the beans in a bowl and cover with water. Leave them to soak overnight.

Drain the beans and put them in a large saucepan with the bacon, onion and garlic. Cover with the water, place the pan on high heat and bring to the boil.

Add the bouquet garni and pepper to the pan and stir well. Lower the heat and simmer the soup for 1½ to 2 hours, or until the beans and bacon are cooked.

Remove the bacon hock and cut the meat into pieces. Remove the bouquet garni and discard. Purée some of the

Bacon, beans and olives combine to make this tasty Bean and Bacon Soup that may be served as a one-dish meal.

beans, using a fork or an electric blender and add to the soup to thicken it. Stir in the bacon pieces and olives. Taste and add salt and more pepper, if necessary.

Pour the soup into individual bowls, sprinkle with the parsley and serve hot.

Bean Curd

Square, custard-like cakes of cooked, puréed and pressed soya beans, bean curd is sold in Oriental provision stores.

The cakes, which are about ½-inch thick and 3-inches square, should be drained and stored in fresh water in a covered jar in the refrigerator. They will keep for up to two weeks if the water is changed every day. There is no substitute for fresh bean curd in Chinese cooking.

Bean Curd and Crabmeat

A Chinese recipe, Bean Curd and Crabmeat will serve 4 people as a main course, or 6 to 8 people as part of a Chinese meal. This dish must be quickly cooked, so before you begin to cook be sure you have all the ingredients prepared and within easy reach.

4 SERVINGS

½ lb. fresh or canned crabmeat
4 cakes of fresh bean curd, about 3-inches square and ½-inch thick
3 tablespoons groundnut oil
1 spring onion [scallion], chopped
1 teaspoon peeled and finely chopped fresh ginger
1½ teaspoons salt
3 tablespoons chicken stock
⅛ teaspoon freshly ground black pepper
½ teaspoon cornflour [cornstarch]
5 teaspoons cold water
5 watercress sprigs

Low Cal

Pick over the crabmeat and discard all bits of cartilage and shell.

Slice each square of bean curd into ¼-inch slices. Cut each slice in half.

Put a heavy, 12-inch frying-pan over high heat for 30 seconds. Add the oil, swirl it about in the pan and heat it for 30 seconds. Turn the heat down to moderate when the oil is hot.

Stir in the chopped spring onion and the ginger. Add the bean curd, salt and chicken stock. Bring to the boil, cover the pan and cook over moderate heat for 3 minutes.

Stir in the crabmeat and black pepper and cook for 1 minute.

Mix the cornflour with the water and add it to the crabmeat. Stirring constantly, cook for 1 minute, or until the crabmeat and bean curd are coated with a clear, light glaze.

Put into a warmed serving dish, garnish with sprigs of watercress and serve at once.

Bean-Curd Skin

Large or small, thin, stiff sheets of dried bean curd, bean-curd skin is available in Chinese provision stores. It requires no refrigeration and will keep indefinitely. There is no substitute for bean-curd skin in Chinese recipes.

Bean Salad

A favourite dish in the southwestern part of the United States, Bean Salad goes well with cold meat or a grilled steak.

4 TO 6 SERVINGS

8 oz. [1 cup] red kidney beans
6 oz. [¾ cup] white beans, such as haricot or butter [dried lima] beans
4 oz. [½ cup] chick-peas
1 red pepper, the white pith removed, seeded and coarsely chopped
1 small onion, finely chopped, or 3 spring onions [scallions], chopped
1 garlic clove, crushed
2 tablespoons chopped fresh chives
2 tablespoons white wine vinegar
6 tablespoons olive oil
1 tablespoon lemon juice

½ teaspoon salt
¼ teaspoon black pepper

Soak the beans and peas in water overnight. Put them in a large saucepan, cover with water and bring to the boil over high heat. Cover the pan, lower the heat and simmer for 40 minutes or until tender. Drain and cool.

In a large salad bowl, combine the beans, peas, red pepper, onion, crushed garlic and chives.

In a small bowl, combine the vinegar, lemon juice, oil, salt and pepper. Mix, add to the bean mixture and toss well.

Refrigerate for about 30 minutes and before serving, leave at room temperature for 10 minutes.

Bean Sprouts

Rich in vitamin C, young sprouts of the mung or soya bean, which are about two-inches long, are a common ingredient in Chinese dishes. Sold fresh and in cans, they are becoming increasingly popular as a vegetable and a salad ingredient in Western cooking.

Canned bean sprouts should be thoroughly drained before using. The heads and tails of fresh bean sprouts can be removed before use, but it is not necessary. The fresh sprouts will keep for up to two weeks if they are stored in water in a covered jar in the refrigerator.

Bean sprouts must be cooked very quickly so they do not lose their crispness.

Bean curd—cakes of puréed soya beans—and bean-curd skin—strips of dried curd—are used in many Chinese dishes.

Bean Sprouts with Ginger

 ①

A deliciously crisp, quickly made vegetable dish, Bean Sprouts with Ginger must be cooked just before serving.

4 SERVINGS

3 tablespoons cooking oil
1 large onion, finely sliced
1-inch piece of fresh ginger, peeled, finely sliced and cut into thin strips
1 teaspoon salt
1 lb. fresh bean sprouts

Heat the oil in a large frying-pan over high heat. Add the onion, lower the heat to moderate and fry for 6 minutes, stirring occasionally with a wooden spoon. Add the ginger and continue frying for another 4 minutes.

Add the salt, stir to mix and add the bean sprouts. Raise the heat and, turning and tossing the bean sprouts, fry them for only 2 to 3 minutes.

This crunchy Bean Sprout Salad is unusual and attractive.

Bean Sprouts with Green Peppers

 ①

A Chinese dish, Bean Sprouts with Green Peppers can be served as part of a Chinese meal or as an unusual vegetable accompaniment to roast chicken or grilled fish. Cook it at the last minute.

6 SERVINGS

2 lb. fresh bean sprouts
2 large green peppers
4 tablespoons vegetable oil
3 tablespoons white wine
2 teaspoons salt
¼ teaspoon monosodium glutamate

Soak the bean sprouts in cold water for 15 minutes. Drain well. Wash the green peppers. Remove the seeds and white pith and cut the peppers into fine, almost threadlike strips.

Heat the oil in a heavy frying-pan over high heat. Add the bean sprouts and shredded green peppers and, stirring constantly, cook for 3 minutes.

Add the wine, salt and monosodium glutamate and, still stirring, cook for 2 more minutes. Serve hot.

Bean Sprout Salad

 ①

This fresh, crunchy salad is ideal to serve with or after grilled fish or chicken, or with other vegetarian salads.

4 SERVINGS

1 lb. fresh or canned bean sprouts
2 oz. canned pimiento, chopped
1 pickled cucumber, chopped
1 tablespoon chopped chives
DRESSING
2 tablespoons olive oil
1 tablespoon wine vinegar
½ teaspoon prepared mustard
2 teaspoons soy sauce
½ teaspoon sugar
½ teaspoon salt

Put the bean sprouts in a salad bowl with the pimiento, pickled cucumber and chives.

Mix all the ingredients for the dressing together, making sure the salt and sugar are dissolved. Pour the dressing over the salad. Toss the salad well and put in a refrigerator or a cool place for 1 hour before serving.